REGULATING

to

DISASTER

HOW GREEN JOBS POLICIES ARE
DAMAGING AMERICA'S ECONOMY

Diana Furchtgott-Roth

Encounter Books · New York · London

First American edition published in 2012 by Encounter Books, an activity of Encounter for Culture and Education, Inc., a nonprofit, tax-exempt corporation.
Encounter Books website address: www.encounterbooks.com

Manufactured in the United States and printed on acid-free paper. The paper used in this publication meets the minimum requirements of ANSI/NISO Z39.48-1992 (R 1997) (*Permanence of Paper*).

FIRST AMERICAN EDITION

LIBRARY OF CONGRESS CATALOGING-IN-PUBLICATION DATA
Furchtgott-Roth, Diana.
Regulating to disaster: how green jobs policies are damaging America's economy/by Diana Furchtgott-Roth.
p. cm.
Includes bibliographical references and index.
ISBN 978-1-59403-616-3 (hardcover: alk. paper)
1. Economic development—Environmental aspects—United States.
2. Green movement—United States. 3. Job creation—United States.
4. United States—Economic policy—2009. I. Title.
HC110.E5F87 2012
331.12'042—dc23
2012003218

To my parents, Gabriel and Ellen Roth,
who in 1967 moved the family from Britain to America,
the land of large cars and long highways, giant refrigerators, plentiful
hot water, and long high-pressure showers. As my father said,
"We have to move here, they even heat the bathrooms."

CONTENTS

Contents

LIST OF FIGURES
AND TABLES

LIST OF ABBREVIATIONS

AFL-CIO   American Federation of Labor and Congress of
          Industrial Organizations
API   American Petroleum Institute
ARRA   American Recovery and Reinvestment Act of 2009
BEA   Bureau of Economic Analysis
BLS   Bureau of Labor Statistics
BTU   British Thermal Unit
CAFE   Corporate Average Fuel Economy
CAP   Center for American Progress
CBO   Congressional Budget Office
CDC   Centers for Disease Control and Prevention
CEERT   Center for Energy Efficiency and Renewable
          Technologies

CFL	compact fluorescent light bulb
CIA	Central Intelligence Agency
CSG	Council of State Governments
DOD	Department of Defense
DOE	Department of Energy
DOJ	Department of Justice
DOL	Department of Labor
DOT	Department of Transportation
DSCC	Democratic Senatorial Campaign Committee
EIA	Energy Information Administration
EISA	Energy Independence and Security Act of 2007
EPA	Environmental Protection Agency
ERCOT	Electric Reliability Council of Texas
ETA	Employment and Training Administration
FEC	Federal Elections Commission
FFB	Federal Financing Bank
GAO	Government Accountability Office
GDP	Gross Domestic Product
HUD	Department of Housing and Urban Development
IEA	International Energy Agency
ILO	International Labour Organization
ITC	International Trade Commission
ITUC	International Trade Union Confederation
LED	light-emitting diodes
LEED	Leadership in Energy and Environmental Design
LIUNA	Laborers' International Union of North America
LMI	Labor Market Improvement
LPO	Loan Program Office of the Department of Energy
MACT	Maximum Achievable Control Technology
MW	Megawatt
NERA	National Economic Research Association
NGO	nongovernmental organization
NRC	National Research Council

OECD	Organisation for Economic Co-operation and Development
OMB	Office of Management and Budget
PERI	Political Economy Research Institute
RPS	Renewable Portfolio Standard
SEC	Securities and Exchange Commission
SEIU	Service Employees International Union
UAW	International Union, United Automobile, Aerospace, and Agricultural Implement Workers of America
UN	United Nations
UNEP	United Nations Environment Programme
USGBC	U.S. Green Building Council
USGS	U.S. Geological Survey
USW	United Steelworkers
WTO	World Trade Organization

1

INTRODUCTION

The date was June 6, 2012, the setting an ornate hearing room in the Rayburn House Office Building, where the full House Government Reform and Oversight Committee was investigating definitions of green jobs. Chairman Darrell Issa, a California Republican, was questioning John Galvin, acting commissioner of the Bureau of Labor Statistics, on the meaning of the 3.1 million green jobs his agency had recorded in data released in March.

"If you sweep the floor in a solar powered facility, is that a green job?" Issa asked. The answer was yes. Issa then ascertained from Galvin that hybrid bus drivers have green jobs, along with all the other bus drivers and workers who put gas in buses. Employees at bicycle shops also have green jobs. So do workers at antique dealers, at the Salvation Army used clothing recycling centers, and at used record stores, because these count as recycled goods. Garbage men have green jobs, and so do oil lobbyists engaged in advocacy related to environmental issues.

As a witness at the hearing, I explained that since the white paper cup placed before me on the table had a "Power to Save Energy" logo, then employees who produced it had green jobs, because the product met the BLS definition of "environmental compliance, education, training and public awareness." If the paper cup had been pure white, without the logo, its producers would not have green jobs.

When the Bureau of Labor Statistics can define producers of cups with environmental logos—but not without—as having green jobs, along with oil lobbyists, the definition becomes increasingly meaningless. The 3.1 million green jobs are a matter of relabeling, not creating new opportunities for Americans to move up the career ladder. And with slow economic growth and job creation, and unemployment rates above 8 percent for over three years, everyone agrees that Americans need more jobs.

The administration may tout 3.1 million green jobs as a large number, but 3.1 million shows a lack of imagination and ambition. In addition, it falls short of the 5 million promised by President Obama on the campaign trail in 2008. If BLS can "create" green jobs by simply relabeling existing jobs as green, why stop at 3.1 million? If oil lobbyists can bask in the social approbation of a job labeled as green, why should not every American enjoy the same approval? Saying that everyone has a green job would actually be less arbitrary than randomly picking 3.1 million Americans and labeling their jobs as green.

In contrast to the fuzzy number of 3.1 million green jobs, some numbers in the economy are treated with the utmost precision. The BLS issues the monthly estimate of jobs created in the economy, derived from a survey of 400,000 businesses, every month, then revised for two consecutive months. Finally, about a year later, the figure is benchmarked against an aggregate count of jobs for accuracy. Another example is tax return data. Both companies and households face severe penalties for cheating on tax returns. The number has to be absolutely correct, and if mistakes are found in an Internal Revenue Service audit, people can go to jail. Corporations that report financial information to the Securities and Exchange Commission must meet exacting standards and sometimes undergo multiple audits.

Given the government's ability to closely monitor numbers, it is even more surprising that the BLS publishes such an inexact 3.1 million green jobs number. It is a sign that the issue is not taken seriously, that the search for green jobs is just window-dressing to appeal to some environmental constituency. When the government plays around with numbers to this extent it is a recipe for disaster. Someone is trying to trick the voter. In Chapter 2, we will see that the Environmental Protection Agency plays games with the costs and benefits of the Mercury and Air Toxic Standards for Power Plants rule for the same reason.

In contrast to the exacting nature of other information, the green jobs numbers are arbitrary. No one will go to jail if the number is 1 million, 2 million, or 5 million green jobs. Everyone knows that the numbers represent a form of fiction.

How did we descend to this 3.1 million green jobs number?

President Obama has been vocal in advocating government funding of green jobs and clean energy, but legislation to promote "green jobs" began with President George W. Bush. In 2007, President Bush signed into law the Energy Independence and Security Act, which included as Title X the Green Jobs Act, sponsored by then-Representative Hilda Solis, a California Democrat.[1] Solis became secretary of labor in 2009, and took charge of implementing the legislation she pioneered.

The Green Jobs Act authorized funding for green-collar job training in the areas of retrofitting buildings, installing solar panels and setting up wind farms, and building energy efficient buildings, among others.

The bill authorized funds for states to offer grants for labor management training programs and apprenticeships, in order to coordinate green jobs programs with union officials.[2] Other sections contained incentives for construction of green buildings, with particular reference to federal buildings.[3]

The green jobs movement is also blooming among international organizations in Europe and Asia. The Green Jobs Initiative was launched jointly by the United Nations Environment Programme, the International Labour Organization, the International Organization of Employers, and the International Trade Union Confederation. Through conferences and recommendations, their mission "supports a concerted effort by governments, employers and trade unions to promote environmentally sustainable jobs and development in a climate-challenged world."[4]

The rationale behind these conferences, besides giving participants attractive "climate change" credentials, is the perennial concept that economic progress is harming the planet. Today's bogeyman is global warming. In the 19th century, British economist Thomas Malthus forecast that population growth would result in an exhaustion of the planet's resources, resulting in the description of economics as "the dismal science." And dismal indeed is the view that the world is running out of resources, that our air is getting dirtier, and that we are making our planet uninhabitable through excessive emissions of carbon—a situation that can only be solved by government choice of more expensive alternative energy technology.

Many scientists believe that released CO_2 gas either makes the atmosphere more like a greenhouse or that it gets absorbed by the oceans and acidifies them.[5] Rather than a shortage of fossil fuels, they believe that there may be no longer enough buffering capacity in the seas and the sky to hide the results of CO_2 released by humans and protect us from the consequences.

Is Planet Earth getting warmer through man-made emissions of greenhouse gases, or due to natural causes beyond human control? If so, is warming harmful rather than beneficial? On cold winter days, many would find a little more warmth welcome. It might even lead to lower heating bills and fewer carbon emissions. I leave it to the scientific community to battle out the pros and cons of the climate change debate. But it is certain that, if global warming needs to be mitigated, there are less expensive ways of reducing these emissions than by green jobs policies.

Some scientists, including Dutch Nobel Prize–winning atmospheric chemist Paul Crutzen, believe that altering some features of the Earth's environment would be a more cost-effective and efficient way to combat global warming.[6] This is termed "geoengineering." Geoengineering would be less disruptive to business activity, less threatening to employment, and most likely relatively inexpensive. Most important, it would reduce warming even if large countries such as India and China did not agree to reduce their emissions.

The geoengineering approach could be a less-expensive substitute for, or supplement to, industrial carbon reduction policies such as green jobs policies. One form is solar radiation management, which would theoretically diminish the warmth caused by the sun's rays by injecting fine sulfur particles or other reflective aerosols into the upper atmosphere to reflect incoming radiation.[7]

Another method involves spraying clouds with saltwater to increase their reflectance. Clouds seeded with saltwater would be thicker and would reflect more heat back toward the sun, away from Earth.[8] Cooling effects—as well as other, adverse consequences—have been observed after volcanic eruptions.

A third proposed technique makes the surface of the planet more reflective by brightening structures and painting roofs white, as well as by increasing the reflectivity of deserts and oceans.[9]

Successful geoengineering would permit the Earth's population to make smaller reductions in carbon use and still achieve a retarding effect on global warming, if that is what is desired, but at a lower cost to economic activity.

Geoengineering solutions are less expensive than carbon reduction. Some estimate that the discounted cost of enhancing clouds' reflectance through saltwater spraying for 200 years could cost $300 million to $1.8 billion.[10] The discounted global benefits over the same period would be $4 trillion to $10 trillion.[11] These costs are small in comparison to the economic damage that could result from reduced use of carbon fuels and the high cost of non-carbon substitutes, such as solar and wind power.

Furthermore, if India and China do not agree to cut their carbon emissions, proposed dramatic cuts in American carbon emissions alone would not solve the problems of climate change. But geoengineering solutions would still be effective, even against the effects of greenhouse gases not resulting from human activity.

It is unlikely that India and China will embrace carbon cuts. They are free from cuts in the Kyoto Protocol, which set limits on thirty-seven industrialized countries' emissions of greenhouse gases, chiefly carbon dioxide. Signatory governments agreed to reduce their emissions by at least 5 percent below 1990 levels by 2008 to 2012. President Bill Clinton signed the agreement in 1997, but the Senate refused to ratify it, citing potential economic damage. Neither did India and China support limits on greenhouse gases at the 2011 meetings in Durban, South Africa.

Although geoengineering could provide a less-expensive alternative to mitigating effects of global warming, it is astonishing how little federal funding is dedicated to it. There was no funding for geoengineering research in President Obama's 2013 budget.[12] A Government Accountability Office (GAO) study published in 2010 found that $950,000—less than $1 million—was spent on research on solar radiation management in fiscal years 2009 and 2010.[13]

In comparison, billions of dollars are spent on conservation and renewable energy, such as wind and solar, and in 2010 Congress discussed imposing trillions of dollars as taxes on carbon emissions. To address concerns about global warming and climate change, it is not necessary to impose industrial policy on the economy. Yet that is what policymakers are doing.

What is occurring in Washington, DC, is the unequivocal support of green technologies, without looking into the substance of their operations. This has created an unfair advantage for those in certain industries. Those engaging in the traditionally least-productive section of the green process, such as solar panel manufacturing and installation, receive praise and funds, while hydrofracturing (known as "fracking") for natural gas and oil production or raising the efficiency of the internal combustion engine are is dismissed. Nuclear power is green, but trucking nuclear waste is not, even though it is necessary for the plant to produce power.

The supernova bankruptcy of Solyndra, Inc., the solar panel manufacturer that received a $535 million Department of Energy (DOE) loan guarantee, has focused attention on unproductive investments in the DOE loan program. Since 2009, the DOE has made thirty-four commitments totaling $34.7 billion.[14] Of this, the DOE has provided $13.6 billion in loans to solar and wind production companies that were virtually guaranteed enormous profits as a result of their agreements with utility companies to purchase their energy output. The *New York Times*, in an article in November 2011, termed these "a gold rush" of loans, because the recipients had guaranteed buyers to purchase expensive energy.

One example of why "gold rush" is so apt is the $1.6 billion DOE loan guarantee to BrightSource Energy, a politically-connected corporation whose chairman, John Bryson, became Obama's Secretary of Commerce in October 2011. Peter Darbee, CEO of Pacific Gas and Electric, personally spoke to Obama on BrightSource's behalf in 2010, because PG&E needed solar power to meet California's growing requirements for renewable energy in electricity production.

PG&E has committed to buying all the power from Bright-Source, no matter how much it costs, in order to fulfill California's requirement, signed into law by Governor Jerry Brown in April 2011, that 33 percent of electricity be generated by renewables by 2020. Colorado has a similar requirement. This is gold for BrightSource, but a loser for Californians, who must pay higher electricity costs. The U.S. Energy Information Administration has estimated that the average levelized cost for natural gas-fired plants entering service in 2017 is $69 per megawatt hour, compared to $157 per megawatt hour for solar-powered plants, so households have far higher electricity bills using solar power. Between bankruptcy and corporate welfare, the question arises: Is there even one Energy Department loan that makes any sense?

Worthwhile loans, presumably, would "make a difference" by funding companies that otherwise could not flourish. Corporate welfare does not meet this standard. Neither should venture capital disguised as loans.

Any evaluation of green initiatives should include estimates of slowdown in economic activity and the number of jobs lost due to these initiatives, as well as the potential benefits. If a state introduces a renewable energy standard, traditional energy producers will lose business and jobs. There is only so much total electricity that a market demands. By requiring some to be produced by a more expensive, renewable source, less will be produced by traditional suppliers, thus leading to economic losses for prior providers.

The same principle holds true in the manufacturing fields. If the government supports a wind manufacturer, companies that manufacture other forms of energy, such as oil and gas, will feel the pinch. A lower demand for oil and gas, even one that is non-market determined, leads to a shrinking of economic activity and a smaller workforce. Jobs are lost because of green policies, and they must be counted to determine the full costs and employment resulting from green jobs.

The remainder of the book is divided as follows. Part 1, consisting of Chapters 2, 3, and 4, reviews the definitions of green jobs and the problems of the green laws and regulations advanced to promote them, from agencies as diverse as DOE, the Environmental Protection Agency (EPA), the Department of Transportation (DOT), and the Department of Housing and Urban Development (HUD). Green jobs in modern times came about through an alliance of unions and environmentalists, including activists Bracken Hendricks, Joel Rogers, and Leo Gerard, who launched the modern green jobs movement.

Part 2, containing Chapters 5, 6, and 7, shows the damage caused by green theology put into practice, including the fatally flawed green studies that are used to persuade the public that "investments" in green jobs lead to higher employment. One example of a failed investment is the story of Solyndra, the solar panel firm awarded guaranteed loans over the objections of career officials in the Office of Management and Budget (OMB). Solyndra has come to epitomize the costs of industrial policy. But Solyndra is not the only example. Government funds are wasted on wind power, both in America and abroad, and traditional sources of power generation, such as coal and natural gas, have to increase or decrease their power generation to balance intermittent levels of wind power.

Part 3, consisting of Chapters 8 and 9, shows the larger implications of green jobs policies both globally and morally. Unfortunately much mandated equipment, such as solar panels and wind turbines, is made abroad and imported. China, with its massive wind farms and solar arrays, derives less than one percent of its electricity from renewables. So all that America gains from this costly venture is moral superiority. Our economies are sick; we have higher unemployment; our young college graduates cannot find jobs. But we can brag that we are saving the world.

In conclusion, Chapter 10 describes the emergence of the New American Revolution, the oil and gas that are beginning to power America's economy. Now, North America is the fastest-growing oil producing region in the world, with the potential to overtake Russia and Saudi Arabia in a few years. The United States has become the world's largest exporter of refined petroleum products.

On July 15, 2010, President Obama attended the groundbreaking of the Korean LG Chem battery plant, which received a grant of $151 million from the Energy Department. He said, "Because of a grant to this company, a grant that's leveraging more than 150 million private dollars, as many as 300 people will be put to work doing construction and another 300 will eventually be hired to operate this plant when it's fully up and running. And this is going to lead to growth at local businesses like parts suppliers and restaurants. It will be a boost to the economy of the entire region."[15]

LG Chem was supposed to be fully operational by 2012, supply batteries for the electric Chevy Volt and Ford Focus, and employ 300 workers. But as of May, 2012, the plant employed 220 workers and had not yet begun production. Other battery companies are also in trouble. Ener1 of Indianapolis used $55 million of a $118 million grant and is now bankrupt. A123, a Michigan company whose groundbreaking was also attended by President Obama, received $249 million and now has substantial cash losses.

Obama concluded his speech at the battery plant in Holland, Michigan, by saying, "This is a symbol of where Michigan is going, this is a symbol of where Holland is going, this is a symbol of where America is going." But if these plants are a symbol, then America is stalled. More hopeful symbols are America's new discoveries of oil and natural gas. Jobs producing refined petroleum products, or fracking for natural gas, might not fit the BLS definitions of green. But they are a booming part of the economy, and are generating more green dollar jobs by drawing manufacturing back to America.

PART I

THE ELUSIVE GREEN JOB

2

GREEN LEGISLATION, GREEN REGULATIONS

More than Afghanistan, more than healthcare, more than sports teams, Americans care about jobs. It is not hard to understand why. Many Americans are out of work, especially younger Americans, and those with jobs worry that they may lose them. The American dream that tomorrow will always have more economic promise than today is fading.

Drive through Delaware, and you might see an enormous automobile manufacturing plant. At least, it used to be an automobile manufacturing plant. Today, its doors are closed, its structure decays. A few years ago, thousands of Vice President Joe Biden's constituents had well-paying jobs at the plant. Today, they have lower-paying jobs—if they are lucky. The less fortunate ones are simply unemployed.

America is filled with relics of the economy we have lost. We see them every day: the skeletons of factories; the remnants of automobile showrooms; the shuttered shopping malls; young people who cannot find any job, much less jobs as good as those held by their parents. The tombstones silently shriek. They remind us of an economy that was prematurely murdered by an arrogant group of assassins whose government-centered political and financial futures could only be made by outlawing and killing the market-oriented economy that had served America so well.

Displacing a productive economy with government programs is neither new nor unusual. In 1850 the French economist Frédéric Bastiat wrote an essay entitled "That Which Is Seen, and That Which Is Not Seen."[1] What is seen, according to Bastiat, are the jobs directly created by the government, and what is not seen are the workers displaced by the effects of increased taxes, tariffs, and government regulation.

Bastiat wrote, "When an official spends for his own profit an extra hundred sous, it implies that a taxpayer spends for his profit a hundred sous less. But the expense of the official is seen, because the act is performed, while that of the taxpayer is not seen, because, alas! he is prevented from performing it."[2]

With resonance today, Bastiat explains, "The State opens a road, builds a palace, straightens a street, cuts a canal; and so gives work to certain workmen—this is what is seen: but it deprives certain other workmen of work, and this is what is not seen."[3]

But even Frédéric Bastiat did not anticipate how disruptive government programs could be. Rather like Bastiat's government, the administration claims that mandated green technologies will create jobs. Call it contemporary science fiction with moral overtones: if you believe in the moral imperative of green technologies, they will create more jobs. They may create some, but they displace many others.

Tax revenues for subsidizing green jobs, such as installation of insulation and energy-efficient windows, and producers of renewable energy, such as from sunshine and wind, create jobs in those sectors but leave less to be spent on other activities.

America is following in the trails leading nowhere that other nations have blazed. In Spain, economics professor Gabriel Calzada Alvarez of the Universidad Rey Juan Carlos has calculated that his country has spent $714,000 per green job.[4] Higher energy costs have driven away jobs in metallurgy, mining, and food processing, so more than two jobs have been destroyed for every job created. Even in sunny Spain, solar power accounted for less than 3 percent of 2010 electrical production.[5] In June 2012, Spain was negotiating with the European Central Bank for a bailout, its unemployment rate was 24 percent, and youth unemployment was over 50 percent.

Don Quixote may have tilted at windmills, but he was positively rational compared to modern governments that seek to create new economies out of green technologies. The sad reality is that nowhere have green technologies led to more jobs.

Today, we can see the visible scars and victims of the government's war against the market economy. We are those victims.

REDUCING OIL PRODUCTION IN THE GULF OF MEXICO

On May 27, 2010, President Obama, with the support of the Secretary of the Interior Ken Salazar, issued a six-month moratorium on all drilling below 500 feet, including halting the issuing of new permits to drill in the Gulf of Mexico. Secretary Salazar cited a panel of fifteen experts backing his decision, claiming they had supported the moratorium.

On June 8, 2010, eight of the fifteen experts wrote a letter to Senator Mary Landrieu, a Democrat from Louisiana, angrily stating that they had supported only a draft version of the moratorium, one that would halt new drilling below 1,000 feet. In the letter, they claimed the report presented to the president was modified after they had signed off on its initial recommendation of temporarily suspending drilling below 1,000 feet. They concluded, "he [Secretary Salazar] should not be free to use our names to justify his political decisions."[6]

Independent oil and service companies instantly fought back, and on June 22, 2010, Judge Martin Feldman ruled against the moratorium, holding that it was too broad and failed to take into account the economic effects on the Gulf Coast. On July 12, 2010, Secretary Salazar issued a revised moratorium basing restrictions on technology and drilling configuration rather than on water depth.[7] Even under the revised moratorium, the economic effects on Gulf Coast residents were pronounced.

Results from the Gulf of Mexico moratorium were immediate. Production of crude oil in federal waters dropped over 8 percent in the year ending June 2011, compared with the year before. Even though production in the Gulf of Mexico is highly variable, and subject to hurricanes, the 2010 season was benign in the Gulf, with no massive interruption in production.[8]

This decline in production amounted to about 134,500 barrels of crude oil per day, at realized prices of $80 per barrel, for a total of over $3.9 billion.[9] But even these numbers do not paint an entire picture of the damage.

At the time, a major group of discoveries was being announced in the lower tertiary Gulf of Mexico. These discoveries were concentrated near the edge of U.S. territorial waters, with the most prolific in Keathley Canyon and other "hot" areas in Alaminos Canyon and Walker Ridge.[10] In fact, in September 2009, British Petroleum (BP) had announced the discovery of one of the largest oil fields in the world, Tiber, drilled by the now infamous Deepwater Horizon, whose next assignment would be its last.[11] With the first exploratory well drilled in the Gulf after Macondo, in June 2011, ExxonMobil confirmed that it had found a large discovery before the moratorium, but waited to make the announcement until engineers could drill further to appraise the prospect.[12]

However, these massive exploration and appraisal projects were not as much affected as were current producing areas that were under development. In issuing the moratorium, the government issued a blanket decree against all wells, which meant that exploration and appraisal wells (those drilled to confirm the extent and size of a previous discovery) were put under the same ban as development wells (wells driven in a proven reservoir).

Development drilling is what drives current oil production, as it takes many years to bring online projects like Macondo from the exploratory phase to the development phase. The government's ban delayed the development of massive projects like Chevron's Jack, Anadarko's Lucius, and countless others from drilling wells that would bring production online quickly.

More than anything, the government needs to provide a clear regulatory outlook on the future. Regulations have undergone a chaotic transformation that has yet to be clarified, with the Bureau of Ocean Energy Management, Regulation, and Enforcement taking over the duties of the former Minerals Management Service.

As of June 8, 2012, the active deep water rig count in the Gulf of Mexico was 48, finally surpassing the level at the time of the BP oil spill.[13] But since the moratorium was lifted in October 2010, the pace of permit approvals remained significantly slower than it had been prior to the incident for a full year.[14] Furthermore, the average approval time for a plan increased from the 2006-2010 average of 61 days to 102 days as of April 2012, a 67 percent increase.[15] Without clarity and certainty, America will miss out on future investments.

PLAYING RUSSIAN ROULETTE WITH THE AMERICAN ECONOMY

In the game of Russian roulette, a person puts a single bullet in a pistol with six chambers, spins the revolver, and points the pistol at his head. It is a self-defeating game: not only because of the risk and uncertainty involved, but also because there is no upside to playing. The individual is better off not to play at all, much less to play on repeated occasions.

Mandating green jobs to the American economy is rather like playing Russian roulette. Our economy is better off left alone.

Uncertainty is harmful when the government advocates laws and rules such as green technologies with no upside. These mandated technologies look rather like Russian roulette, except with six bullets rather than one loaded in the pistol.

Of course, uncertainty is an inherent part, and a valuable part, of any economy. No risk means no reward. But rewards only come when there is uncertainty about the magnitude of potential upsides. Yet there are no possible upsides for green technologies.

Because Congress and the administration are mandating and subsidizing more costly green technology, businesses and consumers are reducing some economic activity and investments. Some investments are going overseas, and some are simply not being made anywhere. The result is lost jobs. Businesses are hiring more temporary workers, but not permanent workers. Consumers are wary of spending because they are afraid of tax hikes and further shrinkage of the values of their homes and their retirement savings.

As an example of the Russian roulette of green technologies, consider the American Clean Energy and Security Act, cosponsored by Democratic Representatives Henry Waxman of California and Edward Markey of Massachusetts. The bill, proposed in the iiith Congress, would have raised energy prices.[16] Sometimes known as the cap-and-trade bill, it would have imposed strict new efficiency standards on automobiles and appliances, required firms to use nonexistent technology, and mandated greenhouse gas emissions per person back to 19th-century levels by 2050.

Its companion in the Senate was the Kerry-Lieberman bill, sponsored by Senators John Kerry, a Democrat from Massachusetts, and Joseph Lieberman, an Independent from Connecticut.[17]

The Waxman-Markey bill was a lose-lose proposition for the American economy and the American people. Everyone would lose; it was only a question of how quickly. Like Russian roulette, the best option for America was not to play at all. Yet Markey, then-chairman of the House Energy and Environment Subcommittee, declared that the bill would "create jobs by the millions, save money by the billions, and unleash energy investment by the trillions."[18] Then-House Speaker Nancy Pelosi said it was about "jobs, jobs, and jobs."[19]

Yes, the cap-and-trade bill would perhaps have created a few jobs building more expensive energy, such as solar panels and windmills, and inventing the technology to comply with the government's new requirements. But the bill's $800 billion plus price tag came from new taxes, higher prices for cheaper energy such as oil and gas, and increased borrowing. This would have reduced jobs elsewhere, leading to certain job losses, rather like in Bastiat's example.

The 1,200-page bill would have increased the price of energy by setting allowances for greenhouse gas emissions and mandated new standards for energy production and use. The bill would have raised $846.6 billion over 10 years while adding $821.2 billion to federal spending.[20]

The bill required that greenhouse gas emissions in 2012 not exceed 97 percent of 2005 emissions, declining to 17 percent of 2005 emissions by 2050.[21] Meeting these standards now is technologically impossible without radically reducing our standards of living, but Congress was hoping that technology would magically appear as needed.

The mechanism for this was a cap-and-trade program under which the Environmental Protection Agency (EPA) would issue allowances to emit greenhouse gases at a steadily declining rate through 2050. Under this program, when emissions exceed a firm's allowance, or cap, it would have to purchase allowances from the government or other firms, a tax under another name, driving up costs that would be passed on to consumers.

Electric utilities would have been given free allowances to encourage them to support the bill. Oil and gas would have been particularly hard hit, because they are responsible for 35 percent of emissions yet were allocated only three percent of the free allowances.

Just as the increases in oil prices in the 1970s brought about an increase in unemployment, such legislation could usher in years, perhaps decades, of lower economic growth and higher unemployment than would be the case otherwise.

Economists Steven Davis of the University of Chicago and John Haltiwanger of the University of Maryland have analyzed extensively the effects of the oil price increases between 1972 and 1988.[22] Although their research deals with the effects of oil price increases, it is also applicable to increases in the price of energy, which would be the effect of Waxman-Markey.

Davis and Haltiwanger find that oil price increases resulted in more jobs lost than jobs gained in almost every industry sector of the economy. The largest oil shock, in 1973, caused an estimated 8 percent decline in manufacturing employment over the following two years.

Oil price increases have larger effects on economic activity than oil price declines, Davis and Haltiwanger calculate, a finding shared by other economic studies. In other words, when energy prices increase firms lay off workers, but when prices decline, the workers are not hired back as fast.

Davis and Haltiwanger also find that higher energy prices are more likely to suppress employment than monetary shocks. Many politicians fret over the harmful effects of recent American monetary policy but overlook the even greater danger to employment from cap-and-trade bills.

Cap-and-trade is but one of many forms of green technologies promoted by the administration. Each one is bad for the economy. Some proposals are worse than others, but the differences range between having one bullet in the pistol and six bullets in the pistol. None has an upside for the economy; they only have a downside. The right choice for America is not to find the least bad of the bunch, the pistol with only one bullet rather than six bullets pointed at our head. The right choice for America is not to play Russian roulette at all and remove from government those who recommended these suicidal games in the first place.

DESTROYING AMERICAN JOBS THROUGH NEW ENVIRONMENTAL PROGRAMS

The nonpartisan Congressional Budget Office (CBO) agreed. In May 2010, the CBO issued a report entitled "How Policies to Reduce Greenhouse Gas Emissions Could Affect Employment."[23] The report concluded that "job losses in the industries that shrink would lower employment more than job gains in other industries would increase employment, thereby raising the overall unemployment rate."[24]

The CBO report shows that emissions reduction programs would cause job losses in coal mining, oil and gas extraction, gas utilities, and petroleum refining. In addition, workers' wages adjusted for inflation would be lower than otherwise because of the increase in prices due to the cap-and-trade program. The CBO concludes that some workers, therefore, would leave the labor market, because at the new lower wages they would prefer to stay home.

Any reader of the CBO report would realize that it is not in the interests of American workers to embark on an emissions reduction program, especially with high unemployment rates and slow economic growth, as was the case during most of 2009 and 2010. According to the CBO, "While the economy was adjusting to the emission-reduction program, a number of people would lose their job, and some of those people would face prolonged hardship."[25] Workers laid off in declining industries would find it hard to get new jobs.

The CBO report further points out that, "In cases in which a shrinking industry was the primary employer in a community, the entire community could suffer."[26] The tax base would dwindle and real estate would lose its value as unemployed workers moved elsewhere. The community's personal income would diminish and real estate values would fall as the jobless moved away.

W. David Montgomery, senior vice president of National Economic Research Associates (NERA) and former assistant director of the CBO, estimates that the measures proposed by EPA, including the Clean Air Transport Rule, utility, water, and coal ash regulations would increase electricity prices by 1 percent to 3 percent in 2015 and 3 to 5 percent in 2020, compared to what they would be without the regulations.[27] And that does not even account for inflation.

By 2035 electricity prices would rise to 7 percent to 9 percent higher than what they would be without regulations, again not considering inflation. Montgomery concludes that EPA regulations would cause a reduction of total macroeconomic investment by about $150 billion from 2010 to 2015, which, following the logic of Keynesian models, would result in a net destruction of over 1 million jobs.

Montgomery also gives a grim portrait of the future of total labor compensation in America under proposed EPA regulations. Montgomery finds EPA regulations would lower total labor compensation by a quarter of a percentage point by 2015. This decline of between $100 and $150 in average worker compensation would rise to about $200 of average lost wages in 2020. The slow recovery of wages is a result of a productivity growth increasing at a slow rate, itself resulting from diverting resources and investment away from industries damaged by strict environmental regulations.

The coal mining sector would experience the greatest losses of output and employment by 2015, at a 20 percent decrease in real output. Electricity, heavy industry, and energy-intensive sectors would experience the next greatest losses. Coal mining would decline as coal-fired power plants are retired, and electricity use would fall due to higher prices. Auto manufacturing, heavy industry, and energy-intensive industries would be weaker because of lower demand for their products, resulting from higher prices. Iron and steel would also suffer under new EPA regulations. Montgomery's predictions accord with the documented negative effects of the 1990 Clean Air Act Amendments on electricity and primary metals industries.

OZONE RULE OUT, MERCURY RULE IN

On September 2, 2011, President Obama admitted that environmental regulations have negative employment consequences. He instructed the EPA to refrain from adopting stricter standards on ozone,[28] just after the Department of Labor (DOL) reported that in August 2011 there was no net growth of jobs in the United

States.[29] The data were later revised to show that the economy created 104,000 jobs in August, but, at the time, there were fears that the economy was going into another recession.[30]

Obama's action amounted to an admission that imposing new, more costly regulatory requirements on business may conflict with hiring additional workers, now most Americans' primary policy goal.

In blocking the ozone rule, Obama declared, "I have continued to underscore the importance of reducing regulatory burdens and regulatory uncertainty, particularly as our economy continues to recover. With that in mind, and after careful consideration, I have requested that Administrator Jackson withdraw the draft Ozone National Ambient Air Quality Standards at this time."[31]

The phrase "at this time" shows that the hold is temporary and that the rule can move forward at any time. Even better would have been to withdraw it entirely. And why stop at one regulation or seven? Why not put a hold on more regulations? They create a climate of uncertainty, damaging economic growth and employment, and inhibiting employers and investors.

The ozone regulations would have required power plants, factories, and automobiles to reduce emissions in order to lower permissible levels of ozone in the atmosphere. They would have lowered the standard for permissible ozone from the current level of 0.075 parts per million set in 2008 to a range of 0.060 to 0.070 parts per million in 2020, depending on the final regulation. Before 2008, the maximum level permitted was 0.084, set by President Bill Clinton in 1997.[32]

Moving from 0.075 ppm to 0.070 might not seem like a large step, but 515 of the 675 counties required to measure ozone are now out of compliance with the weaker rule. If the standard were 0.060 now, EPA estimated that 660 counties would be out of compliance. Counties would have to phase in the new rules in 2014 and be fully compliant by 2031.[33]

The EPA has estimated that it would cost $19 billion to $90 billion a year for America to comply with the new ozone standard, an amount that it juxtaposed to projected health benefits of $13 billion to $100 billion annually. With a 0.060 standard, for example, EPA estimates that there would be 58,000 fewer cases of asthma and 2.1 million fewer missed days of work and school.[34]

Whereas the costs to Americans in terms of new designs for automobiles, more expensive technology for power plants, and movement of additional manufacturing plants to China are clearly predictable, the savings in healthcare costs are murkier.

Take asthma, for instance. America's air has been gradually getting cleaner since 1980,[35] as EPA's own data show, but the number of children with asthma has risen. According to the Centers for Disease Control (CDC), 3.6 percent of children had asthma in 1980, and almost twice that, 7.5 percent, in 1995.[36] Now, using a slightly different measure, 10 percent of children have asthma. CDC acknowledges that "the causes of asthma remain unclear and the current research paints a complex picture," yet the EPA forecasts 58,000 fewer asthma cases from ozone reductions.

Although Americans escaped the cap-and-trade bill and the ozone regulation, they were not so lucky with mercury. The Mercury and Air Toxic Standards for Power Plants rule will raise electricity rates all over the country, particularly in the battleground states of Illinois, Ohio, Indiana, Florida, and Michigan.

The rule was released the Wednesday before Christmas, 2011, when few were paying attention, and was announced by EPA Administrator Lisa Jackson at the National Children's Hospital in Washington, DC, with the hospital's CEO and the national volunteer chair of the American Lung Association delivering remarks. Jackson said that this costly initiative is for the children, and that millions of children will be protected. She talked about how fifteen years ago her son spent his first Christmas in hospital, suffering from asthma.

Jackson said nothing about the costs. EPA's state-by-state interactive map showed benefits for each state, but no costs (costs were buried in the 510-page Regulatory Impact Analysis for the Final Mercury and Air Toxics Standards report). To sweeten the rule, she estimated that it would create 46,000 new construction jobs and 8,000 utility jobs.

The Mercury and Air Toxic Standards for Power Plants rule will make electricity generation far more complex and expensive, especially in the eastern half of the United States. It will require the closure of many coal- and oil-fired power plants, and placement of emissions control equipment on others. Forty-five percent of American electricity was produced by coal in the first quarter of 2011, but it declined to 36 percent in the first quarter of 2012.

The EPA will restrict power plants' and boilers' emissions of "heavy metals," including mercury, arsenic, chromium, and nickel, and acid gases, such as hydrogen chloride and hydrogen fluoride. Most people's eyes glaze over when they hear about EPA's new Utility Maximum Achievable Control Technology rule. But when they hear that it will raise their electricity bills, they pay more attention.

Maximum Achievable Control Technology means that plants and boilers have to use the most stringent methods possible to get the heavy metals out of the air, even if these methods cost billions and the benefits are worth far less—as is the case with the new utility rule. That is why many plants will have to close.

Susan Dudley, director of the Regulatory Studies Center at George Washington University, wrote in the *National Journal* on December 19, 2011, "If the enormous public benefits EPA predicts from these mercury standards were real, they would justify the cost to Americans of almost $11 billion per year. Unfortunately, they are not."

Dudley explains that the EPA derives its benefits by assigning high values to reducing emissions of fine particles (not air toxics or acid gases) that will occur as a side effect of the required controls on mercury. But the EPA already regulates these particles through other rules. Through sleight of hand, the EPA calculates almost all of the benefits for this rule from particle reductions that fall well below the levels it has already established as safe in other proceedings.

Mercury and arsenic are well known to the public as toxins, and in certain doses they can be lethal. But the new EPA rules will push emissions caps unnecessarily low, driving up generating costs and the price of power to industry and households, and forcing some boilers and plants to shut down.

The EPA estimates its new rules would cost households and businesses $10 billion a year in 2016. Industry groups have estimated the costs at $40 billion to $120 billion for full compliance, with many older coal and oil-fired plants forced to close. Illinois, Ohio, Indiana, Missouri, and Michigan are the hardest-hit, because they are home to the oldest plants with the fewest emissions controls.

These additional costs would come on top of those to be imposed, starting around 2015, by the EPA's other planned standards for carbon, water, coal ash, and particulates.

The benefits, calculated at $33 billion to $81 billion each year, starting from 2016, supposedly come from improvements in Americans' health, mostly from decreases in asthma—the same health benefits used to justify the ozone rule. The EPA forecast 130,000 fewer asthma cases from its mercury rule, mostly from fewer particulates. This is more than twice the amount of asthma cases, 58,000, saved by the ozone rule. But, just as with ozone, these projected benefits are "guesstimates," gains that are hard to specify given that other factors, such as obesity and lack of exercise, are in play.

Table 2-1 shows which states rely on coal and oil for electricity generation and therefore would face the highest costs under new environmental regulations. In 2010, twenty-one states used coal for more than half of their electricity generation. Eight states, including Kentucky, Indiana, Ohio, Missouri, and West Virginia, use coal to generate more than 80 percent of their electricity. They would face the highest costs under new environmental regulations.

The Russian roulette of new regulations means higher electricity prices for these parts of the country, which are already suffering from declining manufacturing. North Dakota and Texas would be adversely affected, not only because of the amount of coal that they use, but also because it tends to be lignite, or brown coal, which is dirtier. Power plants using lignite would find it more expensive to comply with new regulations.

THE INCANDESCENT LIGHTBULB BAN: NO JOKE FOR AMERICAN WORKERS

In the name of energy savings, in 2007 then-Representative Jane Harman, a California Democrat who resigned in February 2011, and Representative Fred Upton, a Michigan Republican, introduced legislation outlawing the 130-year-old lightbulb.[37] The bill was rolled into the 2007 Energy Independence and Security Act, the same law whose Title X, the Green Jobs Act, sponsored by then-Representative Hilda Solis, inspired the BLS green jobs count.[38] Incandescent lightbulb plants closed, and jobs went to China.

As of January 1, 2012, Americans were no longer able to buy 100-watt incandescent lightbulbs, the kind Thomas Edison invented and the only kind many of us know—and prefer. Incandescent lightbulbs are being phased out by wattage over a two-year period, starting January 2012. The 100-watt bulbs were the first to be outlawed, by act of Congress, followed by 75-watt bulbs in January 2013, and 60- and 40-watt bulbs in January 2014.[39]

Incandescent bulbs were made in America, in plants such as Osram Sylvania's Kentucky facility,[40] but the vast majority of the new fluorescent bulbs are made in China, because twisting the glass into a the spiral shape of a compact fluorescent lamp or CFL is labor-intensive. One American plant, Neptun Light, opened in Lake Bluff, Illinois, with funding from the stimulus program, but that is the exception rather than the rule.[41]

It is unlikely that more CFL plants will open in America because of the high labor costs. It is not that CFL plants have moved offshore; CFLs were never made in America. The main producers of CFLs—Philips, Sylvania, and General Electric (GE)—make their bulbs in China or Poland.

Calls to repeal the incandescent lightbulb ban are coming from consumers, who prefer incandescent lamps. Congress, in the fiscal year 2012 appropriations bill passed in December 2011, inserted a provision preventing the administration from spending funds to enforce the lightbulb ban, but it is still in place. As this book goes to print, consumers who want to stock up have a few months left to buy 75-watt bulbs, and just over a year to buy 60- and 40-watt bulbs.

Without traditional lightbulbs, Americans will be left to choose between three different types of new bulbs: CFLs, halogens, and light-emitting diodes, or LEDs. All three cost more than but are also said to last longer than incandescent bulbs. As with hybrid cars, they carry a higher purchase cost but supposedly lower operating costs over time.

But CFLs, LEDs, and halogen bulbs all have disadvantages. The new bulbs are expensive. Today a conventional 75-watt bulb costs 60 cents on Amazon.com, compared with $2.50 for a CFL and $9.75 for a halogen. The LED is not yet available in a 100-watt size. The energy-efficient versions are supposed to last longer, but many people prefer not to pay the greater upfront cost. Or, if they have rooms they use infrequently, they do not see the point of put-ting in long-life bulbs.

Plus, many people do not like the light cast by fluorescents, even though these bulbs are the least expensive of the alternative energy set. Some say the bulbs cast a yellow or blue tint, flicker, hum, or cause headaches. Furthermore, CFLs present disposal problems because they contain mercury. The EPA gives detailed instructions for disposing of the new bulbs.[42]

If a CFL breaks, the EPA instructions include leaving a room for fifteen minutes and turning off forced air heating and cooling. Then, bulb remnants should not be swept up with a broom or vac-uum cleaner but rather carefully scooped up using stiff paper and placed in a canning jar or sealed plastic bag. Afterwards, sticky tape or wet wipes should be used to collect the last fragments. This is not something most people want to do when they drop a lightbulb. They just want to sweep it up, throw it in the trash, and get on with their day.

Even when a CFL bulb reaches the end of its natural life, it cannot be placed in the garbage, according to the EPA. It must be turned in at special recycling centers. The EPA has links to recy-cling centers on its website.

The government requires companies to reduce mercury emis-sions with its new Mercury and Air Toxic Standards for Power Plants rule, discussed above, but it has no qualms about bringing mercury into people's homes with the incandescent lightbulb ban.

Consumers vote with their wallets, and according to the National Electrical Manufacturers Association, by the fourth quarter of 2011 only 17 percent of bulbs sold were CFLs, while the rest were incandescents.[43] Consumers should be free to choose the lightbulbs they prefer. If Congress believes that consumers should conserve energy, it can impose a tax on the model bulbs whose use it would discourage, or on electricity in general.

The argument that consumers are irrational, that they do not want to pay more upfront for a better, longer-lasting, product, does not square with reality. Consumers buy many expensive goods, ranging from luxury cars to the latest smart phone. When consumers want something, they buy it. And they do not seem to want fluorescent bulbs.

To push the matter further, the Department of Energy (DOE) created the "L Prize" a $10 million award for creating a green, affordable lightbulb. The winner was Philips, with a bulb for retail sale at $50.[44] If consumers did not want green bulbs before, there is no logic in expecting they will pay an even higher price for them now.

ETHANOL: AN UNREALISTIC MANDATE

For over thirty years, taxpayers funded ethanol subsidies, paid to corn growers and ethanol producers, amounting to nearly $6 billion last year.[45] On December 31, 2011, the 45 cents per gallon subsidy expired, along with the 54-cent tariff for imported ethanol. What now keeps the ethanol industry afloat is the mandate for the American economy to consume ethanol.[46]

Ethanol, as most motorists have learned, is a corn-based additive that stretches gasoline, so reduces gasoline needed to operate vehicles. But the gasoline-ethanol blend, currently 10 percent ethanol, lowers vehicles' gas mileage, leaving motorists with higher fuel bills.

In addition, federal ethanol subsidies are responsible for avoidable greenhouse gas emissions and for diverting corn from the food pipeline. The diversion raises corn, meat, and other food prices in the United States and all over the world.

Congress, in the 2007 Energy Independence and Security Act, agreed to require the use of 15 billion gallons of ethanol or other renewable fuels in 2012, up from 5 billion in 2007, with quantities gradually increasing to 36 billion gallons in 2022.[47]

Still, America is having difficulty absorbing the required 15 billion gallons of ethanol. In 2022 the total of 36 billion gallons is supposed to be totally derived from uneconomic sources. Sixteen billion is supposed to be derived from cellulosic ethanol, and the remainder from corn. These substances are not produced in commercial quantities. Since mandating the impossible is impossible, the EPA was given the authority to relax the requirements. The actual volume of cellulosic biofuel required by EPA for 2012 is 8.65 million gallons, instead of 500 million gallons, as set out in the 2007 act.[48] However, producers will be forced to pay $6.8 million in fines for failing to meet the mandate's requirement in 2011.[49]

To make matters worse, as the EPA wrote,

The Renewable Fuels Standard (RFS) program requires producers or importers of renewable fuel to generate fuel credits, known as Renewable Identification Numbers (RINs), in proportion to the amount and type of renewable fuel they produced or imported. The RFS Program also requires that non-renewable fuel refiners and importers, known as obligated parties, and renewable fuel exporters obtain valid RINs and retire those RINs each year by submitting them to the EPA.[50]

While the EPA indicates at least two companies have been creating fraudulent RINS (Clean Green Fuels and Absolute Fuels) it states in its question-and-answer section that "The Renewable Fuel Standard (RFS) regulations are clear that invalid RINs may not be used for compliance. The EPA does not certify or otherwise validate RINs. In providing regulated parties with the flexibility of purchasing RINs to meet RFS requirements, the EPA stated that the buyer must beware."

Even without the complication of fraud, complying with the 2012 mandate is difficult. Ethanol is costly to ship, because it separates from gasoline in the presence of water. So, unlike gasoline, blends of ethanol and gasoline that motorists put in cars cannot be transported through pipelines. Instead, ethanol is shipped by rail and mixed with gasoline near the point of distribution. With high gasoline prices, motorists are driving less and purchasing more fuel-efficient cars, reducing gasoline-and ethanol-consumption.

The EPA's solution? Force more ethanol consumption, by allowing ethanol levels in gasoline to rise from 10 percent to 15 percent for cars from model years 2001 onward. Since higher ethanol blends are harmful to older car engines—some believe to newer engines also—gas stations would have to operate different pumps for the 10 percent and 15 percent blends. And if a motorist put the 15 percent blend in an older car by mistake—an accident that would likely occur frequently—the engine would be damaged.

Ethanol was not supposed to be harmful. In the 1990s, when Congress passed legislation mandating the use of oxygenated fuels, using ethanol for energy was going to be win-win. The United States can grow so much corn, the argument went, that the country could divert some for gasoline and thus reduce tailpipe carbon emissions and become less dependent on foreign oil producers.

Alas, in the real world, unintended consequences arrive all too often.

Consider the link between ethanol and greenhouse gas emissions. Many scientists now believe that the production of ethanol causes more harmful emissions than it prevents. Other research has shown that substantially increasing our use of ethanol is not cost-effective, because the United States has neither the infrastructure nor the vehicles to use it efficiently.

The more ethanol we produce, the more greenhouse gases are generated in that production. This occurs because rising corn prices encourage farmers all over the world to transform their land from forests and fallow fields to corn, thereby losing trees and shrubs that capture airborne carbon dioxide.

A BETTER ALTERNATIVE

What is needed is a bill such as the Regulatory Accountability Act of 2011, sponsored by House Judiciary Committee Chairman Lamar Smith of Texas and Ohio Republican Senator Rob Portman. The bill would in most cases require an analysis of the costs and the benefits, which would have saved Americans billions of dollars.

The bill seeks to check agencies such as the EPA. The House bill, cosponsored by Democratic Representative Collin Peterson of Minnesota, passed with a 253–167 vote in December 2011 and is waiting for passage in the Senate.

The bill would provide greater transparency and cost-benefit scrutiny to the most expensive rules and would generally require the least burdensome option, rather than the most expensive. In addition, it would require a more rigorous process for costly rules, including formal hearings at which substantive evidence would have to be provided.

The bill requires cost-benefit analysis to be undertaken in rulemakings (proposed rule, final rule, and judicial review) and requires high-quality data to be used in the analysis.

Following the analysis, agencies are required to select the "least costly rule considered during the rule making . . . that meets relevant statutory objectives" unless "the additional benefits of

TABLE 2-1
Electricity Generation by State, 2010

State	Coal %	Petroleum liquids %	Natural Gas %	Nuclear %	Hydro-power %	Solar %	Wind %	Biomass %	Geothermal %
AL	42.3	0.1	25.7	25.6	6.1	0.0	0.0	0.2	0.0
AK	6.5	13.8	58.9	0.0	20.6	0.0	0.2	0.0	0.0
AZ	38.9	0.1	26.6	28.0	5.9	0.0	0.1	0.1	0.0
AR	47.2	0.1	20.7	25.5	6.4	0.0	0.0	0.1	0.0
CA	0.9	0.0	49.3	17.4	18.3	0.4	3.6	2.8	7.0
CO	67.8	0.0	22.2	0.0	3.4	0.1	6.6	0.1	0.0
CT	7.9	1.2	34.2	50.8	1.3	0.0	0.0	2.3	0.0
DE	45.7	1.0	51.0	0.0	0.0	0.0	0.0	2.3	0.0
DC	0.0	100.0	0.0	0.0	0.0	0.0	0.0	0.0	0.0
FL	26.8	2.7	56.5	10.8	0.1	0.0	0.0	1.1	0.0
GA	54.5	0.1	17.6	25.2	2.5	0.0	0.0	0.0	0.0
HI	15.8	78.2	0.0	0.0	0.3	0.0	2.4	0.9	2.0
ID	0.0	0.0	15.6	0.0	78.8	0.0	4.2	0.6	0.8
IL	46.2	0.1	2.5	48.4	0.1	0.0	2.3	0.4	0.0
IN	92.0	0.1	4.9	0.0	0.4	0.0	2.4	0.2	0.0
IA	71.4	0.2	2.6	8.1	1.5	0.0	15.9	0.2	0.0
KS	67.1	0.1	5.8	19.7	0.0	0.0	7.1	0.0	0.0
KY	93.2	0.1	1.7	0.0	2.7	0.0	0.0	0.1	0.0

TABLE 2-1 (continued)
Electricity Generation by State

State	Coal %	Petroleum liquids %	Natural Gas %	Nuclear %	Hydro-power %	Solar %	Wind %	Biomass %	Geothermal %
LA	32.1	0.1	37.1	25.0	1.5	0.0	0.0	0.1	0.0
ME	0.5	1.4	49.9	0.0	25.4	0.0	4.1	16.7	0.0
MD	54.2	0.7	6.7	32.5	3.9	0.0	0.0	0.9	0.0
MA	20.2	0.7	58.5	14.0	2.4	0.0	0.0	3.0	0.0
MI	59.5	0.2	11.0	26.8	1.1	0.0	0.3	1.5	0.0
MN	52.2	0.1	7.8	25.8	1.2	0.0	10.0	2.4	0.0
MS	25.9	0.1	55.6	18.3	0.0	0.0	0.0	0.0	0.0
MO	81.3	0.1	5.2	9.7	1.7	0.0	1.0	0.0	0.0
MT	63.1	0.0	0.3	0.0	31.1	0.0	3.1	0.0	0.0
NE	65.2	0.1	1.2	30.9	1.3	0.0	1.2	0.1	0.0
NV	20.1	0.0	67.0	0.0	6.1	0.6	0.0	0.0	6.1
NH	13.9	0.2	24.1	49.2	6.7	0.0	0.3	5.4	0.0
NJ	10.0	0.3	37.2	50.8	0.0	0.0	0.0	1.2	0.0
NM	70.8	0.1	23.2	0.0	0.7	0.0	5.0	0.1	0.0
NY	9.7	1.0	35.6	31.0	18.6	0.0	2.0	1.4	0.0
NC	56.6	0.2	6.7	32.2	3.7	0.0	0.0	0.5	0.0
ND	81.9	0.1	0.0	0.0	5.9	0.0	12.1	0.0	0.0

OH	82.4	0.2	5.0	11.1	0.3	0.0	0.0	0.2	0.0
OK	43.5	0.0	47.4	0.0	4.1	0.0	5.2	0.0	0.0
OR	7.6	0.0	28.7	0.0	55.8	0.0	7.2	0.7	0.0
PA	48.5	0.2	14.2	34.2	1.0	0.0	0.8	0.7	0.0
RI	0.0	0.1	98.0	0.0	0.0	0.0	0.0	1.8	0.0
SC	36.7	0.1	10.6	50.8	2.3	0.0	0.0	0.4	0.0
SD	32.8	0.1	2.2	0.0	56.7	0.0	8.3	0.0	0.0
TN	52.5	0.3	2.7	34.4	10.3	0.0	0.1	0.0	0.0
TX	39.8	0.0	41.0	11.2	0.3	0.0	7.1	0.1	0.7
UT	81.0	0.1	15.1	0.0	1.9	0.0	1.1	0.1	0.0
VT	0.0	0.0	0.1	73.5	19.0	0.0	0.2	7.1	0.0
VA	35.2	1.7	23.9	37.5	2.1	0.0	0.0	1.3	0.0
WA	8.5	0.0	10.5	9.2	66.0	0.0	4.6	0.7	0.0
WV	97.4	0.2	0.2	0.0	1.1	0.0	1.2	0.0	0.0
WI	64.0	0.1	8.8	21.4	2.0	0.0	1.8	1.1	0.0
WY	90.6	0.1	0.2	0.0	2.2	0.0	6.8	0.0	0.0
U.S. Total	46.1	0.6	22.6	20.3	6.4	0.0	2.4	0.7	0.0

Source: Total Electricity Sector Generation and Its Constituent Parts by State, for the Year 2010, U.S. Energy Information Administration Power Monthly, released March 2011, http://38.96.246.204/electricity/monthly/index.cfm.

the more costly rule justify its additional costs."[51] The exception is only available for public health, safety, and welfare regulations.

The bill insures a more rigorous standard of judicial review regarding costly rules (those with an estimated effect of $1 billion or more), such as the mercury rule.

As Obama and Congress express their concern with America's slow economic growth and high level of unemployment, thousands of federal workers are quietly working around the clock in Washington, DC, to unintentionally destroy jobs. The passage of the Regulatory Accountability Act of 2011 would end the current regulatory game of Russian roulette, and bring the costs and the benefits of their actions into the open.

3

THE GREEN JOB
THEOLOGY

For several years, the public has been told that "green energy"—an expansive term that embraces renewable energy, pollution reduction, and conservation—will create jobs in America, lots of jobs, and that the federal government must subsidize green energy to create these jobs.

But no one knows what green jobs are.

Neither the federal government nor state governments can agree on the function or characteristics of a green job, although so many people seem to want them. Some green jobs, such as home insulators, have been around for decades and are being relabeled as green jobs. Other jobs, such as manufacturing electric vehicles, are green jobs, but come at the expense of ending other auto industry jobs. Jobs in clean coal production are green jobs, but jobs in coal mining are not.

Not only is there no clear federal definition of a green job, but states have their own definitions. This means that federal grants to states to create green jobs do not produce even results.

No wonder, then, that America has not succeeded in creating many green jobs. Instead, federal and state governments work hard at relabeling traditional jobs, in an attempt to convince themselves and the public that such jobs exist. Meanwhile, the cost to the taxpayer rises.

Green jobs are part of a new social ethic of employment. A job is good; a green job is better. A green job gives us virtue, a dispensation for the other shortcomings of our life. We may have moral shortcomings; we may earn little; our lives and the society around us may be disintegrating. But if we have a green job, we have a virtue beyond reproach. We can wear it on our sleeve. We print it on a bumper sticker to place on our Toyota Prius if we are wealthy enough to afford one, or on our Ford Focus if we are not.

Green jobs are not only more virtuous than other jobs. As it turns out, green jobs sometimes are eligible for government subsidies; call it a political advantage over other jobs. Yet green jobs often are not economically viable. Stated differently, green jobs may be morally superior, but they are economic disasters, a waste of taxpayer resources, and a drain on the federal budget. In school, our children are taught to aspire to green jobs and to eschew opportunities that lack green virtue. The world, so they are taught, is about to end, and only a brave new world order of obedient green job holders can save it. Never mind the economic malaise and social decay that permeate our lives. Green jobs can save us.

Our children may grow up economically insecure, but they are psychologically secure in knowing that their economic sacrifices are saving the world. They are morally superior to their parents, who grew up in a generation that never knew green jobs.

But were their parents really so different?

FROM DIRTY JOBS TO GREEN JOBS IN ONE GENERATION

It is the 1960s, and Tom, Dick, and Harry Doe are brothers. They each have jobs, but they come home dirty and tired. Tom works in a garbage dump, moving trash to a landfill. Dick works installing insulation in home attics. Harry is a janitor at a hydroelectric dam.

Their wives think that the brothers are in dirty, dead-end jobs.

Fast-forward to the 21st century. Tom, Dick, and Harry each have children, Tom Jr., Dick Jr., and Harriet. Just as did their parents, each still comes home dirty and tired. Tom Jr. works in a landfill. His state calls it soil conservation, and says that his job is a green job. Dick Jr. installs ceiling insulation. His state calls it weatherization, and designates it a green job. Harriet is a janitor at a hydroelectric plant. The state calls it waste management for renewable energy, another green job.

President George W. Bush and President Obama both have said that green jobs are the future of America. In the course of one generation, Tom Jr., Dick Jr., and Harriet have moved from dirty, dead-end jobs to green jobs and the future of America. Ain't America great?

Nations that are serious about economic growth and employment count the absolute number of new jobs added to the economy. Creating new jobs is hard work. It is a lot easier to simply redefine an existing job as a new job, a distinguished job. Let us call it a "green job." And to show we have made progress, let us say we have made lots of green jobs. Our government may not be good at creating jobs, but it excels at relabeling existing jobs as green jobs.

How many jobs has our government relabeled as green? Let us try to count them. First, let us visit the Bureau of Labor Statistics at the Department of Labor, and see what types of jobs it has labeled as green and how many it has created.

The Federal Oracle of Green Jobs

In the 1960s, America did not define a green job. The 1970s best-seller by Charles Reich, *The Greening of America*, was about cultural revolution, not green jobs.[1]

As we shall see in Chapter 4, it was only in 1999 that Alan Durning created green-collar jobs. Of course, before green jobs there were Green Berets, the Green Bay Packers, and even a comic book character called the Green Hornet. Mr. Green Jeans was the sidekick to Captain Kangaroo, but few parents would want their children to grow up to be Mr. Green Jeans.

Green has not always been a color associated with a job well done. In the 1960s, a "green" worker was a euphemism for an inexperienced and unproductive employee: "John won't be able to keep up with the assembly line at the factory. He is too green." Or perhaps after a night on the town: "Jerry looks a little green around the gills." No, in the 1960s, to call a worker "green" was not a compliment.

Today, America sees the color green as a positive value, even in workers. Children are taught that green is good, whether it is recycling, the environment, or the color of an advertisement. Some schools have green roofs, and no doubt some school districts will one day discover the virtue of painting school buses green.

But it is not just our education system that is enamored with the color green. So too is our federal government.

The Bureau of Labor Statistics of the Department of Labor (DOL) is responsible for the federal definition of green jobs under

Title X of the Energy Independence and Security Act of 2007. Few Americans have heard of the Bureau of Labor Statistics, which goes by the acronym of BLS.

In the Theology of Green Jobs, however, the BLS is an important temple and its workers the anointed oracles. For it is the BLS that bestows the government seal of approval on certain jobs to be virtuous green jobs. In contrast, other jobs languish in moral inferiority, without the benefit of government subsidies. President Obama's transportation policy is based on green jobs, with funds siphoned off from the Highway Trust Fund to mass transit. The federal government gives tax subsidies to electric vehicles, both for companies to produce them and Americans to buy them.

The BLS takes its responsibility seriously. It has defined green jobs either as "jobs in businesses that produce goods or provide services that benefit the environment or conserve natural resources," or as "jobs in which workers' duties involve making their establishment's production processes more environmentally friendly or use fewer natural resources."[2]

The BLS has compiled a list of 333 detailed industry groups that can be classified as green. Many jobs in those industries qualify as green jobs, and those who are employed in those industries can be counted as "green workers."[3]

Included are long lists of potential jobs that might qualify.[4] The BLS aggregated the number of jobs within the renewable sources industry, such as wind, biomass, geothermal, and solar. Within the private utility industry, there were a total of 65,700 jobs counted as green. Of these, 4,700 jobs were in renewable energy. Wind energy generated the most with 2,200 jobs. Biomass followed wind energy as the second highest producer of jobs with 1,100 jobs, followed by geothermal, with 600 jobs, and solar power, with 400 jobs. The manufacture of energy efficient products, and those that pertain to pollution reduction and recycling, account for 45,791 green jobs across a wide range of manufactured products.[5]

Of course, jobs in conservation, such as organic farming and land and water management, qualify as well.

In order for the firms in that industry to be considered "green," they have to meet one of five goals, namely (1) Energy from Renewable Sources, (2) Energy Efficiency, (3) Pollution Reduction and Removal, (4) Natural Resources Conservation, or (5) Environmental Compliance, Education, and Training and Public Awareness. BLS describes examples of work in the particular industries that might classify the people performing such jobs as "green workers."

In agriculture, for instance, one of the major categories of workers are the 36,611 organic farmers and growers, who are credited both with achieving natural resource conservation and creating energy from renewable sources. The biggest economic contributors from this category are likely to be producers of corn. Farmers who produce corn to eat are not counted as green workers. But when they produce corn for ethanol—and the Department of Agriculture (USDA) estimates that for the 2010/2011 marketing year 45 percent of the U.S. corn crop was used for ethanol—they have a green job.[6]

What if the farmer produces some corn to eat, and some corn to make ethanol, as countless corn producers do? By USDA definitions, the farmer has a green job. As long as the farmer sells at least some corn to ethanol producers, he is green.

In the Theology of Green Jobs, a farmer who grows hundreds of acres of corn to feed Americans or starving people around the world has not yet risen to the sufficient moral level to be labeled a green worker. But if the farmer were to sell some corn to a processor to produce ethanol to fuel a Cadillac SUV on the other side of America, the farmer is elevated to the virtuous title of green worker.

The 20,605 organic producers of fruits and vegetables count as green jobs, but owners of large farms do not. Unlike most green workers, many organic farmers are low-paid and unskilled. Information on the number workers in this area is imprecise, since farming is a seasonal workforce with highly varying annual demand. Similarly, businesses that purchase locally produced food are considered green—but not if they import food from other countries.[7]

What if a business sells some locally produced food, and some from overseas? Just as with corn producers, if even a few workers are engaged in selling local produce, then the business can count itself as virtuously green. Calculations do not include self-employed workers, however. Hence, if an employee of a green farm strikes out on his own and becomes self-employed, then a green job is lost—even if he is selling organic produce.[8]

With farming, it is possible to calculate the percentage of employment that is dedicated to ethanol or organic produce, but in other areas the numbers are not so clear. One example is "wood chips used for biomass." How many workers are employed in the timber industry to create wood chips? Wood chips are largely a byproduct of milling, and milling is not considered a green job. Yet, according to the Labor Department's definition, the 33,214 wood product-manufacturing jobs are considered green because companies sell the wood chips for biomass.

Electricity production is another gray area. The 4,665 men and women who produce renewable energy are clearly green. But what about increasing the efficiency of a power plant that uses fossil fuels, such as oil, coal, or natural gas? After all, since the introduction of electricity, its production has been getting gradually more efficient, as new technology replaces old.

Unfortunately, increasing the efficiency of traditional energy sources, such as a new gas-fired power plant, does not qualify as a green job. Similarly, those who increase the efficiency of electricity transmission networks, thus reducing the electricity lost in transmission, are not considered green either. The only exceptions are if engineers are specifically working on "smart grids," or working to reduce heat loss at refineries or chemical plants.

Those energy efficiency operations that qualify as green jobs include construction of Leadership in Energy and Environmental Design (LEED) certified structures, installation of energy efficient windows, and manufacturing and repairing Energy Star appliances. LEED certifications, granted by the U.S. Green Building Council (USGBC), a nonprofit organization,[9] and Energy Star certifications granted by the Environmental Protection Agency (EPA) and the Department of Energy (DOE),[10] are national standards.

It is puzzling to learn that the 81,950 "green" construction workers are doing a different kind of job when installing a gas-insulated window rather than a traditional pane window. According to Brett McMahon of Miller and Long Construction, installing a "Lo-Flo" toilet is a green job, but installing a regular toilet is just plumbing.[11] Workers who do such non-green jobs are just as necessary as those performing green jobs, and they would be needed even if there were no concept of a green economy.

Another puzzling class of green workers is the 241,877 employed in public transportation. Buses and trains are classified as "green," but taxis are not. However, in many cases building and operating a rail line uses more energy than does operating a bus system. And in other cases, it makes more sense to take a taxi than a bus. Further, if rail service is green, should not planes be included? The carbon emissions of planes per mile travelled are substantially less per mile of travel than those of cars.[12]

Many industries in the federal government's categories border on the absurd. Table 3-1 shows a few examples.

People who work in museums have worthy green jobs, but only in environment and science museums. There are 22,510 people with these so-called green jobs. A job in an art gallery is not a green job. The securities and commodity exchange industry counts as green—but only for emissions allowance trading. News syndicates employing 23,197 people are green—as long as they

TABLE 3-1
Industries Where Green Goods and Services Are Classified

	Title	Examples
712110	Museums	Environment and science museums
712130	Zoos and Botanical gardens	Botanical gardens, zoos
551114	Managing offices	Headquarters for environment-related companies
541810	Advertising agencies	Environment advertising for public awareness
541820	Public relations agencies	Environmental public relations for awareness
541922	Commercial photography	Environmental photography
523130	Commodity contracts dealing	Emissions allowance trading
523140	Commodity contracts brokerage	Emissions allowance trading
523210	Securities and commodity exchanges	Emissions allowance trading
515120	Television broadcasting	Environmental content for TV broadcasting
515210	Cable and other subscription programming	Environmental content for cable distribution
519110	News syndicates	Environmental news media
511130	Book publishers	Environmental or training books/manuals
511140	Directory and mailing list publishers	Industry association directories or mailing lists
511199	All other publishers	Environmental or association calendars, etc.

Source: Bureau of Labor Statistics: Industries Where Green Goods and Services Are Classified, http://www.bls.gov/green/final_green_def_8242010_pub.pdf, August 24, 2010

publish environmental media. Book publishers are green, if they issue environmental books or training manuals. Does this book qualify as an environmental book, since it is about green jobs, so does this make Encounter Books a green company? Am I, writing these words, doing a green job?

One has to wonder why the federal government has burdened itself with making these distinctions between green jobs and less virtuous jobs. Surely someone in the environmental movement could manage the classification system without imposing the cost on the federal government, just as a private organization such as Weight Watchers classifies foods by point values based on nutritional content.

The green job designations have more psychological than economic effects. These labels are unlikely to change the behavior of businesses or consumers—although they do serve an advertising and public relations function. Businesses want to be more efficient to cut their costs, and consumers do the same, seeking products to help them reduce their fuel bills.

The entire exercise of the BLS as the Oracle of Green Jobs is an attempt to justify government initiatives, while in practice doing nothing to make America more efficient. The sector that has gained jobs is the federal bureaucracy, with bureaucrats creating reams of memos and manuals. This does not help to contribute to any of the major goals of green jobs outlined by the BLS.

The Lesser Temples of Green Jobs in the States

One of the charming aspects of the Green Job Theology is that no one has a monopoly on the virtuous occupation of labeling some jobs as green and others not. BLS is the most important temple, but states also have their own bureaucracies of green job definitions: you may call them the Lesser Temples of Green Job Oracles. These lesser temples have not done any better than the federal temple at crafting green jobs definitions. Many states, including Arizona, Idaho, Maryland, and others, have drawn upon or simply adapted the BLS definition.

The DOL's Employment and Training Administration (ETA) released a Solicitation for State Labor Market Improvement (LMI)

Green Jobs Grants in July 2009, which led many states to form consortiums and study the green jobs within their states and regions.[13]

The Northern Plains and Rocky Mountain Green Job Consortium (Utah, Montana, Wyoming, South Dakota, Nebraska, and Iowa) defined a green job as "one in which an employee produces a product or service that improves energy efficiency, expands the use of renewable energy, and/or supports environmental sustainability."[14]

Another consortium, the Mid-Atlantic Regional Collaborative, consisting of Maryland, Virginia and the District of Columbia, concluded that

Green jobs are jobs involved in economic activities that help protect or restore the environment or conserve natural resources. These economic activities generally fall into the following categories: Renewable Energy; Energy Efficiency; Greenhouse Gas Reduction; Pollution Reduction and Cleanup; Recycling and Waste Reduction; Agricultural and Natural Resources Conservation; Education, Compliance, Public Awareness and Training.[15]

Louisiana and Mississippi partnered in surveying green jobs in their states in 2009. To be a green firm in Louisiana or Mississippi, employees must spend more than 50 percent of their time in one of seven green activity categories, specifically renewable energy; energy efficiency; greenhouse gas reduction; pollution prevention and cleanup; recycling and waste reduction; sustainable agriculture; natural resource conservation and coastal restoration; and education, compliance, public awareness, and training supporting the other categories.[16]

Alabama created its own definition of green jobs: those jobs related to the identifiable green activities of "increasing energy efficiency; producing renewable, clean transportation and fuels; agriculture and natural resource conservation; pollution prevention and environmental cleanup; and research, consulting and environmental support."[17]

Other states that have written their own definitions include Pennsylvania and Oregon. Pennsylvania defines green jobs as "those that promote energy efficiency, contribute to the sustainable use of resources, prevent pollution and reduce harmful emissions or clean up the environment."[18] Oregon has a similar definition.[19]

Some states have lengthy and highly specific definitions. For example, California's extensive working definition is based on the following **GREEN** acronym:

Generating and storing renewable energy
Recycling existing materials
Energy efficient product manufacturing, distribution, construction, installation, and maintenance
Education, compliance and awareness
Natural and sustainable product manufacturing

New Jersey has perhaps the most accurate definition: "It turns out that, in most cases, a green job is not an entirely new job, but a traditional job that contributes to reducing carbon emissions or pollution or otherwise benefiting the environment."[20]

Some definitions of green jobs specify that green jobs should be full-time positions that pay a living wage. Wisconsin gave out grants to companies to create green jobs, which it defined as "full-time jobs in businesses that manufacture clean energy products (for example wind, solar, biofuels, and advanced electrical storage systems) or otherwise help reduce the consumption of fossil fuels."[21]

TABLE 3-2
Time Spent on Green Work, Northern Plains and Rocky Mountain Consortium

Percent of Time Dedicated to Green Work	Number of Workers	Percent of Workers
1%–49%	65,607	41
50%–99%	35,609	22
100%	41,423	26
Not reported	19,241	12

Source: Northern Plains and Rocky Mountain Consortium. *The Northern Plains and Rocky Mountain Consortium Final Report.* 2011. http://researchingthegreeneconomy. org/docfolder/publications/The%20Northern%20Plains%20&%20Rocky%20Mountain%20Consortium%20Final%20Report.pdf

But most state definitions, following the lead of the Labor Department, do not clarify how much time must be spent on "green activities" to qualify a position as a green job. This means either that the person's entire workday is focused on such green activities, or that having one green duty bumps a job into the green category.

A report of the Northern Plains and Rocky Mountain Consortium found that only 26 percent of employees reported spending all of their efforts on green activities, and only 48 percent of employees reported spending half or more of their time on green activities. In other words, more than half of employees counted as green are not spending half their time on green activities.

Universities are examples of the easy creation of so-called green jobs. Many colleges have environmental studies programs and would therefore qualify as providing green goods and services under North American Industry Classification System (NAICS) code 611310, "colleges and universities."[22] Some have renamed their civil engineering departments "Departments of Environmental Engineering," and some ask their cafeterias to compost scraps. But these actions do not require hiring new employees.

Would the people who instituted composting be counted as new green workers because they instituted this new system as one of their duties? Would the workers who now put food scraps in a compost heap rather than a trash bag count as green workers? What about the social media coordinator who announces this practice as a victory for the environment on the college's Facebook page? The list of potential relabeled jobs goes on.

The ambiguity of the definitions of green jobs is one reason why efforts to create them have been so unsuccessful.

Taxpayers Spend Billions to Create a Few Green Jobs

Green jobs may not be different, but they do not come cheap. The American Recovery and Reinvestment Act of 2009, known as the stimulus bill, provided the DOL's Employment and Training Administration (ETA) with $500 million for grants in research and training for green jobs.

The ETA's definition of green jobs was "jobs associated with products and services that use renewable energy resources, reduce pollution, and conserve natural resources." Grants were issued through the Energy Training Partnership, Pathways Out of Poverty, and State Energy Sector Partnership.

At a hearing on November 2, 2011, before a House Oversight and Government Reform subcommittee, the inspector general of the DOE and an assistant inspector general of the Labor Department testified that funds authorized by Congress to create green jobs had not been spent or, if spent, had yielded meager results.[23]

Elliot Lewis, the DOL's assistant inspector general for audit, testified that an audit of the DOL's green jobs training program showed that only 2.5 percent of individuals originally enrolled were still employed in the jobs for which they were trained six months after the start of their job as of June 30, 2011.[24] Whether they had gone on to other jobs, green or otherwise, or become unemployed, the DOL's tracking system did not say.

Gregory Friedman, inspector general of the DOE, testified that as of late October, 45 percent of funds appropriated by the 2009 American Reinvestment and Recovery Act (the stimulus bill) for green energy had not been spent, because few "shovel-ready" projects existed.

The testimony of the two inspectors general shows why green jobs programs have not succeeded in increasing employment. Instead, government money is either wasted or unspent.

Take the green jobs training sponsored by the DOL's Employment and Training Administration (ETA). As of June 30, 2011, ETA had awarded $490 million of the $500 million provided by Congress for the program. The funds were awarded to state workforce agencies, community colleges, and nonprofits. Green jobs were defined as those "associated with products and services that use renewable energy resources, reduce pollution, and conserve natural resources." ETA money trained some workers in green jobs such as hybrid- and electric-car auto mechanics, weatherization of buildings, and solar panel installation. Other workers received job referrals, training in basic workforce readiness skills, and credentials and support services to overcome employment barriers.

Yet, almost three years after Congress passed the Recovery Act, grantees had spent only $257.3 million, about half of the funds earmarked for them. Elliot Lewis's testimony showed that as of June 30, 2011, out of 53,000 people who were served by the ETA programs, 47,000 enrolled in training. Of them, 26,000 completed training, and 8,000 found jobs.

On April 2, 2012, in response to a request from Iowa Senator Chuck Grassley, a Republican, ETA Assistant Secretary Jane Oates provided updated outcomes and expenditures data through December 31, 2011. Ms. Oates's data showed that 8,400 found new jobs by June 30, 2011, and of them, 5,400 were employed six months later on December 31, 2011.[25] In other words, of the

53,000 who had participated by the end of the second quarter of 2011, 5,400 were still employed in their new positions by the end of the fourth quarter of 2011, or 10.2 percent.

By December 31, 2011, combined expenditures of the Energy Training Partnership, Pathways Out of Poverty, and State Energy Sector Partnership totaled $257.3 million, or $47,754 per new job retained more than 6 months.

The number employed by the green jobs program is less than 8 percent of ETA's target of 69,717. Another $243 million is left unspent. The program does not appear to be on track. In its defense, Assistant Secretary Oates told the House Government Reform and Oversight Committee on June 6, 2012, "Many of these grants have ongoing training activity, with some of the programs not finishing until 2013. As the economy continues to strengthen and growth industries emerge, we have encouraged grantees to modify training plans and curricula to meet the needs of local green energy employers."[26] But this appears unlikely.

The DOE had similar problems spending its recovery funds, according to Friedman. Out of the Energy Efficiency and Conservation Block Grant Program, almost a third, or $879 million, had not been spent as of March 31, two years after enactment. In Energy Delivery and Energy Reliability, $2.6 billion, or 57 percent, was unspent.

Even more disconcerting, when the funds were spent, the work was often of poor quality. In one state audit, nine out of seventeen weatherized homes failed inspection due to substandard workmanship. One subcontractor gave preference to relatives and employees, even though the target population was elderly and handicapped residents.

Friedman said, with regard to weatherization programs, that "the main abuses were charging for work that wasn't completed or done at all, abusing priority sequence, premiums for things that could have been gotten for a lower cost."

He explained that state and local governments were unprepared to receive the grants. "Not to make light of a serious situation, but it was like attaching a lawn hose to a fire hydrant," he said. "The governments were overwhelmed."

It is not only agency inspector generals who found that stimulus funds did not create jobs. In a series of reports titled "Green Jobs Created or Saved by the Recovery Act," the Council of State Governments (CSG) came the same conclusion. During the first two quarters of stimulus (July to December 2009), and the sixth quarter (October through December of 2009), CSG concluded that the DOL programs created 1,365 jobs. This is almost identical to the assistant inspector general's report of 1,366 jobs created in the entirety of the stimulus program up until June 20, 2011.

The International Movement for Green Jobs

The green jobs movement is not confined to the United States. The Theology of Green Job virtue can be found in practically every country around the world. Curiously, most countries have their own government Oracles of Green Job definitions. The international oracles do no better than their American counterparts.

In Australia and New Zealand, green jobs are defined as "managers, professionals and technicians who work in green organisations or who have green skills and responsibilities within other organisations that may not be considered as green; [or] service, clerical, sales and semi-skilled workers who work in green organisations."[27]

In Britain, a parliamentary report states that "The transition to a low carbon economy will require a 'greening' of the whole of the economy. As such, all jobs will need to be 'greened' to some extent."[28]

A 2010 Report of the British House of Commons, titled "Green Jobs and Skills: Government Response to the Committee's Second Report," notes that

DWP's [the Department for Work and Pensions] Future Jobs Fund aims to create up to 10,000 'green jobs'. For the purposes of this fund a "green job" can be defined as one that provides a good or service that helps move the economy to lower carbon emissions and greater resource efficiency. This includes jobs in environmental sectors (including recycling, waste management, environmental consultancy and monitoring), renewable energy technologies (including wind, wave, geothermal and biomass) and emerging low-carbon sectors (such as alternative fuels, CCS, carbon finance and building technologies).[29]

However, in a flash of wisdom unseen in America, the original report, "Green Jobs and Skills," cautioned the government about the possibility of displacing other workers through green employment initiatives, saying "jobs will have to move from carbon-dependent sectors to low carbon sectors as economic growth shifts."[30] In Japan, the prime minister ordered the environmental minister to draft a Green New Deal in 2009 including funds for green jobs creation. Also, Japan's National Parks Program has a green worker program that has created green jobs.[31] It gives the following examples of operations undertaken:

- Elimination of alien species
- Repairs of mountain trails eroded by rainwater and overuse
- Burning off fields for the maintenance of grassland landscapes.

International organizations have their own sets of definitions. In a joint study, the International Labour Organization (ILO) and the United Nations Environment Programme (UNEP) define green jobs "as work in agriculture, industry, services and administration that contributes to preserving or restoring the quality of the environment."[32] A 2010 Report by the Organisation for Economic Cooperation and Development (OECD) states that "green jobs are defined as jobs that contribute to protecting the environment and reducing the harmful effects human activity has on it (mitigation), or to helping to better cope with current climate change conditions (adaptation)."[33] Eurostat, the statistical arm of the European Commission, uses the OECD's definition.

The GHK Group (Gilmore Hankey Kirke), in a study commissioned by the European Commission, concluded that, under a core definition based on organic agriculture, renewable energy, water extraction and supply, and sustainable forestry, Europe has 4.4 million green jobs. Under a broader definition, including all agriculture and forestry, fishing, mining and quarrying as well as all electricity generation and water supply and extraction, the number of green jobs is 21 million, over four times higher.[34]

Which number to believe is a matter of theology.

Conclusion

Green jobs were not a term of art, much less a fashion statement, in recent centuries. Neither Samuel Johnson nor Noah Webster would have known what they are. But in the 21st century, green jobs are all the rage. Yet many European countries are cratering on the brink of economic disaster, America's growth is slowing. In uncertain economic times, most people, in America and elsewhere, just want a job, any job. They do not care if it is green, red, white, or blue. Spending taxpayer dollars counting or creating green jobs shows the irrationality and waste associated with current government policies.

4

THE GENESIS OF
THE THEOLOGY
OF GREEN JOBS
MOVEMENT

Today, we Americans worship at the temple of green jobs, listen to the prophets of green jobs, and trust in the coming of green jobs. A generation ago, Americans would have been deeply skeptical of green jobs. Why is our generation different?

Perhaps green jobs theology was the natural result of events commonly felt by all Americans: natural disasters or economic paralysis created by dislocation of natural resources. Yet it is difficult to point to a single set of events that led to the green jobs theology.

Alternatively, perhaps the green jobs theology was the calculated construction of clever people, those who had much to gain by the green jobs theology. Who might benefit from the green jobs movement? That is an easy question to answer: union leaders and environmentalists.

Unions want more membership dues to support the costs of leadership and to pay for the pensions and healthcare of retiring members. To attract new members, unions need jobs for rank-and-file members—and energy intensive, dirty jobs, at that. Environmentalists want to preserve the environment, and they want the public at large to share that goal. For much of the 20th century, unions and environmentalists had different goals and were deeply suspicious of one another, but now they share a common cause. Green jobs have only been around for about a decade. How did this come about?

THE ORIGINS OF GREEN-COLLAR JOBS

Labor unions and environmentalists have reasons to mistrust each other, but both have politics that slant left. Both believe that more government control is better than less government, and both regard corporations with suspicion. Given their similar politics, could unions and environmentalists be friends? Could a political movement enhance both groups? The answer came not so much from politicians or even union leaders or environmentalists but rather from writers.

Sometimes valuable information comes from the dog who did not bark in the night, as in Arthur Conan Doyle's short detective story "Silver Blaze" in *The Memoirs of Sherlock Holmes.*[1] In the case of green jobs, the dog who did not bark is Charles Reich's *The Greening of America*, a bestseller in 1970 and 1971. The book says not a word about green jobs. It is about the student countercultural revolutions of the 1960s, an attack on the American Corporate State.

Reich criticizes jobs not for destroying the environment, but for their rigidity. He writes, "Jobs and occupations in the society are rigidly defined and controlled, and arranged in a hierarchy of rewards, status and authority. An individual can move from one position to another, but he gains little freedom thereby, for in each position he is subject to conditions imposed upon it . . ."[2] Students protesting in the 1960s were concerned with self-fulfillment, not with green jobs.

It was not until 1999 that the term "green-collar" was born, when author Alan Durning wrote *Green Collar Jobs* in response to the changes of the economic base in the towns of northwestern America.[3] In its initial context, the term "green collar" and "green jobs" signified the shift from traditional resource extraction industries such as timber, coal, oil, and gas, to more environment-friendly industries such as tourism and sustainable forestry.

Durning asked whether jobs and the environment must be substitutes for one another (as he believed is happening in the Northwest with the disappearance of traditional forestry work in favor of more high-technology jobs), or whether it is possible to make the two complementary. Durning saw the rise of the Information Age as creating "industries that spin wealth not by moving more timber or steel . . . but by moving electrons, or stimulating neurons, in more profitable ways." As a result of the job losses in traditional blue-collar sectors, he wrote that the dawn of the Information Age had resulted in negative consequences for the poor, creating wider income disparities than ever before.

Green Collar Jobs did not cause the modern green jobs movement, which, as will be seen, has political and social agendas not discussed in Durning's book. However, the call to "do something" about protecting the environment and creating jobs was echoed by the green movement in the early years of the 21st century.

The catchy phrase "green-collar" soon attracted attention and began to unite certain unions and environmentalists, who stand together behind the green flag in the formation of a grass-roots and political movement that aims to unite the dual causes of creating jobs for the unemployed and solving the perceived problem of climate change.

Supposedly a bridge between labor interests and environmental interests, the green jobs movement was intended both to create more jobs and to protect the environment. That is a program that both labor and environmentalists could support. But what if the green jobs movement actually lost jobs while doing little or nothing to improve the environment? As it turns out, that is exactly what has happened with the green jobs movement. And, as it also turns out, both labor and environmentalists still support the green jobs movement. In labor and environmental politics, sloganeering is sometimes more important than results.

APOLLO: A ONCE AND FUTURE DEITY SEEKING TO SPEND BILLIONS OF DOLLARS

The Greek deity Apollo was god of knowledge and predictor of the future. A real Apollo would foresee green jobs for what they are, harmful for labor and with little good for environmentalists. Supporters of green job initiatives might reasonably shun the image of Apollo. A real peek at the future cannot be good. But a particularly clever supporter of green jobs might try to buy the image of Apollo without letting Apollo even speak. Supporters could create a conflict for Apollo by using his image. And that is exactly what green jobs supporters did.

Travel from Durning's 1999 *Green Collar Jobs* to 2003, when Bracken Hendricks, an environmental protection advocate who served as a special assistant to Vice President Al Gore, was laying the foundation for the green jobs movement. He gave a speech at the Take Back America Conference sponsored by the Campaign for America's Future and the Institute for America's Future. In what was to be the seed of the green jobs movement, Hendricks announced the creation of the Apollo Alliance for Energy Independence.

The green jobs movement began through a coalition of union leaders and environmentalists, and was designed to operate for their joint benefit. In 2001, the Apollo Alliance was made up of two major lobbyists: a group of union officials and environmentalists, and the Center for American Progress (whose former vice president for energy policy, Kate Gordon, remains on the Apollo Alliance Advisory Board). Union members of the Board include Leo Gerard, president of the United Steelworkers (USW) union; and Gerald Hudson, vice president of the Service Employees International Union (SEIU). Environmentalist board members include Mindy Lubber, president of Ceres; and Carl Pope, former executive director of the Sierra Club.[4]

The Apollo Alliance "offers a bold vision to catalyze the transition to a clean energy economy."[5] Its goals are to reduce dependency on foreign oil (without using domestic oil, of course), cut carbon emissions, and create jobs in the new "green" sector. Hendricks, like Durning, raised the issue of the supposed "choice" we are forced to make between jobs and the environment. Though this 2003 speech was delivered before Apollo Alliance discovered the phrase "green jobs," it encapsulated the green mission Apollo has vigorously assumed since 2007.

In his initial 2003 speech at the Take Back America Conference, Hendricks announced that ten labor unions had endorsed the new Apollo Alliance. The Alliance was officially launched the following year by far-left activist and professor Joel Rogers and environmentalist Dan Carol, who approached United Steelworkers (USW) president Leo Gerard with the proposition to merge their respective interests. Apollo Alliance, with Hendricks as its executive director, quickly strengthened its position by receiving endorsements from 200 supporting organizations.[6]

Apollo Alliance was, until its merger with the BlueGreen Alliance, the unofficial leader of the green-collar workforce movement. Formed in 2001 in response to 9/11 by the progressive organizations Institute for America's Future and the Center on Wisconsin Strategy, it sought to launch a clean energy revolution in the United States. Shortly after its creation, the Alliance expanded into many states, promoting its "Ten-Point Plan" for reducing the country's dependence on foreign oil.

The Apollo Alliance was created to serve the interests of these charter members. Green jobs advocates are the ones who stand to gain the most from green legislation and subsidies. Can it really be possible that green-collar jobs are objectively best for America when all of the movement's major supporters are interested parties, who stand to be the sole beneficiaries of such an agenda?

Hendricks promised that the Apollo Alliance will end what he saw as a dichotomy between the environment and the economy, as well as provide "a meaningful role for government acting in the public interest."[7] Even at its outset, it is clear that the green jobs movement's motive was to hide behind a green scepter in order to garner support from the government, which will then grant subsidies to labor unions and issue mandates to get more work for the unions represented by the Apollo Alliance.

Hendricks proposed spending $300 billion over ten years in order to create 3 million "good" jobs, with the goal of increasing the country's national energy diversity, promoting high performance building, investing in domestic manufacturing, and rebuilding public infrastructure.

In 2007 Hendricks, together with Congressman Jay Inslee, a Democrat from Washington State, wrote *Apollo's Fire: Igniting America's Clean Energy Economy*,[8] in which they laid out the manifesto of the Apollo Alliance, proposing that federal policies can solve two of the country's pressing issues: global warming and unemployment. The book's title, like the name of the Apollo

Alliance coalition, reflects the authors' cry for policymakers to have the same vision and leadership to solve the green crisis as was present in the Apollo program that landed a man on the moon in 1969.

But what will be the cost to achieve this vision of "solving" the environmental and social problems? Many of the green companies Inslee and Hendricks proudly endorsed in their book as likely winners, such as SkyPower, EarthFirst, VeraSun Energy, Aventine Renewables, and Pacific Ethanol, have since gone bankrupt. Inslee and Hendricks, disappointingly, never enumerated the enormous risks of spending billions of taxpayer dollars. Achieving this vision of a green future would, as a result, cost billions of taxpayer dollars.

REGULATING HIRING TO PROMOTE GREEN JOBS

As the Apollo Alliance was achieving fame, in 2006, San Francisco State University urban studies professor Raquel Pinderhughes began to document growth of local green-collar jobs in the San Francisco area. She found more than 100 firms and institutions, covering 22 sectors, including hazardous materials cleanup, solar installation, home performance (including insulation and weatherization), public transit jobs, landscaping, and bicycle repair services.

Pinderhughes defined green-collar jobs as "blue-collar work force opportunities created by firms and organizations whose mission is to improve environmental quality."[9] Pinderhughes analyzed the trend in San Francisco Bay Area laws and programs designed to improve environmental quality. These include policies "related to zero waste, energy and water conservation, residential solar energy, whole home performance, local procurement, open space, and strengthening local food systems." At the same time, she observed an increase in the number of Bay Area residents who chose to spend money on goods and services that are beneficial for the environment.

Pinderhughes and the Apollo Alliance thought that "Wall Street [has] overwhelmed the political process" and that the "free market solutions that rule our economy today" have proven to be insufficient to solve the nation's great labor and environmental needs.[10]

They believed that government should offer rewards to firms who improved environmental quality. Plus, green-collar jobs ought to provide workers with "good" career-track jobs with secure wages and benefits. In this new world, unions would be the main suppliers of workers in green industries. Hiring requirements would be needed to ensure that green-collar jobs were available to workers with limited education and skills. Government subsidies should fund training for green jobs.

Sound familiar? Yes, because the idea was codified in the Energy Independence and Security Act of 2007.

In 2007 Pinderhughes released a comprehensive study titled *Green Collar Jobs* in which she analyzed the capacity of green businesses to provide high-quality jobs for workers who find it difficult to find jobs.[11] Much of the information and data produced in this report were provided by the not-so-disinterested Apollo Alliance.

Pinderhughes concluded that green-collar jobs are good jobs, for they provide workers with "living wages," many benefits, and opportunities for career advancement. Green-collar jobs have low barriers to entry, and they make up for workers' limited skills by providing workers with job training.

According to Pinderhughes, people with barriers to employment are interested in green-collar jobs, and green-collar employers are enthusiastic about the prospect of hiring low-income local residents for green jobs. A sense of responsibility, a good attitude, punctuality, basic communication skills, and a strong work ethic are a few qualifications green-collar employers expect.

Pinderhughes explains that providing assistance to workers with barriers to entry is imperative and would come about through job-training programs. The target population for green jobs would be eighteen- to thirty-five-year old men and women with limited education and labor market skills, who could be trained in three- to six-month programs.

Pinderhughes also argues that the need for a green-collar sector arises from the economic, educational, and racial inequalities that exist in Bay Area cities, particularly because black, Latino, and Asian residents suffer significant levels of poverty and are worse-off than white residents, primarily due to inequalities of access to high-quality education and employment opportunities. She writes:

> Providing low-income residents with access to living wage jobs is a critical step towards alleviating poverty, unemployment, and racial inequality. In this context, the deliberate cultivation of green collar jobs for men and women with barriers to employment provides city staff, staff in job training programs, and green business employers with a unique opportunity to work together to bring the benefits of green economic development to low-income residents and communities.[12]

However, Pinderhughes neglects the essential component of the changes she advocates, namely, the cost to the economy. She is not alone, for every author of green literature fails to inform the reader exactly *how* their green initiative will be paid for, and what we must give up in order to support a new, hypothetical, and unproven sector of the economy.

When reading any green literature, one encounters promises that appear too good to be true. And if results are as great as Hendricks and Pinderhughes suggest, why must the green-collar sector be imposed on society through policy? For example, as discussed in Chapter 2, Americans are forbidden to buy incandescent light bulbs. Why do green jobs not grow naturally through the rational decisions of Americans? Why is it assumed that normal Americans behave irrationally when choosing what to buy and where to work—but green jobs advocates and government officials are never irrational and never make mistakes?

THE AFL-CIO: IF YOU CAN'T BEAT THEM, JOIN THEM

In the middle of the first decade of the 21st century, America was hemorrhaging union manufacturing jobs. And the American Federation of Labor and Congress of Industrial Organizations (AFL-CIO) knew it. Then came the political movement for green jobs, likely causing even more traditional manufacturing jobs to flee. What should the AFL-CIO do? Fight against green jobs to protect traditional unionized jobs in the manufacturing sector? Or join forces with the politically attractive green jobs movement?

History shows that the AFL-CIO, confronted with a political challenge from the environmentalists, chose to switch rather than fight. If you can't beat 'em, join 'em.

By 2007 labor unions, which had traditionally been opposed to global warming legislation, no longer fought against the supposed gains to be had in a new green economy.

Leo Gerard, president of the USW and vice president of the AFL-CIO, became "outraged by melting ice caps, rising sea levels, and killer hurricanes" and committed to "corporate accountability" for all the messes their greenhouse gas belching had made.[13] Overwhelmed by the depopulated steel industry, which, according to the Labor Department has shrunk from 850,000 to 57,000 workers,[14] Gerard saw a golden opportunity with the Apollo Alliance. Apollo promised a ten-year, $300 billion program to further its cause of creating millions of jobs and cleaning the environment. Thus, linking the causes of solving global warming and rejuvenating the disappearance of middle-income jobs, Gerard jumped on board Apollo.

Gerard won the support of the AFL-CIO and other labor leaders at the Apollo Alliance.[15] Union leaders argued that Apollo would ensure that American workers would benefit from, rather than be adversely affected by, efforts to reduce greenhouse gas emissions.

What is surprising is that the merger of unions and environmentalists was not inevitable. Efforts to fight global warming have had potentially negative consequences for organized labor, whose members are facing job losses. President Obama's decision in January 2012 not to approve the Keystone XL Pipeline cost the economy many union construction jobs, and the Laborers International Union of North America (LIUNA) came out against the decision.[16] Other unions, such as the Service Employees International Union (SEIU) and International Union, United Automobile, Aerospace and Agricultural Implement Workers of America (UAW) supported the president.[17] (This will be discussed further in Chapter 10.)

The coal and auto industries are but two industries that have suffered from green legislation. Although boilermakers and sheet metal workers might appear to gain some jobs from the expansion of solar and wind energy—even though the reality is quite different—they are losing other jobs, and will likely lose many more.

Until 2006, the AFL-CIO had stayed off the global warming bandwagon, refusing to state that climate change posed any risk.[18] However, by early 2008, with the Apollo Alliance promising millions of green jobs, the AFL-CIO changed its position and began to support for "a new industrial policy, an environmental economic development policy . . ."[19] In its March 2008 Executive Council statement, the AFL-CIO made it clear that its continual support was conditional on Congress unambiguously "establishing an environmental economic development policy that . . . protects the interests of working families . . . [and protects] workers' wages and benefits. . . . "[20]

Specifically, organized labor's acceptance of the crusade against global warming was contingent on its own increased welfare from such legislation. This is why the Apollo Alliance and, as will be discussed below, the BlueGreen Alliance, have been the backbones of the green jobs movement. For it is far from inevitable that organized labor and environmentalists should see eye-to-eye on their respective agendas. This is precisely why the Apollo Alliance's green jobs movement has garnered so much strength. It unites two independent large, vocal armies by promising to cater to both—a union whose consequences reverberate across every other sector of the American economy (not least, taxpayers), diminishing the resources of those sectors in order to accommodate the green jobs activists.

GREEN JOBS AND PRESIDENTIAL POLITICS

The BlueGreen Alliance is another major player linking labor unions and environmental organizations in the green jobs movement. Launched in 2006 by the USW and the Sierra Club, the BlueGreen Alliance is an environmentalist advocacy organization operating under the banner of "Good Jobs, A Clean Environment, And a Safer World."[21]

On July 1, 2011, the BlueGreen Alliance merged with the Apollo Alliance. A press statement released on May 26, 2011 explained, "Together, the BlueGreen Alliance and the Apollo Alliance project will engage with labor, environmental, business and community leaders across the country to advance a bold vision of how to transform our energy future and, at the same time, create good jobs and rebuild our economy."[22]

However, in the 2008 presidential primaries, BlueGreen, still independent, called on the candidates to commit to reducing carbon emissions by 2 percent every year, increasing green-energy based manufacturing jobs by 2 percent, and rewriting American trade laws to advance labor and environmental standards.[23]

BlueGreen seeks to accomplish its goals through federal and state legislation. It supports the anti-trade view that the government should impose tariffs on imports.[24] Such a policy would provide a windfall for unions, but it would be disastrous for American consumers, who would see prices rise, and for some of those employed with non-union jobs. If the country's goal is to create increasing numbers of jobs, then such trade policies as sponsored by green jobs advocates would have the effect of undermining the efficiency of the American economy.

The modern green jobs movement arose during the 2008 presidential election from the alliance of unions and environmentalists that sought to persuade policymakers to impose a green mentality on the entire country.

As green jobs etched their way into the platforms and campaign promises of the presidential candidates, then-Senator Barack Obama said that green jobs were "central to . . . [his] energy plan," and called for a $150 billion investment in green-collar jobs. Candidate Hillary Rodham Clinton declared she wanted to "put money into clean-energy jobs, green-collar jobs" in order to "jump-start" the jobs in America, and termed renewable energy employment the "jobs of the future." A third Democratic candidate, former Senator John Edwards, said that he would "create 150,000 green-collar jobs a year."[25] [26]

The green jobs Kool-Aid was bipartisan. Senator John McCain, the Republican presidential candidate, called for research and development of green technology, saying it would be the "path to restore the strength of America's economy."[27]

With Obama's victory, green jobs came into their own. In February 2009 the president signed the American Recovery and Reinvestment Act, which, as mentioned in Chapter 3, provided $500 million in direct green jobs grants, with provisions to create jobs in the industries of "energy, utilities, construction, and manufacturing, as well as job training."[28] In addition, Obama devoted nearly $60 billion in indirect stimulus funds to the new green-based economy.[29]

A crack in the BlueGreen Alliance and Apollo project developed on January 20, 2012, when the Laborers Union withdrew from the Alliance due to the president's failure to approve the Keystone XL Pipeline.[30] However, most unions continued to support Obama, despite the lost job opportunities from Keystone XL.

ELEVATING GREEN JOBS TO WHITE HOUSE STATUS

To coordinate the environmental and organized labor initiatives, in March 2009 President Obama appointed environmental advocate and attorney Van Jones as special advisor for green jobs, enterprise, and innovation at the White House Council on Environmental Quality. Jones resigned six months into his tenure after it was revealed that he had been an admitted communist and that his name was listed on a 9/11-conspiracy website, and because of a recent statement in which he used a crude term in a speech to describe Republicans.[31] [32] Since Jones's departure, the "green czar" position has remained unfilled.

Named one of the "Heroes of the Environment" by *Time* Magazine in 2008, Jones has been one of the most influential and outspoken champions of green-collar jobs.[33] In 2007 he founded Green for All, a nongovernmental organization (NGO) whose mission is to "help build a green economy strong enough to lift people out of poverty."[34]

Jones's book, *The Green Collar Economy*, appeared in 2008. Jones proposed a "Green New Deal" to save the economy. The Green New Deal would be "an economic stimulus package on steroids," he wrote.[35] He argued that for too long the government has been partners with the "problem makers" (such as warmongers, polluters, and incarcerators), granting them all billions in tax breaks. Now, Jones insisted, is the time for the government to become partners with the "problem solvers," that is, the progressive organizations that he represents.

In other words, despite the government's gloriously poor record of picking winners in the past, Jones was confident that this time around the government would get it right, if it could but follow his plan. Jones tells us that the good news is found in a new, green-collar economy, "one that will create good, productive jobs while restoring the health of our planet's living systems." The "good old days" of capitalism are over, he informs us, but by adhering to his gospel "the solution for the economy is simple."[36]

As for paying for his green revolution, Jones suggested that the government should guarantee bank loans to green industries while they are "experimenting" with new methods of environmentally friendly practices, Solyndra-style. Jones wants taxpayers to subsidize and essentially bail out the new green sectors if they end up failing. Whether or not taxpayers support the Green New Deal is immaterial; Jones knows what is best for the economy, so taxpayers need only offer their purses for assistance.

It is no coincidence that Jones was "green czar" while the White House was pressuring the Department of Energy (DOE) to approve the Solyndra loan guarantee. In his book, Jones called for the institution of a federal revolving loan fund to issue low-interest or long-term loans to risky startup green companies.[37] He imagines that the government ought to proclaim "no credit, no problem" to any new company which thinks green. Both of these methods entail the government spending billions of dollars.

Even if we assume government officials are completely unbiased in their spending and have perfect knowledge, so as to only grant loans to those truly worthy and promising companies, would government funding really result in a better outcome than if entrepreneurs invested a tax break into their business, or if consumers spent the funds themselves?

Another way of funding the green crusade, according to Jones, is to require the government to attach green strings to government-subsidized programs. Recipients of subsidies would have to meet certain green standards. As Jones states, this "would have a profound and immediate effect on the overall 'greenness' of local economies."[38]

Once again, Jones seeks to put government officials on a pedestal from which they can dictate to consumers what is best for them, commanding that we all go green, or else. Helping the environment and creating jobs is indeed a noble goal, but what makes Jones's "'greenness'" somehow inherently superior to, say, an initiative to subsidize dog owners or scuba divers?

FUNDING GREEN JOBS WITH TAXPAYER DOLLARS

The origins and history of the green jobs movement are defined by the consistent proclamation by its advocates of one of the biggest economic sophistries, namely the broken window fallacy described by Frédéric Bastiat over 150 years ago.[39] Bastiat wrote that some may think that a child who throws a rock through a shop window is unknowingly doing a tremendous service for his community, for the shopkeeper now has to hire someone to fix his window, who in turn must purchase supplies, hire workers, and will spend the money he earns fixing the window on goods and service he desires.

On the surface, it seems that the shopkeeper's broken window is a blessing, for it apparently enriches countless number of workers and producers. But this overlooks that the shopkeeper was going to do something else with the money which he spent mending his window. Before the window was broken, the shopkeeper has money and a window. After the window is broken, he just has his window. He has already spent his money, so he can no longer invest it into his business by, say, hiring a new worker or retiling his floor. Society is therefore worse off than before the window was broken, by exactly the value of the window.

The situation with green jobs is precisely the same. If the government "breaks the window" of a non-green company and gives its value to a favored green company, society gains the value of the artificially created green company and the jobs that come with it, but loses the value of the company that was destroyed in order to support the green company. Society will be poorer because distribution of scarce resources by central government planners is inherently more inefficient than by the free market, in which resources are distributed by the efficient signals of prices. In a centrally planned economy, biased policymakers distribute scarce resources.[40]

True to their progressive foundation, Apollo Alliance released in 2008 *The New Apollo Program,* which called on the federal government to "invest" billions of dollars into such things as energy efficiency, renewable energy, and mass transit. It gave strategies to develop opportunities for American workers in the new clean energy economy. This strategy relied on the $800 billion "rescue" package issued by Congress in 2009. Indeed, Senate Majority Leader Harry Reid claimed,

This legislation is the first step in building a clean energy economy that creates jobs and moves us closer to solving our enormous energy and environmental challenges . . . The Apollo Alliance has been an important factor in helping us develop and execute a strategy that makes great progress on these goals and in motivating the public to support them . . . The Alliance deserves applause for its efforts to help shape and pass this bill.[41]

The New Apollo Program outlines the Alliance's intentions to "generate and invest $500 billion over the next ten years . . . to transform America into the global leader of the new green economy."[42] Despite its awe-inspiring goals, the Apollo Alliance has admittedly accomplished literally nothing of value in the two years since the stimulus package was signed into law. Among its so-called "achievements" of the year 2010 are calling for a national Transportation Manufacturing Action Plan that creates "good jobs" and increases investment in public transit and cleaner freight movement; making the economic case for federal climate and clean energy measures; and investing in domestic clean energy manufacturing.

This last achievement is the Apollo's seal of approval for the Investments for Manufacturing Progress and Clean Technology (IMPACT) Act, proposed by Senator Sherrod Brown of Ohio, that would "authorize $30 billion to establish state-level revolving loan funds to help small and medium-sized manufacturers retrain workers, retool facilities for clean energy production and become more energy efficient." In other words, the IMPACT Act would, as Van Jones would have it, allow the government to "invest" $30 billion on risky and unproven new businesses. The only merit these companies have to deserve this charity is their claim to be "green." Plain and simple, the IMPACT Act would be a case of pork barrel spending.

These so-called "achievements" of 2010 are matched only by the Apollo Alliance's self-described glorious "clean energy victories across America." These victories are, in reality, only theoretical goals and plans for the future. Apollo reports not even one single green job throughout the entire country as actually having come about yet because of its efforts. The most it has to show for itself is in Los Angeles, where "at the close of 2010, the first class of trainees graduated and are prepared to begin the big job of retrofitting 1,000 city-owned buildings." We are ever anxious to hear whether this valiant project ever came to fruition.

The future-expressing auxiliary verb "will" (as in "will create") is present in each "victory" in the nation-wide list, meaning that these so-called triumphs are, in truth, merely heartwarming hopes for the future. Over $800 billion of "rescue" and two years later Apollo cites among its achievements *not one* single green job having yet been created.[43] And that is after its December 2008 Apollo Economic Recovery Act report that predicted that in *one year* "650,000 direct jobs and 1.3 million more indirect jobs" would be created throughout the country.[44]

Even Van Jones, when asked in 2009 by *Newsweek* to point out any actual returns on the $60 billion of the stimulus devoted to green jobs, had little of substance to boast about:

> Right now I'm in Indiana, and there's a conference for weatherization workers. Usually there are about 700 people at it; today there are 3,200 people and a good chunk of them are newly trained weatherization workers, going out and cutting energy bills. I'm looking at a lot of people who are fired up and ready to go. You're also starting to see employers making different decisions because of the stimulus package. You have companies like Siemens, [which] announced a couple months ago that it's going to be building a turbine plant, hiring hundreds of workers

just because they recognize the [government's] commitment to clean energy.[45]

The "green czar" admits that $60 billion later the extent of
his success is a large turnout at a conference and that "a lot
of people . . . are fired up and ready to go." Is this the type of
success we would hope for with a $60 billion taxpayer-funded
stimulus?

Alan Durning, author of *Green Collar Jobs,* jumped on the
bandwagon of the current green jobs campaign in 2008, in an
article entitled "Climate Fairness." He argues that climate change
is "not an egalitarian menace: everyone will not suffer equally.
Perversely, those people and nations least to blame for causing
it are the most vulnerable to its impacts."[46] Durning quotes his-
torian Eduardo Galeano, who mentions the odd and humorous
(though alas, absurd) economic logic that "the division of labor
among nations is that some specialize in winning and others in
losing."[47]

Durning further writes:

This epic injustice gives the lie to the argument that stopping climate change is "just" an environmental issue.
Indeed, it makes arresting climate change as much a
social priority as an environmental one.

And it argues for climate solutions that are not only
efficient and effective but also fair. A certain amount of
climate change is already unavoidable. Inevitably, it will
punish the blameless. Because climate change takes
disproportionately from the poor, we should design our
climate solutions to help the poor disproportionately. In
other words, climate solutions should make working families and poor nations economically whole.[48]

Durning asserts that climate change directly causes greater inequality between the haves and have-nots. And though this belief is found in his 1999 book on the northwest United States economy, Durning takes it a few steps too far in this article into making this a universal rule, especially since he offers no evidence to substantiate the claim that climate change affects only the poor and not the rich. Van Jones has made this supposed direct relation between climate change and inequality the central article of his creed and the uniting point for the call to action to "solve" all social injustices by "solving" the global warming issue.

What is perhaps most disturbing in the plethora of green literature is how liberally the word "solve" is used. One green article, written by Eric de Place, audaciously informs the reader that to solve all of our economic woes, we need to "follow a simple three-step program: (1) cap carbon, (2) auction the permits, (3) rebate all the revenue on a per capita basis." And then, without the least bit of humility, proudly enlightens us with: "Problem solved."[49] The third step, de Place admits, is predicated on the "wealthiest income quintile [taking] a small hit." In other words, he wants the wallets of America's "rich" to become the playground of politicians and special interest groups trying to throw darts in a pitch-black room.

But it is not only the wallets of the rich. Such a policy would raise the costs of energy for everyone, not just the wealthy. Arguably, the wealthy would be in a better position to bear these costs than the poor would be. Is it right to support this special-interest scheme of gambling with hardworking Americans' money just because some think that it is for the communal good? What knowledge and skill does the Apollo Alliance have to run an entire economy that others lack?

In 2010 Durning wrote another article charging climate change as "penalizing people of color":

Typical African-American households, for example, have carbon footprints just 80 percent the size of their white counterparts. So African Americans have created less of the problem of a warming planet, but bear more of the burden.[50]

Underlying the green jobs campaign is the old proposition and rallying cry that the poor deserve certain entitlements. As will be shown later, the labor unions that support the Apollo Alliance will, ironically perhaps, be the net losers of such legislation and charity.

DEFENDING THE FAITH: ATTACKS ON GOVERNMENT SKEPTICS OF GREEN JOBS THEOLOGY

Green jobs theologians have little patience with skeptics, particularly those in the federal government. Consider, for example, the Congressional Budget Office (CBO), hardly a bastion of market principles. In late 2011, CBO reached the remarkable finding that President Obama's stimulus program had created millions of new jobs in the third quarter of 2011,[51] even though the American economy actually lost 8.8 million jobs in the recession, which it had yet to make up.[52] Claiming that a government program created millions of jobs when the economy had yet to gain back the millions of jobs lost would appear to be logically consistent with green jobs theology. CBO is hardly an obvious target of abuse by green jobs advocates.

But in 2010, CBO published a briefing paper that concluded that green job gains would not offset other job losses from environmental policies.[53] In green jobs theology, the CBO paper was worse than heresy. It was an attack on the foundation of the theology itself. In 2010, the green jobs apostle Durning wrote a piece titled "Rebutting CBO's Climate Policy and Jobs Paper."[54]

Rather than frontally assault the CBO, a frequent defender of government regulatory and spending programs, Durning insists that CBO has made a few minor mistakes. He goes on to claim that, "properly understood," the CBO paper should instill confidence into us that that a clean-energy path is the best option for a high-employment future. To solve what he sees as a flawed conclusion made by CBO, Durning corrects the "simplifying but false assumptions" made by the report.[55]

As if he were the great Houdini himself, Durning informs us that if we only "take away some of the assumptions above, 'slightly lower' employment surely starts to look like 'increased employment.'" What is more, Durning predicts that by following his advice the nation will return to full employment by 2050. Predicting the state of the economy in forty years and that it will take forty years to return to full employment is obviously absurd.[56]

Even if we assume Durning does possess the prophetic ability to predict employment levels in the year 2050, once again he (like all the authors of green literature) fails to inform us of the costs of his programs. Surely if all society cared about was employment levels, the government could hire unemployed Americans to dig ditches and fill them up again at $40 per hour. This scenario implies that those who are currently employed in other sectors at less than $40 per hour might be tempted to quit their jobs and join the ditch diggers.

Of course, such an implication is absurd, because bringing it about would entail the enormous cost of sacrificing every other thing of value in society except for fruitless employment. Scarce resources would be allocated to inefficient enterprises, and while everyone is starving and doing meaningless work, all we would have to show for it would be a line of well-formed ditches.

Though an exaggeration, this scenario illuminates the implications of the green-collar jobs movement. Groups such as the Apollo Alliance, the BlueGreen Alliance, and Green for All lobby want the government to take resources away from other sectors of the economy to have them distributed to themselves, regardless of the costs involved. If the government were to provide green startup jobs with billions of taxpayer dollars, and ensure loans in case they fail, then the "good jobs" of the green-collar workforce might indeed increase temporarily, just as its advocates proclaim, before failing like Solyndra.

But this supposed green success would be at the cost of billions of dollars from other sectors of the economy. Even if we assume one of our green gurus is spot-on in his tactics of masterminding the entire economy of the United States in order to solve the three issues of global warming, unemployment, and social inequality all at the same time, society as a whole would have to accept a lower standard of living on an unprecedented scale.

Furthermore, what would result is a world in which consumers and producers lose all liberty. For by advocating the attachment of green strings to funded programs, Durning, Hendricks, Jones, and their ilk are essentially making the authoritative decision that green-collar jobs are somehow innately superior to any other job. Regardless of the beliefs of the other 150 million American workers, we would be forced into accepting green as the only worthy worker color. If neither the inadequacy of any one central planner to map out an entire economy nor the waste of billions of taxpayer dollars raise suspicions about the green jobs movement, then surely the loss of our freedom in choosing occupations, businesses startups, and products to purchase should be too high a cost to bear.

PART II

GREEN THEOLOGY
IN PRACTICE

5

FATALLY FLAWED GREEN STUDIES

How do advocates of government investment in green technology convince the government to play along? Green technology advocates produce so-called economic studies that turn logic on its head. These studies find that green technologies will increase economic growth and job creation.

Such studies have many flaws, including a failure to account for the economic activity displaced through investment in the new, green world; failure to account for the economic costs of higher energy prices; using multiple erroneous assumptions; falsely claiming the development of new industries; and falsely claiming higher numbers of well-paying jobs.

The Political Economy Research Institute (PERI), the Center for American Progress, Global Insight (GI), and the Center for Energy Efficiency and Renewable Technologies (CEERT)—all make the same fundamental errors.

FAILURE TO ACCOUNT FOR ECONOMIC COSTS OF HIGHER ENERGY PRICES

There is no better place to start than a report entitled "New Jobs—Cleaner Air: Employment Effects under Planned Changes to the EPA's Air Pollution Rules,"[1] released in February 2011, by James Heintz of the Political Economy Research Institute (PERI) and Ceres, a national coalition of investors and environmental groups, under contract to the Environmental Protection Agency (EPA).

Given that it was an EPA-funded report, its conclusion—that new EPA clean-air standards will result in millions of new jobs created through investments in pollution controls, as well as new plant construction replacing older, less-efficient coal plants in the country—should come as no surprise.

In response to which, one might ask: If such EPA regulations will create so many jobs, why not ban emissions altogether? That might create even more jobs.

Environmental regulations that favor one sector over another are examples of government showing favoritism and picking winners. Even if the government were able to allocate resources most effectively (history has proven that it does not), green studies do not take seriously the opportunity costs involved in economic decisions.

PERI observes that new environmental regulations would lead to the installation of modern pollution controls and the building of new power plants, creating a wide array of skilled construction and professional jobs. Some new jobs might be created, but as Frédéric Bastiat showed in 1848, far more uncounted jobs will be lost.[2] Based on recent estimates that the power sector will invest almost $200 billion total in capital improvements over the next five years, PERI estimates that total employment associated with these investments will total 1.46 million jobs over the next five years, or about 290,000 jobs per year.[3]

These are both dramatic and misleading claims. If businesses are compelled by the government to make $200 billion in so-called "investments" to comply with environmental regulations, it stands to reason that some jobs will be directly created. But requiring $200 billion in spending on environmental "investments" means that $200 billion will not be invested in other areas, which by economic logic and necessity would have had a higher return than the government-mandated spending. (If the mandated spending had had a higher return, the government would not have needed to mandate it.)

Most green studies fail to consider the costs of prematurely retiring approximately 39,000 MW coal-fired power plants, building other plants, and instituting mandated pollution control equipment.[4] [5] This is estimated to cost about $200 billion in utility capital expenditures between 2010 and 2015.

Even in a $15 trillion economy, $200 billion in spending is substantial. To misallocate it away from productive investments to less worthwhile activities is an enormous loss to the economy. Nowhere does PERI account for these overwhelming losses.

Moreover, PERI does not address the enormous harm to the American economy from higher electricity prices, due to added costs of environmental regulations. Someone must pay the $200 billion, and that someone is the consumer of electricity. As noted in Chapter 1, higher energy and electricity prices have a predictable downward effect on economic activity.

PERI goes further, claiming that it knows exactly where these so-called "investment" benefits will accrue. According to PERI, states that will see the biggest job gains from this construction activity include Virginia, Tennessee, Illinois, North Carolina, and Indiana.[6] These happen to be states with substantial coal-fired electricity production today.

PERI uses a simple, static multiplier predicting the number of jobs created through EPA regulations. If an investment of $200 billion creates about 1.5 million jobs, then an investment of $400 billion would naturally create 3 million jobs, and so on, *ad infinitum.* PERI does not account for the cost of regulation and the destruction of other sectors of the economy, especially energy-intensive industries that will move oversees as a result of the higher production costs that follow from regulation.

The "multipliers" used by PERI's model fail to take into account the changes in the economy caused by higher energy prices. They ignore the effects of higher electricity costs on the return on capital investment and willingness to invest. They ignore losses to consumers, who must use less energy as a result of higher prices, and who will have less to spend on other goods and services. Finally, they completely ignore the costs involved in transferring resources from one industry to another.

PERI considers only one set of assumptions characterized by uncertain factors, such as natural gas prices, performance of capacity markets, and discretionary EPA actions. Therefore, without taking into account alternative assumptions that would lead to different conclusions, it is impossible to get an accurate sense of the prospect of sufficient energy or its costs.

USE OF MISLEADING ASSUMPTIONS

Green initiatives are often supported by studies that claim to have an economic foundation. But these studies are littered with flaws, in addition to those discussed above.

PERI, for example, assumes that its green initiatives would eliminate all labor shortages. That is a breathtaking assumption, one that would solve many of the economic problems of the world. However, if reducing the unemployment rate were so easy, it should have happened by now. PERI does not appear to appreciate that there will always be a certain level of unemployment as workers transition between jobs and move in and out of the labor force. It is irresponsible for green reports to assume every unemployed worker to be perfectly skilled and capable.

PERI supports the 19th-century English Luddite fallacy of maximizing jobs by praising new pollution control industries because they will be characterized by employing more workers per dollar of output. However, such low labor productivity is inefficient and slows down economic growth. Real economic growth is epitomized by the exact opposite, namely more output per worker. Lowering average labor productivity results in high costs for both employer and consumer, not to mention lower real wages and fewer benefits for employees.

Green studies never compare multiple ways to "stimulate" the economy. An economy contains thousands of industries, and it seems irresponsible and misleading that green studies should neglect analyzing the many sectors to calculate the most productive use of stimulus funds. Simply insisting that "a green economic recovery is needed to bring our nation's economy back to its full capacity," as PERI does in "Green Recovery: A Program to Create Good Jobs and Start Building a Low-Carbon Economy," does not make it true.[7] "Full capacity" is not even defined in this report.

Another study, by Global Insight (GI), analyzes the current and future green jobs prospects in major U.S. cities.[8] According to the study,

The economic advantages of the Green Economy include the macroeconomic benefits of investment in new technologies, greater productivity, improvements in the U.S. balance of trade, and increased real disposable income across the nation. They also include the microeconomic benefits of lower costs of doing business and reduced household energy expenditures. These advantages are manifested in job growth, income growth, and of course, a cleaner environment.[9]

The claim that a green economy would have greater productivity is, as we have seen throughout the book, false. Imposing alternative energy requirements on businesses and households raises costs, lowers income, and substantially decreases the amount of productivity per worker. In order for real disposable income across the nation to rise due to a green economy, it would have to be the case that alternative clean energy resulted in lower costs—in which case it would not need a mandate.

The study by the macroeconomic consulting firm GI includes a listing of many "green jobs" that are not obviously green. Over half the jobs are in engineering, legal research, and consulting—not necessarily green jobs. Another 10 percent are in government administration. Many jobs are not directly associated with the generation of a single kilowatt-hour of "green" power or a single BTU of "green fuel." Such a dubious method of calculating the number of green jobs leaves much room for manipulation and exaggeration of the statistics, as we saw in Chapter 3.

The GI study also depends on very aggressive assumptions for efficiency. It assumes "a reduction of energy consumption by the current stock of residential and commercial structures by 35 percent over the next three decades. Other research has established that such a reduction is technically feasible."[10] This is unrealistic, because growing societies use more energy and more electricity, rather than less. Think of the electricity needed to power the new flat screen TVs, computers, iPods, and iPads.

In practically any other field, such as health, the military, natural resources, or education, a government-sponsored study that reached the impossible result that a government program would raise every conceivable economic indicia would be met with some skepticism if not scorn. Economic studies, after all, are not written as simple-minded fairy tales in which everyone lives happily ever after.

But in the area of green policies, the distinction between economic studies and fairy tales vanishes. Everyone does live happily after.

FALSE CLAIMS FOR DEVELOPMENT OF NEW INDUSTRIES

A consistent theme of studies supporting green regulations is the development of new, domestic green industry. Surely, one is led to believe, the development of a new American industry will have enormous economic benefits.

But recent history conclusively demonstrates that environmental regulations and mandates do not create successful new domestic industries. On the contrary, although U.S. businesses and consumers are forced to endure the costs of the imposition of such regulations and mandates, some anticipated benefits never materialize, and others are reaped by other countries.[11]

For instance, in 2010, U.S. wind turbine imports were $1.2 billion and exports were $142.1 million, and in 2010 just over half (51.2 percent) of the wind turbines installed in America were manufactured by domestic companies.[12] From 2009 to 2010, U.S. imports of wind-powered generating sets decreased by 46 percent, while exports increased by 21 percent. Still, American exports remain at less than 10 percent of global exports.[13]

In contrast, China is becoming the world's largest manufacturer of wind equipment, controlling almost half of the $45 billion global market for wind turbines. Much of this equipment is exported to America.[14] As we will discuss in Chapter 6, U.S. solar manufacturers are either going bankrupt or relocating to China because of the higher costs imposed by regulations. But PERI assumes that all equipment purchased with mandated investments, or mandated by government agencies, would carry the label "Made In America" and be produced with American raw materials.[15]

The GI study also reports that green manufacturing will create and sustain a viable domestic industry. According to the study,

> The technology of wind electricity is relatively new, but the manufacturing base for its production is very similar to past products. Every state in the country has firms and a labor force with experience making products similar to the blades, 10 gearboxes, brakes, hubs, cooling fans, couplings, drives, cases, bearings, generators, towers and sensors that make up a wind tower.[16]

Yet America imports a significant share of its new wind turbine equipment, international wind manufacturers are more numerous than American ones, and American solar industries are moving offshore. It is not obvious that new domestic technological sectors will be able to compete with established and trusted international producers. New domestic green producers, facing higher labor and energy costs, will be at a disadvantage.

FALSE CLAIMS OF ADDITIONAL WELL-PAYING JOBS

It is not enough to falsely claim that environmental regulations will lead to a new industry. EPA apologists also claim that regulations will lead to *more* jobs and to *better* jobs.

The real danger of green studies is that they proudly report that many new and better jobs will be created due to new mandates and incentives to use higher-cost technologies, but fail to relate the unseen (though very real) destruction of existing industries. This is dangerous chicanery in that not-disinterested parties can easily gain support for harmful economic policies through this deception. To be sure, there are real gains to be had through a cleaner environment. However, the error results from pretending that gains necessarily imply net gains, which they do not.

For instance, Senator Tom Carper, a Democrat from Delaware, referring to the PERI report, released the following statement on February 8, 2011,

It's clear that clean energy investments . . . will not only save thousands of lives and save billions of dollars in health care costs, but will also create almost 300,000 jobs every year. Over five years, it is estimated that clean air regulations will create as many as one and a half million good paying jobs. In Delaware alone, over 6,000 jobs are expected to be created.[17]

Even if we assume Senator Carper is correct in his predictions, he fails to consider the net effects of such environmental regulations. If 300,000 jobs are created every year at the expense of 500,000 lost jobs, it would not benefit America.

The Center for Energy Efficiency and Renewable Technologies (CEERT) discusses the economic effects of achieving California's stated goal of a 33 percent Renewable Portfolio Standard (RPS) by 2020. The authors object to the efforts of the California Public Utilities Commission to protect consumers against the higher energy prices that would result from the use of alternative energy. The CEERT study does not give any cost estimate for reaching the 33 percent goal by 2020. California did not reach its goal of 20 percent by 2010, so the goal for 2020 seems beyond its capability. It would come at the expense of every other sector of the state's economy if it does attempt to reach its 33 percent goal.

The CEERT study lacks meaningful data, reporting without any evidence that a 33 percent RPS could create up to 400,000 construction/manufacturing jobs developing renewable technologies in California. No empirical evidence is offered as to how this number was calculated.

Mindy Lubber, president of Ceres, declared in her foreword to the February 2011 study, "Americans can expect significant economic gains from implementing these new EPA rules in the form of highly-skilled, well-paying jobs that will help us clean up and modernize the nation's power plant fleet. Hundreds of thousands of new jobs will be created in each of the next five years—a welcome boost as the country recovers from a severe economic downturn."[18]

Heintz agreed. "Our research demonstrates that robust employment growth will take place alongside efforts to reduce harmful emissions," he said. "The Eastern and Midwestern states we studied will experience a net gain of jobs, once all investments in pollution control and new generation capacity are completed. We need to move beyond the outdated idea that environmental protection compromises the ongoing growth of our economy."[19]

Another flaw can be seen in PERI's calculations of direct and indirect jobs created through EPA regulations. The ambiguity of the term "green job" has already been discussed in Chapter 3. PERI classifies as green jobs steel workers who produce materials that can be used for both pollution control equipment and coal-fired boilers. In other words, a steel worker who on one day is counted among the evil pollution-causers could the next day find himself among the environment-savers. Therefore, a new "green job" is not even being created.

Simply put, the PERI report attempts to demonstrate that EPA regulations will create net new jobs. However, the PERI report, like other studies examined in this chapter, offers insufficient proof due to faulty models and questionable premises. Underlying such arguments is the myth that the government can regulate the economy to success rather than to disaster and generate higher employment by increasing the cost of technology.

Another perspective comes from Harvard economists Dale Jorgenson and Peter Wilcoxen. They demonstrate that regulations issued through the Clean Air Act raised costs to households and businesses and reduced growth in labor productivity, wages, and employment. Specifically, they find that environmental regulation caused a 2.6 percent reduction in GDP in the 1980s, and a full 3 percent reduction by 1995 when the Clean Air Act Amendments were fully implemented.[20] The Act inhibited net growth because it shifted investment into less dynamic industries at the expense of successful industries, which were penalized by higher energy costs.

PERI admits that a small number of jobs in coal-fired power plants would be sacrificed in favor of green industries. This hardly reaches even the tip of the iceberg, though, when considering the net destruction brought about by new EPA regulations. Coal production and coal mining industries would also suffer. Consumers would have to pay more for electricity, lowering real income of every household in the country. And further, since scarce resources would be taken from successful industries in favor of theoretical and unproven green ones, worker productivity would decrease throughout the economy. Employers would then lower wages accordingly.

Increased electricity costs would compel energy-intensive U.S. industries to raise costs, which will diminish their market share, lead to job cuts, and ultimately become overtaken by international industries. Job losses in domestic energy companies will result, followed closely by job and profit losses in the rest of the economy because of higher energy costs. Consequently, the costs of green initiatives would be most destructively borne by millions of American consumers and workers.

Hence, we must always ask ourselves *at what cost* we are willing to achieve any economic goal. Unfortunately, all green studies conveniently leave out the question *at what cost?*. One report critical of green jobs remarks that pro-green jobs studies "are cost-benefit analyses without any cost considerations."[21] In other words, the favorable future outcomes acclaimed in green jobs studies presuppose the existence of a utopian society where costs simply do not exist.

W. David Montgomery, senior vice president of National Economic Research Associates (NERA) and former assistant director of the Congressional Budget Office (CBO), finds that taking PERI's total required expenditure on pollution control equipment and replacement generators and dividing by direct employment yields a cost of $314,000 per direct job.[22] This is certainly an extraordinarily high price to pay for one employee per year. After all, the average employer cost across all occupations, including benefits, was about $50,000 in 2010, ranging from $100,000 for management and professional occupations to $25,000 for service occupations.

Another green study asserts that green jobs will "strengthen career ladders by providing pathways for workers to move up from lower-paying to higher-paying green jobs that can be created on a geographically equitable basis throughout all regions of the country."[23] But, as we saw in Chapter 3, government efforts to create jobs have met with little success. An audit of the Department of Labors green jobs program showed that only 2.5 percent of those enrolled in green jobs programs were still employed by their employer six months after their job started.[24]

GREEN ENERGY AS THE NEW SPACE RACE, RACING TO THE BOTTOM

Kate Gordon, former vice president of energy policy at the Center for American Progress and current director of advanced energy and sustainability at the Center for the Next Generation in San Francisco, has admitted that the aspired "greening" of the economy can only come about "through political leadership and progressive action."[25] She implies that private individuals and businesses have been unwilling to invest their own money in green industries, and therefore it is necessary for politicians to solve this problem by imposing it on the American people through regulation and artificial incentives. Besides being unethical, Gordon's proposition of achieving economic growth through government coercion is a myth.

Gordon has asserted that, "The global clean-tech market is expected to expand to at least $2.3 trillion by 2020, and America must compete for a piece of this pie."[26] This assumes there is $2.3 trillion lying on the table, waiting for someone to come and grab it. If so, why is the only way to achieve the green revolution through political leadership and progressive action? For if there were really so much cash lying on the table, it would hardly be necessary to rely on the government to coerce businesses and individuals to grab it.

On one hand, Gordon condemns "evil" oil corporations for their greed. On the other, she argues that these same gluttonous firms are unwilling to take advantage of an easy $2.3 trillion. She cannot have it both ways. Either she underestimates the greediness of big corporations (unlikely, judging by her affiliation's view of big business), or she exaggerates the potential of green industries (more likely.)

Gordon emphasizes the importance of innovation in strengthening the economy, hence justifies green "investing." However, by favoring strict regulations and central planning, Gordon can hardly be seen as a champion of entrepreneurial activities. The Solyndra story in Chapter 6 shows the disadvantages of government investment.

Gordon idolizes green research as being the new Space Race. Indeed, this is the source of the Apollo Alliance's name. But landing on the moon, or creating the best clean technology, is expensive. In turning a serious economic issue into a childish pursuit of pride, Gordon describes a race in which only one country can win, and every other country loses. If such were the case, it would be justifiable to exert maximum effort to win the prize.

However, the beauty of true economics lies in the fact that one does not need to finish *first* in order to win. Technology produced in one country spreads to others, as Tufts University professor Amar Bhidé has shown in *The Venturesome Economy*.[27] There is no race, only choices. Instead of admitting that America has choices and various ways to victory, green jobs proponents absurdly proclaim the only two options as being either *green* or *failure*.

For a lack of better arguments Gordon, speaking on behalf of the green movement, asserts that "everyone else is doing it so we should, too." However, as we shall see in Chapter 8, China is producing green technology, but not using it for its power generation. Instead, China relies on coal.

In some European countries, people can retire before age sixty and live off a government pension for the rest of their lives. We do not adopt that policy, even though it sounds inviting, because it is too costly—as these same European countries are finding now, with riots and downgrades from ratings agencies. Just because "someone else is doing it" does not imply that we should as well. If the green experiment causes other countries economic disaster, should we follow suit?

Gordon's failure to grasp the concept of comparative advantage can be seen when she asks, "Do we want to be the world's great clean technology consumer, while the rest of the world prospers?"[28] Maybe. If it is cheaper for America to consume clean energy than to produce it, then absolutely. Clean energy is not an end in and of itself. Clean energy is desirable because of the expectation that it will be profitable in the long run. Models to evaluate its effectiveness need to take into account its costs, as well as its benefits.

America may not be the most efficient economy in the world. We may not have the best technology. We may not have the largest green industry or create the most green jobs. But in the race to the bottom of the intellectual heap, in the tournament to develop the least intellectually defensible studies to rationalize green policies, America is likely second to none. It is a dubious distinction.

6

THE SOLYNDRA STORY

There is no better proof of the risks of green industrial policy, or the misuse of "stimulus" funds, than the case of Solyndra, the Fremont, California, solar company. It declared bankruptcy in September 2011 after receiving a total of $528 million in federal loans.

The tangled tale of Solyndra, a startup company that thought it could make solar panels that turn sunshine into electricity and sell them profitably, ably illustrates the perils of "industrial policy," a shorthand phrase for the government's deciding which new industries or startups to support with federal money or loan guarantees or tax benefits.

Both Republican and Democratic administrations have practiced industrial policy under the "green" energy rubric by supporting ventures that promised to pursue renewable, non-carbon-based energy production or energy conservation.

The authority for the Department of Energy (DOE) to issue loan guarantees for innovative, clean energy technologies, the Energy Policy Act of 2005, was passed by a Republican House and Senate and signed into law by George W. Bush. In the 2005 Act, Congress authorized the issuance of $4 billion of loan guarantees in 2007, and $47 billion in 2009 with the objective of encouraging the development of new technologies. [1] [2]

In numerous speeches, President Bush talked up the value of environmental initiatives. In the White House Rose Garden on April 16, 2008, he declared,

> I have put our nation on a path to slow, stop, and eventually reverse the growth of our greenhouse gas emissions. In 2002, I announced our first step: to reduce America's greenhouse gas intensity by 18 percent through 2012.[3]

However, for all of Bush's speeches, no DOE loan guarantees were made during his administration. The DOE wanted to make a loan to Solyndra, but career officials at the Office of Management and Budget (OMB) did not approve it, on the grounds that the project was not financially sound. One might say that in this matter, the administration was more conservative than the president.

When Barack Obama took office in January 2009, he went even further than had Bush to establish his administration's image as pro-environment. In his first address to Congress, on February 24, 2009, President Obama declared,

> To truly transform our economy, protect our security and save our planet from the ravages of climate change, we need to ultimately make clean, renewable energy the profitable kind of energy.

The Section 1705 Loan Program was created by the 2009 American Reinvestment and Recovery Act, which amended the Energy Policy Act of 2005.[4] The 2009 stimulus bill gave the DOE an additional $3.95 billion for guarantees.[5]

The Obama White House followed up by encouraging the DOE to issue loan guarantees for what the Department and the White House regarded as clean energy projects; however, these projects turned out not to be commercially viable. The loans themselves were made through the Federal Financing Bank (FFB), a bookkeeping arm of the Treasury Department, and so the money was lent at below-market interest rates.

Since September 2009, the DOE has made 38 commitments totaling $35.9 billion. Bankrupt companies, such as Solyndra, and the "gold rush" loans account for 40 percent of the funding. What of the rest? Two nuclear power projects, one for Georgia Power and the other for the French company AREVA, received a total of $10.3 billion, 29 percent of the total. Ford, Nissan, and Severstal Dearborn (a subsidiary of the Russian steel company OAO Severstal) received loans totaling $8.1 billion, another 22 percent. Tesla Motors ($465 million) was taken public by Goldman Sachs and today its stock is worth $3.8 billion, while Fisker Automotive ($529 million), struggling to produce its hot $95,000 sports car, has announced layoffs and is renegotiating the terms of its loan.[6]

Is this not all just welfare for a few well-connected corporations? The hope of finding a "worthwhile" loan thus rests on 13 companies that account for just 6 percent of the funding. But the list does not inspire hope. Three loans ($747 million) are for solar manufacturing and two ($237 million) are for biofuels. If geothermal (3 loans, $546 million) comes a cropper, we are down to the last 3.5 percent of the money.

Between 2009 and 2011, Obama made more than twenty visits to companies that touted themselves as "green." These visits amounted to political-industrial barnstorming meant to support green technology industries, encourage public interest in renewable energy, and paint the Obama presidency green.[7]

Like most elected politicians, President Obama was no doubt aware that supporters of green policies, like other Americans, attend political fund-raisers. That is what makes the story of Solyndra so much more interesting.

SOLYNDRA: A FAILURE, LIKE OTHERS

Solyndra was founded in California in May of 2005 by Christian Gronet to produce a less-expensive type of solar panels, devices to convert sunlight into electricity. Its panels consisted of forty cylinders coated with solar cells.[8] A competing technology consisted of flat panels, made of polysilicon. Polysilicon was expensive, and, according to Solyndra, the panels were more costly to install on a building's roof.

By November 2008, Solyndra had raised $450 million from investors and was applying for a loan guarantee from the DOE under the Energy Policy Act of 2005. But the loan was turned down in January 2009 in the waning days of the Bush administration, on the grounds that "there is presently not an independent market study addressing long term prospects for this company" and "there is concern regarding the scale-up of production assumed in the plan for Fab 2," a second factory.[9]

On January 13, 2009, Lachlan Seward, director of the loan program at the DOE, wrote, "After canvassing the Committee it was the unanimous decision not to engage in further discussions with Solyndra at this time."[10] Lachlan was referring to the DOE Credit Committee, which was composed of DOE officials.

When President Obama took office days later, the tone changed. In an e-mail dated March 10, 2009, a senior adviser to Steven Chu, the Secretary of Energy, wrote an unnamed official, "The solar co board approved the terms of the loan guarantee last night, setting us up for the first loan guarantee conditional commitment for the president's visit to California on the 19th." [11] As events soon revealed, March 19, 2009, was a wildly premature target date for a presidential visit. In fact, President Obama did not visit Solyndra until May 2010.

E-mails dated 2009 depict White House and DOE officials rushing to sign off on the project so that Vice President Joe Biden could appear at the Fremont plant in September 2009 to trumpet the administration's support for green jobs. There was confusion about who would go and when, as well as a palpable sense of urgency and hurry. Within the OMB—historically the most fiscally conservative agency in any administration—there was anxiety about premature planning and precedent.

On March 10, 2009, an OMB official whose name was blacked out by the administration before the e-mails were released to Congress wrote, "DOE is trying to deliver the first loan guarantee within 60 days from inauguration (the prior administration could not get it done in four years). This deal is NOT [sic] ready for prime time." [12] Another OMB official wrote on August 27, 2009, "As long as we make it crystal clear to DOE that this is only in the interest of time, and that there's no precedent set, then I'm okay with it. But we also need to make sure that they don't jam us on later deals so there isn't time to negotiate those, too." [13]

Concerns were still apparent later that summer. On August 19, 2009, an unnamed official wrote presciently, "While debt coverage is robust under stress conditions, the project cash balance goes to $62,000 in September 2011. Under the assumption that a small amount of cash is tied up in working capital, the project will face a funding shortfall. Even one day of A/R results in a negative cash balance, for example." [14]

As of August 27, 2009, the loan still had not been approved. A DOE official wrote, "Can you confirm whether there are any issues regarding a closing on Sept. 3 for a Sept. 4 VP event on Solyndra?"[15]

On August 31, 2009, an unidentified OMB official wrote to Terrell McSweeny, domestic policy adviser to Vice President Biden, saying "We have ended up in the situation of having to do rushed approvals on a couple of occasions (and we are worried about Solyndra at the end of this week.) We would prefer to have sufficient time to do our due diligence reviews and have the approval set the date for the announcement rather than the other way around." [16]

Nevertheless, the loan was approved on September 3, and Biden announced it via satellite at Solyndra's plant on September 4.

Solyndra's bankruptcy has been attributed to factors beyond its control, such as falling prices for polysilicon products and lower costs and pricing in China. But documents filed by Solyndra with the Securities and Exchange Commission (SEC) in September 2009, after Biden's visit and ahead of an initial public offering that failed in June 2010, show that the company was fully aware of all the risks. The White House released emails relating to Solyndra at the request of the House Energy and Commerce Committee.

PricewaterhouseCoopers, Solyndra's auditors, also expressed public concern about the company. Reuters reported that, "PricewaterhouseCoopers LLP said Solyndra's recurring operating losses, negative cash flows, $532.3 million stockholder deficit and other factors 'raise substantial doubt about its ability to continue as a going concern.'" The combination of its deficit, operating losses, and negative cash flow raised doubts as to its ability to survive.[17]

Solyndra itself, in its public filing (S-1) at the SEC in September 2009, dutifully offered twenty-two pages of reasons why it might fail. In case anyone missed the point, the report included a table of financial and operating data for 2006–2009, showing six different measures of gross and net losses—not one positive outcome.

On May 24, 2010, Valerie Jarrett, senior adviser to the president, forwarded a blog post by Philip Smith in Cleantech to Ron Klain, chief of staff to Vice President Biden. The report outlines the doubts of Pricewaterhouse Coopers, Solyndra's auditors, about the company. The post stated, "On a pure business analysis you have to agree with the auditors—they are not a going concern."[18] Jarrett said to Klain in an e-mail, "As you know, a Going Concern letter is not good. Thoughts?"[19]

Although Jarrett and Klain knew that Solyndra would go under, two days later, on May 26, 2010, the president visited the newly built Solyndra manufacturing plant in Fremont, California, and declared, "It is here that companies like Solyndra are leading the way toward a brighter, more prosperous future . . . We can see the positive impacts right here at Solyndra."

Why did these two loyal officials allow the president to be put in that situation? Were they careless, or responding to donor pressure?

PUTTING PRIVATE DEBT BEFORE GOVERNMENT DEBT

Fast-forward to January 2011, when Solyndra's cylindrical panels were not competitive. The price of the polysilicon used by its rivals on their flat panels, the product competing with Solyndra, had fallen from about $375 a kilogram in 2009 to around $60, making flat panels far more attractive. First Solar, a U.S. maker of flat panels, could generate solar power for 75 cents a watt, compared to $4 for Solyndra.

Still, when Solyndra came calling, the DOE insisted on throwing good money after bad, to the frustration of an unnamed OMB official. He wrote, on January 31, 2011, "*If Solyndra defaults down the road, the optics will be arguably worse later than they would be today [sic]."*[20] He added that the public might forgive one mistake, due to the complexity of dealing with innovative companies, but not two mistakes.

Events would later show that the Obama administration made a bad bet. Despite an infusion of investor funds and a loan "restructuring" in February 2011 intended to raise additional funds, Solyndra filed for bankruptcy in September 2011 in the District of Delaware U.S. Bankruptcy Court, in Wilmington.

The company had used $460 million of the federal loans by February 2011 to build a second factory near Fremont, California, even though it had excess capacity at its first plant in Fremont.[21] With Solyndra's bankruptcy, the bulk of these funds are lost to taxpayers.

By January 2011, it was clear to many that Solyndra was going to fail. Still, the DOE helped shore it up by allowing it to draw on another $68 million in government loans. In addition, the department signed off on a restructuring agreement that allowed $385 million in government loans to take a back seat to $75 million in new investors' funds. In the restructuring, the $75 million from investors became senior to all government debt except $143 million.[22]

Due to the restructuring, the remaining $385 million in government loans, first issued in 2009, have equal status as bankruptcy claims with $175 million in original investor funds, and can be recovered only after the investors get back their $75 million and the government gets back $143 million. This reduced the value of the $385 million by about a third because the government would not get back all its money—it would likely only get the $143 million.

According to Eric Meltzer, founder of Telecom Capital Corp., "To me, one of the killer points of the restructuring is that the $175 million of investor loans that was made *pari passu* with the government's $385 million is that the $175 million was not a loan to the second factory, Fab2. It was a loan to a different legal entity. It therefore has no right to be rescued at all within Fab2. Yet there it is—seeking at least partial repayment from the liquidation of Fab2. To me, this is amazing."[23] He continued, "Even if all of the various corporate entities were collapsed into one—which should not be the case—the $175 million would be behind all $528 million of government loans, not *pari passu* with $385 million of loans."

Although objections were raised from the OMB and the Department of Justice (DOJ), the DOE paid no heed. On August 16, 2011, an unnamed official wrote in an e-mail to Mary Miller, assistant secretary for financial markets at the Treasury,

The Title XVII statute and the DOE regulations both require that the guaranteed loan shall not be subordinate to any loan or other debt obligation.

The DOE regulations state that DOE shall consult with OMB and Treasury before DOE grants any "'deviation'" from the requirements of the regulations (to the extent such requirement is not specified by the statute) that would constitute a substantial change in the financial terms of the Loan Guarantee Agreement.

But I will bet a quarter that the DOE lawyers have some kind of theory on how whatever restructuring they have done and whatever they are considering doing does not violate these requirements. Can't wait to hear it.

In other words, besides Valerie Jarrett and Ron Klain, many others in government with an eye for detail knew that the Solyndra deal was illegal. Some said as much to Treasury officials. But by August 2011, the taxpayers' money was lent—and effectively gone when Solyndra declared bankruptcy. No other company wanted to buy Solyndra, so its core assets were auctioned for a mere $3.8 million, which represented less than 1 percent of the loan guaranteed by the DOE.[24]

UNCLE SAM'S SELECTIVE CRONYISM

Given Solyndra's candor and the skepticism felt at and expressed at OMB, a question of motive arises. Why did the government pour more funds into Solyndra and accept a subordinate status on the loan? Could it be because one of President Obama's campaign contributors, George Kaiser, was a major investor in Solyndra through Argonaut Private Equity? Kaiser raised between $50,000 and $100,000 in donations for the president, and donated over $50,000, split between the Democratic Senatorial Campaign Committee (DSCC) and Obama for America, according to Federal Election Commission (FEC) records.

Secretary Chu, in hearings before the House Energy and Commerce Committee on November 17, 2011, testified that there was no political influence during the application process, and that no one from the White House had ever contacted him regarding approving or restructuring the loan. He claimed he did not know which DOE official asked via e-mail whether Solyndra's deal would be closed in time for the visit of the vice president. He went as far as to deny that he had known who George Kaiser was at the time he was approving the loan.

The focus of much of the hearing was on the February 2011 subsequent loan restructuring, which made the government's initial funds subordinate to the new $75 million put up by investors. A number of committee members argued that the DOE had violated Section 1702 of the Energy Policy Act of 2005, which states "[t]he obligation shall be subject to the condition that the obligation is not subordinate to other financing." Mr. Chu claimed that his general counsel found that this section only applied to the initial loan guarantee, not any restructuring thereof.

When asked why the DOE did not consult with the DOJ (as at least one Treasury e-mail suggested), Chu replied that it was not legally necessary to consult with the DOJ unless there were a provision in the original terms of the loan subordinating taxpayer dollars. Chu admitted that it was a tough decision at the time, saying if they allowed Solyndra to go bankrupt, the government would not have been able to recover anything. Yet when committee chairman Fred Upton asked how much we would be able to recover now, the secretary replied, "Not much."

It is very possible that White House officials were working with DOE officials without Chu's knowledge. White House visitor logs, reproduced in Table 6-1, show that George Kaiser made several visits to key White House staffers before the loan guarantee for Solyndra was approved.[25] From 2009 to 2011, he made seventeen visits to the White House. Kaiser is chairman and substantial majority owner of Kaiser-Francis Oil Company, chairman and majority shareholder of BOK Financial Corporation (Bank of Oklahoma), which are both based in Tulsa. He has numerous private equity investments through his various ventures.[26] He is the founder of the George Kaiser Family Foundation, which had assets of around $4 billion at the end of 2009.[27]

On August 2, 2012, the House Energy and Commerce Committee issued a report entitled "The Solyndra Failure." It concluded that "George Kaiser, whose fortune funds the GKFF, was closely involved in financial decisions related to Solyndra, often authorizing key disbursements and restructuring proposals, as well as in Solyndra's lobbying, public relations, and government procurement strategies in Washington."

Ken Levit, executive director of the George Kaiser Family Foundation, and Tony Knowles, president of the National Energy Policy

TABLE 6-1
White House Visitor -ccess Records

Name Last	Name First	Appt Start Date	Appt End Date	Total People	Visitee Last Name	Visitee First Name	Meeting Loc	Meeting Room
Kaiser	George	3/12/09 11:00	3/12/09 23:59	3	Goolsbee	Austan	OEOB	468
Kaiser	George	3/12/09 15:00	3/12/09 23:59	3	Rouse	Pete	WH	WW
Kaiser	George	3/12/09 18:30	3/12/09 23:59	3	Higginbottom	Heather	WH	WW
Kaiser	George	3/13/09 9:00	3/13/09 23:59	3	Furman	Jason	WH	WW
Kaiser	George	5/7/09 12:00	5/7/09 23:59	5	Fenn	Sarah	OEOB	196
Kaiser	George	6/25/09 9:15	6/25/09 23:59	3	Pope	David	OEOB	472
Kaiser	George	6/25/09 17:30	6/25/09 23:59	3	Jarrett	Valerie	WH	WEST WING
Kaiser	George	6/25/09 18:00	6/25/09 23:59	2	Emanuel	Rahm	WH	WW
Kaiser	George	11/12/09 10:30	11/12/09 23:59	3	Gordon	Robert	OEOB	287
Kaiser	George	11/12/09 11:00	11/12/09 23:59	3	Pope	David	WH	WW

Kaiser	George	11/15/09 17:30	12/15/09 23:59	3	Farrell	Diana	OEOB	495
Kaiser	George	2/24/10 16:49	2/24/09 23:59	2	Ford	Kim	OEOB	237
Kaiser	George	6/25/10 11:20	6/25/10 23:59	4	Naidoff	Caitlin	WH	WEST WING
Kaiser	George	6/25/10 13:00	6/25/10 23:59	3	Emanuel	Ezekiel	OEOB	279
Kaiser	George	4/14/11 11:00	4/14/11 23:59	3	Rouse	Peter	WH	WEST WING
Kaiser	George	4/14/11 12:00	4/14/11 23:59	3	Gordon	Robert	OEOB	280
Kaiser	George	7/18/11 9:30	7/18/11 23:59	51		Potus	WH	RESIDENCE

Source: "White House Visitor Access Records," http://www.whitehouse.gov/briefing-room/disclosures/visitor-records.

Institute (NEPI), co-founded by Kaiser, also came along on several of these White House visits.[7] Mr. Levit wrote to Steven Mitchell, a Solyndra board member, on February 27, 2010, "They about had an orgasm in Biden's office when we mentioned Solyndra."[28]

Some people present at the meetings have denied that George Kaiser talked with administration officials about a loan to Solyndra, and that the talks centered on various other topics.[7] According to Knowles, "Never in any of those meetings was there any attempt by George Kaiser to discuss or promote the financial relationship between the George Kaiser Family Foundation, Solyndra, and the federal government."[7]

A week later, on March 6, 2010, Kaiser referred to one of these meetings in an e-mail to Mitchell, saying "BTW, a couple of weeks ago when Ken and I were visiting with a group of Administration folks in DC who are in charge of the Stimulus process (White House, not DOE) and Solyndra came up, every one of them responded simultaneously about their thorough knowledge of the Solyndra story, suggesting it was one of their prime poster children."[29] Several months later, on October 6, Mitchell wrote to Kaiser, "In addition, the consensus is that a meeting with the new White House Chief of Staff is the best avenue to approach the administration for support on the DOE front and for assistance in securing any type of procurement commitments from the government and the military."[30]

The episode reeks of cronyism. As Solyndra was cratering, Steve Mitchell detailed in an October 3, 2010, e-mail to George Kaiser his plan to have the Department of Defense (DOD) buy its solar panels over the next three years outside the usual procurement process. Mitchell wrote, "We are also planning to ask the DOD to execute a purchase order to buy our panels—DOD has 3X the rooftops of Wal-Mart and is the biggest consumer of electricity in the US (and wants to buy solar panels). . . . the DOD has the capacity to easily sign a 300MW three-year purchase order for our panels—this would have to be through a "carve out" that occurs outside of the traditional RFP process through GSA."[31]

So the plan was to have taxpayers funnel even more money into Solyndra through a special DOD purchase. Even though this did not happen, the idea that the DOD might bail out individual companies through purchase orders, outside the bidding process, shows the corruption of the system.

THE DEPARTMENT OF ENERGY DIGS A DEEPER HOLE

One might think the DOE would have learned a lesson from the Solyndra bankruptcy in early September 2011. Surely that would have been a good time to halt the DOE's loan guarantee program and understand why this program has become the poster child for cronyism.

Why the haste to put taxpayers at even more risk? No doubt, the administration was aware that the legal authority for the loan guarantee program was going to end in September 2011. Rather than try to understand why the program was defective, the administration, ardently committed to promoting renewable energy, rushed ahead where a more angelic government might have feared to tread.

Twelve companies received loan guarantees in September 2011, including NRG Energy for $1.2 billion, NextEra Energy Resources for a partial guarantee of $1.5 billion, and Abengoa Solar (a second loan for $1.2 billion, following a first loan for $1.4 billion in December 2010). This brought to $16 billion the sum of guarantees issued by the government under the program since 2009, according to DOE spokesman Sonia Taylor.

Some might be Solyndras.

Take 1366 Technologies, located in Lexington, Massachusetts, which received $150 million on September 8, 2011. After announcing it had raised $20 million (about half the amount it would need to build its first factory) in B round financing in October 2010, the company's plan, as stated in an article by Ucilia Wang on GigaOM that month, was to break ground on its first factory in October 2011 and start shipping silicon wafers in 2013. Additionally, 1366 would use the loan guarantee to begin construction of a second facility in 2013. As in the case of Solyndra, 1366's sales are two years in the future, so they would not have sufficient revenue to be able to repay the loans in time.

On its website, 1366 Technologies states, "The science is understood. The material is abundant. The products work. All that is left is to build the largest manufacturing industry in the history of mankind. This is what we intend to do." If that is the case, why could not 1366 Technologies attract private financing? Perhaps because its schedule was unrealistic. Presumably, the October 2011 break-ground date was pushed back because the loan was approved only in September 2011. As of November 15, 2011, neither plant had broken ground, as the details of the lease for the first commercial scale facility were still being negotiated and the location of the second would depend on the first.[32] The original timeline called for the first shipment of wafers to go out in December 2013. That might be difficult to accomplish.

It probably takes months to break ground, one year to build the plant, and then three months to commence production. Of course, there is selling, delivery, and finally collection of accounts receivable. That is bumping up against two years. The loan is interest-only for about two years. But 1366 still has to pay interest, so it will be under financial stress, creating a very Solyndra-like situation.

Although the 2007 Energy Independence and Security Act, another energy bill signed into law by President George W. Bush, mandated cellulosic ethanol consumption, no one has yet worked out how to make it in large enough quantities to make it cheap enough to succeed as a commercial source of energy. Neverthe-less, that 2007 Act of Congress mandates companies to use 250 million gallons in 2011 and 500 million in 2012, gradually increas-ing to 16 billion gallons in 2022. Setting such production targets from Washington has a whiff of Stalinist-style central planning.

The DOE apparently did not learn from the example of Range Fuels, a cellulosic ethanol plant in Soperton, Georgia. It closed in January 2011, without producing any cellulosic ethanol, after receiving $156 million in federal grants and loans in 2007 and 2008 from the Bush administration, $6 million in grants from the state of Georgia, and $100 million from private investors. In January 2012, its remaining assets fetched a paltry $5 million at auction. POET's prospects are similar.

Neither did the DOE learn from the example of Evergreen Solar, which closed its doors and moved operations to China in January of 2011 after receiving $58 million in grants from the State of Massachusetts.[33] It filed for bankruptcy in January 2012, citing lack of financing as the cause.[34]

A smaller company, Beacon Power, was the second of the DOE's 1705 loan programs projects to declare bankruptcy, on October 30, 2011. Beacon Power, an energy storage company, received a $43 million loan guarantee from the DOE on August 9, 2010. Energy storage is the business of devising ways to store for future use the energy generated by the wind and the sun.

The guarantee financed a 20-megawatt flywheel energy stor-age plant that was built in Stephentown, New York. The plant was the first of its kind, using zero emissions flywheel frequency regu-lation services to enable greater use of renewable energy sources like wind and solar in New York State.

One of the challenges of making wind and solar energy useful is storage. Flywheel technology is a way to store energy mechani-cally, so energy produced at one time can be used at another. Briefly, the flywheel is accelerated by electricity to a very high speed. The flywheel sits inside a housing shaft where the goal is to achieve motion with as little friction as possible, thus storing the energy in the motion of the flywheel. When the energy is needed the motion of the flywheel can then be used to drive a turbine, which is used to create electricity. [35]

The Stephentown plant began earning revenue only in January 2011, and achieved its full 20-megawatt capacity five months later, in June 2011. Beacon had $525,000 in revenue in the second quarter of 2011, and a loss of over $6 million from operations over the course of just three months. Revenue for 2010 totaled $896,000. Loss from operations was $22,308,000, and net loss was $22,680,000. [36]

Beacon's quarterly report filed with the SEC on June 30, 2011, showed signs of severe trouble, describing a deficit of $246 million. The company did not expect positive earnings or cash flow until it had deployed a sufficient number of plants, and it did not have the resources on hand to do this without further funding. Some of the revenues generated had to be used to pay back the loan and so could not be used for further expansion. The company estimated that another $5 million to $10 million would be needed to sustain operations.[37]

Beacon planned to raise these additional funds with sales revenue from a new plant to be built in Hazleton Township, Pennsylvania, with the help of an additional $24 million Smart Grid stimulus grant from the DOE, but it did not get the loan.

Instead, four months later Beacon filed for Chapter 11 bankruptcy, characterizing it as "a necessary and prudent step that will allow us to operate our business without interruption."[38] According to Beacon's press release, the plant had not produced enough revenues to cover operating costs.

The company reported to the SEC that at the time of the filing, $39.1 million of $39.5 million drawn from the FFB's loan was outstanding. Unlike the Solyndra case, the DOE loan is first in line to be repaid, followed by a $3.45 million loan from the Massachusetts Development Finance Agency. In February 2012 Rockland Capital bought Beacon for $30.5 million, enabling part of the loan to be repaid.[39]

Bankruptcies are not limited to American companies. In December 2011 the first publicly traded German solar company, Solon, declared bankruptcy, citing competition from low-cost Chinese imports. Other German companies, such as Q-Cells and Conergy, may also follow suit.

MIMICKING FAILED ECONOMIES

Why is the government, under pressure from voters and credit-rating agencies to reduce the budget deficit, issuing these loan guarantees at all?

One answer, we repeatedly hear, is fear of China, the new Red Scare. In the 1950s we were afraid that the Soviet Union might get ahead of us. "We will bury you," threatened Nikita Khrushchev.

Now America is throwing billions of dollars at renewable energy, electric cars, and high-speed rail, projects that are too weak to attract private funding, because we are concerned that China is getting ahead of us and stealing our jobs.

On October 3, 2011, in a TV interview with ABC, President Obama said, "what we always understood was that not every single business is going to succeed in clean energy, but if we want to compete with China, which is pouring hundreds of billions of dollars into this space, if we want to compete with other countries that are heavily subsidizing the industries of the future, we've got to make sure that our guys here in the United States of America at least have a shot."[40]

Jonathan Silver, who was executive director of the Loan Programs Office at the DOE until his resignation in October 2011, testified at a House Energy and Commerce subcommittee on

September 14, 2011 that "no country has been as aggressive as China, which last year, alone, provided more than $30 billion in credit to the country's solar manufacturers through the government-controlled China Development Bank."[41]

Surely we have descended to great depths as a nation when we have lost confidence in our own reason and instead can think of nothing better to do than mimic the actions of a commercial rival.

China is not using solar energy for its electricity production. As of 2008, 70 percent of China's energy came from coal. As we shall see in Chapter 8, wind and solar provide less than two percent of the power for China's electricity.[42] [43] China is producing solar panels and wind turbines to export to America and Europe, but it is not using these technologies because they are a more costly way to generate electricity. Rather, it is importing our coal so it can produce inexpensive energy in its power plants. Another green energy project, China's high-speed rail investment, is on hold after a high-profile accident in Wenzhou in the Zhejiang province in the summer of 2011.[44]

If we are afraid of China's growth, domestic industrial policy is not the answer. Rather, we should improve economic growth through more efficient tax and regulatory policies. The greater threat from China is that, out of fear, America will pursue government loan guarantee programs, which will slow our economy and make it less efficient. America is more likely to best China without government help. America grows when it relies on the strength of market forces, rather than when our government attempts to pick winners. Loan guarantees are not a sign of confidence in markets but the exact opposite, and make no sense in these economic times, when corporations are flush with cash.

Despite substantial government investment and industrial policy, the Soviet Union is no more, and Russia's economy is collapsing. In the 1970s and 1980s, we were worried that Japan, whose government poured money into cars and shipbuilding and high-definition TVs, would race past us. But Japan's growth has been slow for the past two decades.

Brookings Institution scholars Mark Muro and Jonathan Rothwell disagree. While they admit that the loan program has flaws, they say that opponents do not understand the nature of an important clean energy loan program.[45] Even withstanding Solyndra's bankruptcy, they predict the program will ultimately be a positive for America: "The reality is the DOE's loan guarantee program will likely result in minimal costs and large gains for taxpayers—just like many other federal lending efforts."

But the reason that these renewable energy projects need to turn to the government for loan guarantees is painfully obvious. Their prospects are weak, and private investors and lenders do not want to fund the projects. If large gains were on the horizon, private firms would be vying for the opportunity of funding the projects. China and other countries might want to invest in projects that have no business logic, but American taxpayers deserve better.

Some of the new DOE loans may actually be repaid. But, like Solyndra, some will not. The Solyndra case demonstrates that government should not try to pick industrial winners. The temptation for politics to trump sound judgment and waste millions in taxpayer money is always there.

7

GONE WITH THE WIND

In September 2011, the administration received disappointing job creation numbers from the Department of Labor (DOL). What should the administration have done? Cut taxes? Eliminate regulations? No, the administration decided to do what it does best: hold a press conference to announce that it is spending taxpayer dollars on demonstrably useless projects. Even when it is hopelessly lost, the administration knows that faithful journalists will explain to the American public that the administration is trying really hard.

Thus, the administration announced a new plan to spend an additional $43 million not on junkets to Las Vegas—President Obama does not like Las Vegas—but on wind projects. Secretary Steven Chu declared, "The U.S. has an abundant offshore wind resource that remains untapped. Through these awards, the

Department of Energy is developing the critical technology and knowledge base necessary to responsibly develop this resource, enhance our energy security, and create new clean energy jobs."[1] Not surprisingly, not a single major publication observed the obvious: President Obama could have created more jobs by spending $43 million in Las Vegas.

It seems that in the new green theology, the source of transcendental truths is not glitz of Las Vegas but the inhaled smoke of Woodstock. In *The Freewheelin' Bob Dylan* in 1963, Bob Dylan wrote the lyric, "The answer, my friend, is blowin' in the wind." Nearly fifty years later, those words are no longer merely a part of pop culture; they are statement of how the administration intends to create jobs.

Green jobs theology holds that the government can create a booming economy, revive the manufacturing sector, and provide low-cost energy all with one formula: government support for green energy. Just as it has not worked with Solyndra and solar energy, it has not worked with wind.

In America, foreign wind farm operators and/or owners scooped up nearly 40 percent of funding designated for wind turbines in the American Recovery and Reinvestment Act.[2] In 2010, U.S. wind manufacturing managed to post job losses even with stimulus funds.

Other countries, including members of the European Union and China, have been similarly unsuccessful. China exports wind turbines to America but uses little wind energy for itself. Spain, which has invested substantially in wind, has among the highest electricity costs in Europe.

WIND POWER IN AMERICA
America is still a land where the marketplace for ideas is competitive. Not everyone believes the green theology, and not everyone

takes money to support green theology. Consider, for example, the Colorado-based energy analysis company BENTEK Energy. In July 2011, BENTEK released a study entitled *The Wind Power Paradox*, which offered a new methodology to examine the environmental effects of wind power. BENTEK used actual emissions data from grid operators, in contrast to the theoretical realm of computer models and estimates utilized by previous studies.[3]

The study used data from four grid operators: Electric Reliability Council of Texas (ERCOT), Bonneville Power Administration, California Independent System Operator, and the Midwest Independent System Operator, spread throughout the major wind power centers of the country.[4] In total, these grid operators service 110 million customers.[5]

BENTEK's twofold results countered the long-held belief of the green power of wind turbines. Firstly, carbon dioxide reduction levels have been vastly misrepresented and exaggerated by groups such as the American Wind Energy Association (AWEA), which have an interest in promoting wind energy. Secondly, wind turbines are far more costly than were previously portrayed.

Due to the intermittent nature of wind power, traditional sources of power generation, such as coal and natural gas power plants, have to increase or decrease production in a short time frame to balance the power grid. BENTEK describes this "cycling" as the downfall of wind power.[6] Cycling traditional power plants decreases the efficiency of the plant and the environmental control equipment. This disproportionately increases sulfur dioxide, nitrous oxide, and carbon dioxide. The reduction in greenhouse gas emissions from the installation of wind turbines appears to be surpassed by the need to cycle in states such as Colorado and Texas, which maintain renewable energy standards.[7]

Looking at 300,000 hourly records from 2007 to 2009, the BENTEK report offers disturbing conclusions. In California, sulfur dioxide emissions were not reduced at all. Carbon reduction due to wind energy was 0.3 tons of carbon dioxide per megawatt-hour, rather than the 0.8 tons claimed by the AWEA. Bonneville witnessed worse results, just reductions of 0.1 tons of carbon dioxide per megawatt-hour. Sulfur dioxide and nitrous oxide gains were also overstated in the Midwest.

In Texas, which has more wind-generating capacity than any other state, sulfur dioxide emissions were cut by 1.2 pounds per megawatt-hour, not the 5.7 pounds claimed by the AWEA. The size of the reductions in nitrous oxide and carbon dioxide were commensurately lower, too. Texas experienced a 0.7-pound-per-megawatt-hour drop in nitrous oxide and 0.5-ton-per-megawatt-hour reduction in carbon dioxide, far below the AWEA assertion of 2.3 pounds per megawatt-hour and 0.8 tons per megawatt-hour.[8]

Although some believe that any environmental savings are positive, environmental protection must be balanced with responsible economics. Perhaps the most damning conclusion of the BENTEK study was the finding that wind energy is only a cost effective solution to reduce carbon dioxide if carbon is valued at more than $33 a ton.[9] The cap-and-trade scheme that failed to pass Congress in 2010 drew estimates of $13.70 a ton, with a maximum limit being hit at $16.50 by the end of the first phase in 2020.[10] The authors concluded that "CO_2 reductions through wind generation are either so small as to be insignificant or too expensive to be practical."[11]

My Manhattan Institute colleague Robert Bryce came to precisely the same conclusion, noting that producing 20 percent of domestic electricity from wind by 2030 would cost $850 billion, but only reduce global carbon emissions by 2 percent.[12] General Electric (GE) and its partners are investing in an Oregon wind project called Shepherds Flat that received a partial loan guarantee of $1.9 billion, yet projects creating 35 permanent jobs.[13] In Texas, he writes, although wind turbines make up 10 percent of the entire state's summer electricity generation capacity, ERCOT has only rated 8.7 percent of that wind generation capacity as dependable at peak.[14]

Even more troubling, taxpayers often subsidize the shutting down of wind farms. Numerous instances of wind farms being paid to shut down turbines when it is too windy and supply outpaces demand (for example on windy summer evenings) have been reported in Britain.[15] Bonneville Power in Portland, Oregon, decided to temporarily shut down its wind farms when it experienced an energy surplus (due to increased hydropower in the wake of spring storms) in May 2011.[16] And it is not just windy weather that makes turbines an unstable source of energy. Caribou Wind Park, near Bathurst in northern New Brunswick, Canada, was shut down for the second winter in a row in February of 2011 because of turbines freezing solid.[17]

It is not surprising that windmills are unpopular, with objections coming from everyone from farmers to owners of beach houses to Native American tribes. One Wisconsin state senator, Republican Frank Lasee, went as far as to introduce a bill to impose a moratorium on building wind projects until a study was completed responding to residents complaints about the noise pollution brought by turbines.[18] Forty anti-wind groups have joined to form a movement called Ontario Wind Resistance, citing problems such as property devaluation, and negative health effects from sleep disturbance and deprivation caused by noise.[19] In Massachusetts, the Wampanoag Indians opposed construction of wind turbines that would interfere with their rituals and disturb burial ground.[20]

Wind energy generation capacity additions in the United States have been variable and limited over the past five years. Investments in wind power began to grow in 2006, peaking in 2009, but in 2010 and 2011 the United States saw a large dip in new installed capacity. Additions to wind energy generation capacity are down from 9,922 megawatts in 2009 to 6,816 megawatts in 2011. [21] [22]

The peak in 2009 can be attributed to the American Recovery and Reinvestment Act, with investors rushing to capture as large a share of federal funds as possible. One of the largest recipients of stimulus funds was Spanish-based Iberdrola, whose subsidiaries received $975 million for wind energy grants.[23]

What is interesting is to follow where the manufacturing of the equipment took place. A wind turbine consists of four major components: the base, the tower, the nacelle, and the blades, and each of these can be manufactured in a different location. These are shown in Figure 7-1. The blades catch the wind's energy, rotating a generator that is located in the nacelle. The tower holds the electrical conduits, supports the nacelle, and offers maintenance access to the nacelle. The whole structure is supported by the base, which is made of concrete and steel.[24]

The insides of the nacelle are pictured below.

Attempting to estimate the percentage of American wind equipment that is produced domestically is challenging because the International Trade Commission (ITC) does not have independent codes to track the components of wind energy equipment, and certain components are also used in other industries.

Nevertheless, the ITC estimated that 32 percent of the domestic market, by dollar value, for generating sets, towers, and blades was imported in 2009.[25] At the same time the wind industry trade group, the AWEA, estimated the "domestic content" of wind turbines installed in the United States in 2009 to be 50 percent.[26] Clearly, there are several ways to calculate the contribution of domestic manufacturing to U.S. installed wind energy, and the range of estimates between 32 percent and 50 percent reflects this inherent ambiguity.

There are several reasons why U.S. wind equipment imports have been high. Prior to 2005, the U.S. wind industry was negli-

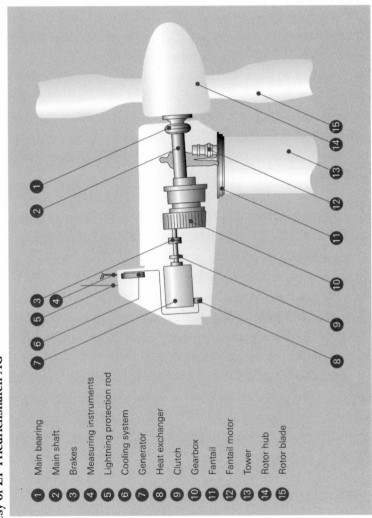

FIGURE 7-1
Image courtesy of ZF Friedrichshafen AG

1 Main bearing
2 Main shaft
3 Brakes
4 Measuring instruments
5 Lightning protection rod
6 Cooling system
7 Generator
8 Heat exchanger
9 Clutch
10 Gearbox
11 Fantail
12 Fantail motor
13 Tower
14 Rotor hub
15 Rotor blade

gible. America first developed a large position in tower manufacture, which was followed by turbine blades. Nacelle manufacture was slower to move to America, where Vestas and Siemens (second and third largest in installations in 2009) [27] opened their first nacelle plants in 2010. [28] [29] That is not to say that the high market share of imports for the major components housed in the nacelle will not still continue.

The U.S. market is also highly fractured. The major U.S. based nacelle producer, GE, has no associated turbine production. Specialized firms control tower production. In summary, production is fragmented among nacelle producers (who do not necessarily manufacture all of the parts in the nacelle), turbine producers, and tower producers.

It is likely that the perceived uncertainty in the U.S. wind energy market made manufacturers hesitant to open up plants in America. There was no certainty that the programs in 2008 and 2009 that led to such a large surge in the dollar value of imports would be continued. In fact, the current fiscal battles in Congress may well lead to cuts in renewable energy subsidies.

Even with continuing subsidies, areas near coasts may continue to see a large market share of imports, because it is less expensive to ship by water rather than rail.

Manufacturers in Europe, where the wind industry is much more mature, clearly were positioned to gain, since the stimulus favored "shovel-ready projects." There was no time to wait for a new U.S. manufacturing capacity to be developed.

THE ROLE OF CHINA

By acquiring Western technology through stringent local requirements and taking advantage of the government's low interest loans, cheap land, and labor, China has become the low-cost, mass producer of manufactured goods throughout the world. The case is no different for wind.

In the case of wind power, foreign companies that wanted to manufacture in China, or import turbines into China, had to comply with the government's changing local content requirements. After years of incremental increases in local manufacturing requirements, with knowledge and expertise slowly being ceded to the state, China made a sweeping move. On July 4, 2005, the National Development and Reform Commission issued Notice 1204, requiring wind farms to purchase equipment in which at least 70 percent of the value was Chinese.[30] Although the order was a potential violation of World Trade Organization (WTO) policies, China believed multinationals would not give up access to the Chinese marketplace, which as of 2009 became the world leader in new wind capacity per year. They were correct.

Market leaders in China, including Spain's Gamesa, which had seen its Chinese market share drop from 35 percent in 2005 to 3 percent in 2010, and Denmark's Vestas, the world's second largest turbine maker, said nothing. The Notice 1204 stood in effect until the summer of 2009, when the Chinese government rescinded the directive due to international pressure.

Unfortunately, this was too late for Gamesa, as by then wind turbines exceeded 95 percent Chinese content, and Chinese manufacturers accounted for 85 percent of the Chinese market. Chinese companies currently control almost half of the world's $45 billion global wind market. In one case, a Chinese supplier outbid Gamesa's American supplier of gearbox frames in regards to cost and quality. The company now buys from China and then ships to the American plant in Fairless Hills, Pennsylvania, for assembly.[31]

Between 2005 and 2010 China looked domestically for a market for wind turbines. Even as the industry boomed, Chinese exports to America remained low, coming seventh overall between 2006 and 2010.[32] Things are rapidly changing though. In late 2010 China began slowing the approval of new domestic wind farms. The installment of thousands of wind turbines has led to a large amount of wind generating capacity, but until they are connected to the electric grid, they cannot provide power to China.

According to Tsinghua University professor Xiangyi Dang, large-scale development of Chinese wind power faces several obstacles.[33] Some of the wind equipment used in China relies on imports and is difficult to renovate and repair. Weather poses continual obstacles. The northern wind farm in China suffers from frost and ice, while the southern wind farm faces storms, constant rainfall and alkaline corrosion.

Further, though the government provides some subsidies for wind energy, these do not make up for the high costs. The power grid construction is less developed than the wind power. There are abundant wind power sources in Inner Mongolia and the northeast areas, but the electricity market is underdeveloped. To use wind farms in these areas requires long-distance electric power transmission. Similarly, China owns a large amount of wind power storage in coastal waters, but the exploitation of offshore wind power is as yet underdeveloped.

Chinese wind manufacturing companies have not slowed their pace, however, and are looking to expand abroad. Sunival, China's largest turbine manufacturer, has recently stated its goal to export as many turbines as they sell domestically and become the largest wind power company in the world by 2015. They have already made a push into the U.S. market.[34]

By partnering with American firms, Chinese companies are attempting to take advantage of federal funds set aside for green technologies. GE, the global market leader in wind power, recently changed to a Chinese gearbox supplier. The AWEA estimates that

50 percent of a typical wind turbine used in the United States is imported.

Take for example Goldwind USA, which appears organically American, with offices in Chicago and dozens of employees. But Goldwind USA is the American arm of Chinese-owned Xinjiang Goldwater Science and Technology Company.[35]

In the company's first major project in Minnesota, Goldwind CEO Tim Rosenzweig stated that an estimated $6.2 million of the $10 million funding went to American workers and parts. Looking purely at expenditures skews the picture. The towers and blades were both manufactured domestically, but the generators, hubs, and turbine housings, parts that require a highly trained skill set and are higher paying, were all manufactured in China. These are the "technologically advanced non-exportable green jobs" the administration hopes to create.

While Xinjiang in Minnesota is a relatively small case, a larger example of Chinese dominance in the United States occurs in Texas.[36] Shenyang Power Group gained exclusive rights to supply one of the largest wind power developments in the United States in October 2009. The agreement includes the manufacture and installation of 240 2.5-megawatt wind turbines over a 36,000-acre development in West Texas.[37] The project received both tax credits and funds from the Recovery Act, adding up to millions of dollars. U.S. Renewable Energy Group, a private-equity group leading the development, detailed how only 15 percent of the 2,800 jobs created would be domestic, with the remaining 85 percent located in China.[38]

Since cost is a major factor in wind turbine installations, especially in the tight credit market, and natural gas provides a less-expensive form of energy, American companies are finding it difficult to compete. With a complete Chinese-made wind turbine running for $600,000, compared to the Western-made equivalent with Chinese parts at $800,000, fully Western manufactured and assembled turbines cannot be competitive.[39]

Although China produces wind turbine components for export, it is not using them for its own electricity generation. China surpassed America in wind power capacity in 2010.[40] But at a January 2011 meeting, officials with the National Energy Administration reported that despite its wind capacity "China still trails the U.S. in the amount of wind power connected to the grid—with only an estimated 31.1 GW grid-tied by the end of 2010."[41] This wastes a significant amount of investment and energy.

For example, at one of the Zhongdian Wind Power Company farms in Jiuquan, Gansu Province, "As many as 80 percent of the turbines were not in operation during a seemingly perfect season for wind generation ... Throughout Guazhou County ... only about a fifth of the installed wind capacity is even connected to the grid. This is the case with almost every wind base across the country."[42]

In Western Inner Mongolia and in northeastern China, abandoned wind power has cost companies millions of dollars in unrealized investment. A rough estimate indicates that one-third of China's nationwide wind power projects have difficulty accessing a grid because local grids cannot use wind-generated electricity.[43]

The less-developed north of China, where the country's most abundant wind resources are located, is having trouble absorbing the high energy demand in the country's central and southeastern regions. The rapidly growing wind farms of the northern regions have also witnessed increased restrictions on grid access in the past few years.

One reason wind power in northern China has been hindered is because of the region's long winters, which can last up to eight months. As heating is a top priority in winter, local grid companies are forced to restrict the amount of wind power in favor of the more stable coal power, so as to make sure the turbines run in full capacity. Wind companies in Inner Mongolia lost some

$77 million in revenue due to the estimated 900 million kilo-watt-hours of reduced generation in winter 2010, according to the Worldwatch Institute.[44] Ironically, China's wind resources are much stronger in winter.

In order to solve the grid storage problems, the wind power produced in the North would have to be transmitted to other regions in China. Unfortunately, the transmission lines currently in use in China's wind-abundant areas have very limited capacity and cannot support the region's rising demand for transmission.

For example, the western Inner Mongolia grid has only two outgoing transmission lines to connect to the Huabei grid. These two lines were built over twenty years ago and are able to transmit far less energy than is needed. Tremendous investment would be needed to build more transmission lines, and it is beyond the means of the small Inner Mongolia Grid company to do so. China's State Grid Corporation, while having the means to help out, lacks the incentive.

Indeed, the reasons why the relatively poor northern regions of China attract so much investment in wind farms has more to do with self-interest than making China the world leader in green energy. Local governments in these regions find that wind power projects are a source of investment, boosting gross domestic product (GDP). Regardless of whether wind farms generate electricity for the grid, new wind installations have a positive effect on local GDP. Access to the national grid is therefore immaterial to the local governments.

Likewise, wind power companies, when investing in wind farms, also have the incentive to overlook potential grid capacity problems. These large state-owned energy companies realize that the central Chinese government is hungry for impressive renewable energy statistics. Therefore, in reporting the large number of wind installations due to their efforts, companies end up as winners in the eyes of the central government. Once they produce the energy they are eager to pin any failings thereafter on the grid companies.

EUROPE

Europe has been credited with leading the way in renewable energy. Spain was especially keen on renewables, particularly wind, and other nations have looked to the "Spanish Experience" in support of their environmental charge.

President Obama, early in his presidency, remarked, "And think of what's happening in countries like Spain, Germany and Japan, where they're making real investments in renewable energy. They're surging ahead of us, poised to take the lead in these new industries."[45] But as mentioned in Chapter 2, research by Gabriel Calzada Alvarez of Universidad Rey Juan Carlos has demonstrated the disastrous results of Spain's push into the wind sector.[46]

Spain's foray into renewable energy began in 1994 when the country created a feed-in tariff scheme for production with renewable resources.[47] The law, which imposed a tariff on imported green technology, was done to protect the infant Spanish industry. As could be expected, it increased the price of energy generated by renewables.[48]

The government would pay back up to 575 percent of the cost of solar plants and up to 90 percent of the cost of wind installations. Finally, the Spanish Parliament passed legislation that reformed Spain's electricity production technology, heavily favoring renewables.[49] Wind producers received a subsidy of €73.22 (about $98 at enactment),[50] between 136 percent and 209 percent of the market price at that time.[51] These laws were part of a set of energy laws mandating that 12 percent of total energy consumption and 29 percent of consumed electricity must come from renewables by 2020.[52]

Calzada Alvarez calculated that over the fifteen-year period when Spain invested in green technology, 2.2 jobs were lost for every job created. Two-thirds of the 110,500 green jobs created were in construction and installation, 25 percent were in administration, and just 10 percent were in maintenance and operation. Since 2000, Spain has spent €571,138 on every green job, with subsidies totaling €1 million per wind industry job. Total subsidies reached €28,671 million, and the extra electricity cost paid by consumers was €7,918.54 million, slowing the economy (about $739,627, $1.3 million, $37,129, and $10,255 million).[53] In 2008, the renewable energy sector employed 0.2 percent of Spain's workforce, and wind accounted for just 10.2 percent of total energy generated.[54]

Currently, Spain has some of the highest energy prices in Europe. This is hurting companies such as Acerinox, the second largest manufacturer of stainless steel in the world, a process that requires large electricity use. Former Acerinox CEO Victoriano Muñoz led the company for thirty-seven years and was a frequent critic of Spain's push into the green economy. In 2002, he noted that the price paid for electricity by consumers had increased 10.7 percent in two years.

In 2004, Acerinox opened two new plants in the United States and South Africa, citing high energy prices as the fundamental reason for his company's move abroad. Consumers in Spain faced a 9.2 percent rise in actual cost per kilowatt-hour in 2006 when Muñoz spoke to the company's shareholders for the last time. He focused on the lack of Spanish competitiveness because of the green energy agenda and predicted the worst was yet to come because of "the continuous reduction of the hydroelectric and nuclear energy production share of the total Spanish electrical system."[55]

As of the end of the first quarter of 2012, Spain's unemployment rate climbed to 24 percent, a Eurozone record.[56] Spain's budget deficit amounted to almost 9 percent of GDP for 2011,[57] with some of this spending accountable to the massive subsidies provided to the green economy drive.[58] [59]

Spain's aggressive push into solar energy also proved fruitless. The government's promise to subsidize the high costs for twenty-five years backfired when companies rushed to invest, raising subsidy costs from $321 million in 2007 to $1.6 billion in 2008. The government's frantic attempt to curb production and decrease subsidies led to the bursting of the bubble, sending panel prices into a free fall and thousands of workers to the unemployment line.[60] In December 2010, Spain initiated a 30 percent cut in solar-powered subsidies following a decision to cap the amount of solar plants that could be installed.[61] In January 2012, Spain ended the subsidies for wind and solar.[62]

Critics may attempt to point to the Spanish experience as a unique case, a flawed framework that created perverse results (although it is similar to current administration plans to rearrange the economy). The opposite is true. Spain has been very aggressive in its promotion of the green economy, and the results are the rule, not the exception.

In Italy, a Bruno Leoni Institute study found that the same amount of capital invested to create a green job would create between 4.8 and 6.9 jobs if spent in the economy generally. As was the case in Spain, the majority of green jobs reportedly created were temporary. At least 60 percent of the 9,000 to 26,000 wind power jobs were lost when the wind turbine became operational. Corruption ran rampant as Italy's mafia claimed the subsidies. In multiple operations numerous individuals were arrested for bribery, fraud, and embezzlement, including the president of Italy's National Wind Energy Association.[63]

Germany attempted to diversify its energy needs by requiring utility companies to buy certain types of renewable produced energy at different rates. The cost of wind-powered energy was

300 percent higher than traditional energy sources. Household electricity rates increased 7.5 percent. Greenhouse gas emissions did decrease, at a price of over $80 per ton for wind power. The carbon price in the European Trading System was $19 per ton at the time. The subsidies exceeded average wages, sometimes as high as €175,000 per worker.[64]

Manuel Frondel, the division chief of the Environment and Resources branch of the economic research institution Rhein-isch-Westfälisches Institut für Wirtschaftsforschung (RWI) based in Essen, Germany, has stated, "Although Germany's promotion of renewable energies is commonly portrayed in the media as set-ting a 'shining example in providing a harvest for the world,' we would instead regard the country's experience as a cautionary tale of massively expensive environmental and energy policy that is devoid of economic and environmental benefits."[65] In May 2010, Germany cut subsidies for green economy freestanding systems (panels installed in open fields rather than on rooftops) by 15 per-cent.[66] In January 2012, Germany announced that it would phase out subsidies for solar power by 2017.[67] In a similar vein, for-mer German Environment Minister Fritz Vahrenholt stated, "For years, I disseminated the hypotheses of the [International Panel on Climate Change], and I feel duped."[68]

If green policies can be said to have succeeded anywhere, it is Denmark. Denmark has become a world leader in the design, manufacture and export of wind technology, with 18 percent of new wind installations in the United States in 2007 provided by Vestas, a Danish company.[69]

Between 2006 and 2010 Denmark represented the main source of imported wind generating sets into the United States by cash flow.[70] Almost $700 million, or three times as much as the second largest U.S. importer, India, was spent in 2010 on Dan-ish made wind-generating sets by the United States.[71] Denmark has continued to be responsible for a disproportionate share of exports in the wind power generation field, but like China its domestic use of wind has not been as successful.

The Danish think tank CEPOS (Danish Centre for Political Studies) concluded that although wind power capacity could generate roughly 19 percent of Denmark's electricity, in practice wind power contributes far less.[72] Due to the sporadic nature of wind power generation, on average over the past five years, only 9.7 percent of Denmark's electricity needs have been met by wind power.[73]

Denmark can afford to have an irregular electricity supply because its hydroelectric heavy neighbors such as Norway and Sweden can quickly make up insufficient power generation or absorb excess electricity.[74] Rather than always be undergenerated, in the last eight years West Denmark has had to export 57 percent of energy generated (45 percent for East Denmark) due to unexpected windy weather.

Along with Spain, Denmark has the highest electricity prices in the European Union.[75] The Danish government's subsidies have led to an employment shift resulting in a $270 million drop in GDP, even with Denmark's remarkable export capacity. Denmark has since moved away from wind power generation. Its state-owned power industry is no longer manufacturing wind turbines, citing no domestic market and falling export demands.[76]

Denmark's Vestas recently laid off an eighth of its 24,000 person workforce and closed four plants in Denmark and one plant in Sweden in an attempt to match Chinese labor costs.[77] Due to subsidies, General Electric (GE), a company with close to 50 percent of the American market share, released its 2011 revenue figures showing an increase from 2010. The company shipped 1,956 wind turbines in 2011 compared to 1,679 in the same period in 2010. The company is selling more units, but each at an additional cost to the taxpayer. As GE chief financial officer

Keith Sherin put it, "The one drag on the whole company all year long was wind."[78]

Many American companies cannot compete with their Chinese counterparts. Normally, this would not matter. Let the lowest-cost producer win. But the involvement of federal stimulus funds changes the story because the rationale for the stimulus was to reinvigorate the American economy. Given the funding and tax breaks swept up by Chinese-American partnerships, with the Americans providing the face of the company but employing few workers, it is apparent why America has high unemployment years after the end of the recovery.

Although seemingly countless and useless billions of dollars of stimulus funds have already been spent, Democrats are calling for yet more, especially for renewable energy. Government aid through low interest loans, grants, mandates, subsidies, tax breaks, tariffs, and presidential praise have not yet succeeded in creating a green economy that bolsters employment, decreases emissions, and lowers energy costs.

Real-world experience has been the opposite. Renewable energy programs such as wind energy have proven unreliable and expensive, as unobtainable as the defeated Rhett Butler and Scarlett O'Hara seeking to find victory in *Gone with the Wind*. Bad ideas do not triumph even if you try them—again and again. The Confederacy will not rise again, and renewable energy will not cure our energy problems. It is time the Obama administration took a skeptical view of green theology and tried a dose of reality. Ironically, the Obama administration claims it likes to work in realities. It has yet to find reality in renewable energy policy.

PART III

MORAL AND GLOBAL IMPLICATIONS

8

GREEN UNEMPLOYMENT FOR AMERICA, GREEN GROWTH FOR ASIA

On a rainy fall day in October 2011, a Washington, DC, think tank, Resources for the Future (RFF), was hosting a conference entitled "Perspectives on Green Economy and Green Growth." Sponsored by the United States Council Foundation and the United States Council for International Business, participants included representatives from Shell Oil, General Electric (GE), the Environmental Protection Agency (EPA), and the Department of Energy (DOE). At the conference Francesca Costantino, the director of the DOE's Office of International Science and Technology Cooperation, told participants that changing to green technologies was a two-step process. First, the government gives incentives to invest in a desired technology. Then, the government requires its use.

This has been the approach of the United States and European governments to wind, solar, and ethanol. But oddly, Costantino's presentation hardly discussed the economic costs of this approach. The vast majority of the attendees understood that shifting technologies was desirable, regardless of the cost.

The voice of reason at the conference was Brookings Institution senior fellow Charles Schultze, who gave a presentation on the disadvantages of the industrial policy that became fashionable in America during the 1970s.[1] With Japan perceived as a major threat to American competitiveness and a successful practitioner of industrial policy, America had to follow in Japan's footsteps. According to Schultze, "The central problem was that the private market was directing investment to the wrong industries. To remedy these problems U.S. companies and the government should develop a coherent and coordinated industrial policy."

Fast-forward to the present day, when industrial policy consists of government actions centered on the energy sector and the problems of global warming and environmental pollution. "And, instead of Japan, today's more limited green version of industrial policy sees China and its fast growing alternative energy industry as a major threat to American technological leadership," said Schultze.

Some people, such as Costantino, might believe that federal incentives for green energy, such as wind and solar, will benefit the United States. Advocates declare that these technologies will result in the production of new systems, creating American green jobs. The theory goes as follows: Congress passes laws requiring the use of certain forms of alternative energy, just as it mandated ethanol and electricity produced from renewables. As a sweetener, Congress subsidizes them, perhaps with refundable tax credits for both businesses and households. Then, Americans produce them, eschewing old-fashioned technologies such as oil and coal.

The result? America will grow faster, winning the modern equivalent of the Race for Space.

On some level, this sounds appealing. But the reality is that in most cases alternative technologies cannot stand on their own without permanent tax credits. And the technology is not Made in America, but Made in Asia. In fact, much mandated equipment, such as solar panels and wind turbines, is made abroad and imported from abroad.

In turn, Asian countries import our traditional fossil fuels and lower their costs of production. This helps Asia to grow and to add jobs even as America and Europe stagnate under higher energy costs. This is a win for Asia, and for all countries that export to America. They get the job of producing the new equipment, but they do not incur the costs of using it.

China's growth has averaged 11.2 percent over the past five years, although it is expected to be 8.2 percent in 2012.[2] [3] As Table 8-1 shows, despite the seemingly significant investments the Chinese government has made in renewable energy, the actual reliance on renewables for electricity generation is negligible. According to the Energy Information Administration, less than 2 percent of Chinese electricity generation comes from renewables such as wind, solar, and biofuels.[4] India, another powerhouse, generates 2.5 percent of its electricity from non-hydropower renewables.[5]

At the opposite extreme, Spain generates 18 percent of its electricity through non-hydropower renewables.[6] These expenditures, along with others, have almost bankrupted Spain, which had a 24 percent unemployment rate as the end of the first quarter of 2012.[7] Its economy shrank by one tenth of 1 percent in 2010, after declining by 3.7 percent in 2009.[8] Germany is next, with 15 percent of electricity derived from such renewables. The United States stands at 4 percent, Canada at 2 percent.[9]

TABLE 8-1
Electricity Generation for Selected Countries, 2010

	Net Renewable (Billion kWh)	Total Generation (Billion kWh)	Renewable as Percent of Total	Hydropower as Percent of Total	Renewable Ex-hydro as Percent of Total
Australia	18.21	241.45	7.54%	5.11%	2.43%
Brazil	429.67	489.53	87.77%	81.92%	5.86%
Canada	360.25	580.58	62.05%	59.94%	2.11%
China	764.54	3964.95	19.28%	18.00%	1.28%
France	78.53	538.96	14.57%	11.53%	3.04%
Germany	104.23	576.76	18.07%	3.26%	14.81%
India	132.36	879.99	15.04%	12.53%	2.51%
Italy	76.19	279.01	27.31%	17.95%	9.36%
Japan	102.84	1013.23	10.15%	7.25%	2.90%
Mexico	46.01	254.36	18.09%	14.44%	3.65%
Russia	167.47	983.20	17.03%	16.73%	0.30%
Spain	94.09	279.65	33.65%	14.95%	18.70%
U.K.	26.25	352.66	7.44%	1.00%	6.45%
U.S.	436.47	4120.03	10.59%	6.24%	4.35%

Source: "International Energy Statistics," U.S. Energy Information Administration, http://www.eia.gov/cfapps/ipdbproject/iedindex3.cfm?tid=2&pid=29&aid=12&cid=AS,BR,CA,CH,FR,GM,IN,IT,JA,MX,RS,SP,UK,US,&syid=2010&eyid=2010&unit=BKWH.

With hydropower, the U.S. share rises to 11 percent. But alternative energy advocates do not include hydropower on their wish list. They describe it as an ecological nightmare because it dams rivers and destroys the movement of fish. Hydropower, by a wide margin, is the largest contributor to renewable electricity production. In Brazil, 82 percent of total power generation comes from hydropower.[10] Many of the major energy consumers of the world economy have yet to adopt renewable forms of power generation that are not hydropower. Hydropower is limited by geographic and meteorological constraints, and meteorological constraints can result in the amount of power generated to vary greatly from year to year. Solar and wind gather a lot of attention, but they have yet to garner a sizable piece of the current world electricity generation portfolio.

But for all of the discussion of non-hydropower renewables over the last decade, the world is still a fossil fuel–driven economy (Figure 8-1), and all major economies in the world are still large consumers of fossil fuel. The United States, Canada, and the Arabian countries are the highest per capita fossil fuel consumers.

The choice between various fuels involves both user demand and domestic supply, especially for fuels where transportation is a higher portion of user cost (coal and natural gas), as is demonstrated in countries such as China and Russia. China is the largest producer and consumer of coal, whereas Russia and the United States are the two biggest producers and consumers of natural gas. Coal, with all of its sulfur and carbon, has witnessed tremendous growth over the previous decade, with China leading the way.

FIGURE 8-1

Top Five Coal-Producing Nations, 2000–2010 Source: "China Dominates Global Coal Production," United States Energy Information Administration, October 4, 2011, http://www.eia.gov/todayinenergy/detail.cfm?id=3350.

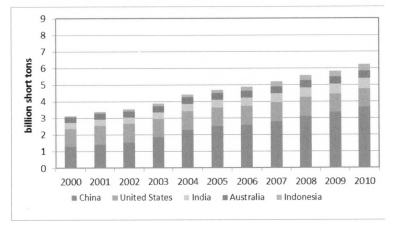

TO EMULATE CHINA, AMERICA SHOULD USE FOSSIL FUELS

Many politicians justify American investment in green technologies on the grounds that we have to catch up to China. China has 9.6 percent capacity of renewable energy, but does not use it.[11] Only a fraction of total renewable energy produced is used, less than 1 percent. For example, while China manufactured 10 gigawatts of solar panels in 2010, less than one gigawatt was installed there.[12]

Not relying on renewables reduces the costs of Chinese manufacturing, allowing it to be far more efficient and globally competitive. China's manufacturing value-added nearly doubled from $893 billion in 2006 to $1,906 billion in 2010.[13] Though America started out with the higher manufacturing value-added figure of $1,712 billion in 2006, it has shown little growth since then, and was overtaken by China in 2010.[14]

China would be even more efficient if it halted subsidies to its renewable market. Currently, the Chinese government subsidizes renewables so that Chinese companies (especially state-owned ones) will get a head start in green technology in expanding their influence in Western markets. Since August 2011 China has been allowing developers to sell solar power directly to utilities at a price of approximately $0.15 per kilowatt-hour. [15] The Chinese government's clean energy initiative has little to do with use in its own markets, and much to do with dominating foreign markets.

Unlike the American government, the Chinese government will only use renewable energy if it is cost effective to do so. European countries consume more than 80 percent of Chinese solar panels, and China shows increased reliance on coal in the future. China now consumes 46 percent of the world's coal, and is the world's largest consumer, according to the Energy Information Administration, compared with 13 percent for the United States (see Table 8-2). Coal fuels over 66 percent of the country's total energy supply.[16] However, China profits from the West's obsession with going green.[17]

Chinese wind energy is still 20 to 40 percent more expensive than coal-fired power, and solar power is at least twice as expensive. Further, the Chinese government charges a renewable energy fee to all residential electricity users, which raises electricity bills by 0.25 percent to 0.4 percent. Industrial users of electricity must pay an additional 0.8 percent. This tax revenue goes to electric grid companies to make up the cost difference between renewable energy and coal-fired power.[18] And much wind power is wasted due to the underdevelopment of grid construction. Solar energy per watt in China costs between $3 and $4, compared to $1 per watt for traditional coal energy.[19]

State-owned banks in China provide substantial funding for renewable energy programs. In 2009 alone, the Chinese government spent $45 billion in upgrading the electricity grid. While the public and private sectors play a role in the renewable energy market, public investment is the dominant of the two because of profitability challenges for private investors.[20]

According to Chi Zhang, chief Asia economist at BP China and a leading expert on renewables, the Chinese government has substantial reserves of cash to fund renewable energy initiatives not necessarily driven by profitability or private-sector participation.[21] Anyone for Solyndra?

A University of Pennsylvania study concludes that "the Chinese government has the funds and willpower to fuel the renewable energy investments necessary to reach its 2020 goal of 15 percent of energy consumption regardless of whether the private sector participates or not."[22] But the study notes that China's initiatives in renewable energy "are largely for pragmatic reasons rather than environmental concerns. . . ."[23]

Although China is already the world leader in the solar power market, both in terms of production and consumption,

TABLE 8-2
Fossil Fuel Consumption for Selected Countries, 2010

	Petroleum (Thousands of barrels per day)	Natural Gas Billion Cubic Feet	Coal Thousand Short Tons
Australia	959	1,141	119,737
Percent of World	1.1	0.99	1.5
Brazil	2,654	890	26,886
Percent of World	3.05	0.77	0.34
Canada	2,237	2,936	52,118
Percent of World	2.57	2.54	0.65
China	9,189	3,768	3,733,733
Percent of World	10.57	3.26	46.9
France	1,814	1,699	16,994
Percent of World	2.09	1.47	0.21
Germany	2,489	3,437	250,695
Percent of World	2.86	2.98	3.15
India	3,182	2,277	759,698
Percent of World	3.66	1.97	9.54
Italy	1,503	2,930	25,235
Percent of World	1.73	2.54	0.32
Japan	4,423	3,718	206,909
Percent of World	5.09	3.22	2.6
Mexico	2,141	2,135	19,413
Percent of World	2.46	1.85	0.24
Russia	2,937	17,495	227,306
Percent of World	3.38	15.15	2.86
Spain	1,440	1,265	18,240
Percent of World	1.66	1.1	0.23
U.K.	1,626	3,330	54,473
Percent of World	1.87	2.88	0.68
U.S.	19,148	24,088	1,048,295
Percent of World	22.02	20.86	13.17
World	86,962	115,454	7,960,922

Source: "International Energy Statistics," United States Energy Information Administration, http://www.eia.gov/cfapps/ipdbproject/iedindex3.cfm?tid=1&pid=1&aid=2&cid=regions& syid=2006&eyid=2010&unit=TST.

solar energy in China accounts for less than 0.01 percent of its total domestic energy.[24] The Chinese government provides subsidies to the solar industry in the form of the Golden Sun Program. These subsidies include 50 percent of grid-connected solar investments and 70 percent of off-grid photovoltaic power investments.[25] China boasted 65 percent of the world's solar water heaters in 2010.[26]

In 2010, one out of every two newly installed wind turbines in the world was installed in China. Secretary general of the Global Wind Energy Council Steve Sawyer has said, "China has become the single largest driver for global wind power development." Among the government tax incentives specifically targeted at this sector is an immediate value added tax rebate (50 percent) applied to selling self-manufactured electric power generated from wind power.[27]

Many of these renewable energy market developments in China can be traced to the enactment of the momentous 2005 Renewable Energy Law, which took effect in 2006. China mandated a provision for Renewable Portfolio Standards (RPSs) (also called "mandated market share"); feed-in tariffs for biomass; "government-guided" prices for wind power; an obligation for utilities to purchase all renewable power generated; and new financing mechanisms and guarantees.[28]

An update to the 2005 Renewable Energy Law was adopted in December 2009 by the People's Congress, and went into effect on April 1, 2010. The update included more detailed planning and coordination between renewable energy producers and transmission planning. This provision deals with the inability of grid storage companies to transmit and store large amounts of wind power being produced.[29]

In addition, provisions were established to guarantee that electric utilities purchase all renewable power generated. Previously, utilities were only obligated to do so if there were sufficient demand on the grid, but now they must always purchase renewable power, with an option of then transferring it to the national grid company for use elsewhere. Utilities face deadlines and penalties for failing to comply with the guaranteed-purchase requirement.

Other recent policy changes in China include raising the goal for total share of renewable energy to 15 percent by 2020, up from the 8 percent goal made in 2006.[30] This may be compared to the European Union's 2008 goal of a 20 percent share by 2020. However, China also changed the wording of their target from "renewables" to "non–fossil fuel sources," which includes nonrenewable nuclear and hydropower. Therefore, it is difficult to predict what the levels of renewable energy will be in 2020.

OUR RIVALS ARE WINNING THROUGH FOSSIL FUELS

America's GDP growth rate has not come close to matching China's since 1989. In 2000, China's GDP growth rate was 8.4 percent, while America's was 4.2 percent. In 2006, China's growth rate of GDP was 12.7, while America's was 2.7. In 2011, China grew at 9.2 percent, while America grew at 1.5 percent, in comparison with a global average of 3.6 percent. Unlike China, which has only recorded one instance of negative growth in 1976, America has seen negative or stagnant growth rates at least 5 times since 1970.[31] [32]

Similarly, over the five-year period from 2006 to 2010, Korea consistently outpaced America's GDP growth rate by two to three percentage points. Over the same period, India's GDP grew faster than America's. Whereas India only saw a downturn in 2008 (descending to 5 percent) the U.S. growth rate followed a steady downward projection from 2006 through 2009.[33]

In 2011 America's unemployment rate was 9 percent, more than double the unemployment rates of 4 percent or less in China and Korea.[34][35] Although our statistical surveys to measure unemployment are more precise, the fundamental difference still exists.

Not all of the differences are due to energy prices, of course. China, India, and Korea have lower labor costs and a different structure of regulation. But these countries are not choosing to adopt non-hydropower renewables on a large scale, as are the United States and many countries in the European Union.

Charles Schultze has written that national energy goals based on industrial policy will fail for two reasons: First, democratic governments are generally not capable of choosing among competing technologies. Second, even if governments knew how to pick winners, parochial interests within the government would exert undue influence on the decision, as was the case with Solyndra.

It is ironic that policymakers are calling for America to invest in alternative technologies to enable us to catch up to China when China uses a tiny fraction of non-hydropower renewables to generate its power. It produces this technology and equipment to sell to us, not for its own use.

If we wanted to be like China, we would use more coal and fewer renewables. We need a president who will say that in order to catch up to China, from now on we will focus on using our domestic reserves of coal, oil, and natural gas—and, by the way, with no more subsidies for renewables. China would then have to sell its solar panels and wind turbines elsewhere.

9

THE OPIATE FOR
THE MASSES:
MORAL SUPERIORITY

Moral superiority. You cannot burn it. You cannot eat it. It will not heat your home or run your car. You cannot buy or sell it. But in America, we have a green energy policy based primarily on moral superiority.

Moral superiority follows no exacting science or engineering to determine which energy policy is morally superior to another. With comparative morality, a government official may be morally superior to a petroleum engineer. The former is good, while the latter is bad. In China, the Cultural Revolution more than a generation ago was inspired by a sense of moral superiority. Millions of people died, and the survivors saw a nation relentlessly harm itself and its future all in the name of moral superiority.

America does not have a Cultural Revolution, but we have new policies, such as green energy, whose foundation is little better. When energy policy is the province of moral superiority, odd outcomes are likely. The immature but morally superior musings of a government official replace the exacting practice of a petroleum engineer.

When government officials rule the world, the world may be a frightening place.

Never mind that such policies will lead to the destruction of efficient and proven energy infrastructure in favor of more costly, inefficient, and sometimes nonexistent green technology. Never mind that higher energy costs will cripple households and businesses alike, resulting in lower growth. Never mind the loss of our freedom to choose the car we drive or the lightbulb we use and the resulting lack of human dignity. In throwing these away, we are left with the fantastical and seemingly heroic feat of saving the world from a carbon apocalypse.

The societal loss incurred as a result of policy by moral superiority is not just that we are led by the whim of one morally superior person, but that we witness open competition of many individuals with childish chest-thrusting seeking to claim the mantel of moral superiority.

A case in point is President Obama's new minimum fuel-efficiency standard, announced in July 2011. The president wants fuel standards to rise from 35.5 miles per gallon in 2016 to 54.5 miles per gallon in 2025, supposedly saving Americans $1.7 trillion over the lifetime of their vehicles and $8,000 per vehicle by 2025. Not to be outdone in the realm of moral superiority, some senators, led by California Democrat Dianne Feinstein and Maine Republican Olympia Snowe, prefer even higher standards, of 62 miles per gallon for cars and 44 miles per gallon for trucks by 2025.[1]

"This agreement on fuel standards represents the single most important step we've ever taken as a nation to reduce our dependence on foreign oil," the president said. "Most of the companies here today were part of an agreement we reached two years ago to raise the fuel efficiency of their cars over the next five years. We've set an aggressive target and the companies are stepping up to the plate."[2]

Senior White House advisor Ron Bloom assures us that he is "confident that the automobile manufacturers will be able to absorb the additional costs and still sell cars for a profit" and that the deal will not affect safety.[3] Billions of car buyers around the world never have insisted on buying such cars; it turns out that the White House is not only morally superior, but also omniscient about what car buyers actually want, even if they do not even know it themselves.

Why does Ron Bloom have the super-human ability to confidently assure automobile corporations that they will be able to "absorb the additional costs" of a minimum fuel-efficiency standard? What gives him the right to inform companies and consumers of the best way to spend their money? How ironic that this should occur in the United States of America, known as the land of the free.

If these fuel-saving technologies are so desirable, why do we need to require Americans to use them? As this book has shown, the answer is that fuel-saving technologies are anything but a bargain. New cars will become significantly more expensive, more people will die in car crashes, automakers will face higher costs and hire fewer workers—but at least people can feel good about themselves.

In truth, the government's fuel-efficiency standards have been textbook studies in unintended consequences. One unintended consequence is that in order to meet the standard, auto companies must either downsize their vehicles or add new technology. New technology means higher car prices, encouraging consumers to keep their existing vehicles longer. And, ironically, old cars generally pollute more than new ones. By enacting Corporate Average Fuel Economy (CAFE) regulations, congressmen were certainly not casting a vote for keeping clunkers on the road, but this is exactly what happened, an unintended consequence.

Further, CAFE restricts consumer choice. Automobile producers, instead of catering to the needs of their customers, are forced to instead concentrate on appeasing Washington's finest. These regulations, enacted in 1975, destroyed the market for the popular but thirsty family station wagon. Despite a demand for the cars, automakers could not comply with the fuel standards.

Another unintended consequence of CAFE was the sport-utility vehicle (SUV) boom in the 1990s. With big wagons now excluded from the market, consumers took advantage of the SUV loophole in the CAFE rules. Ironically, the 1975 fuel-efficiency regulations, aimed at keeping low-miles-per-gallon vehicles off the road, are directly responsible for the growth of the gas-guzzling modern SUV, which in this past decade has been top on the hit list of environmentalists.

Last but certainly not least, lighter cars are less safe. Despite what any environmentalist tells you, it is a matter of physics. Larger, heavier vehicles, the ones that CAFE will end, provide more protection in collisions because they have more mass to absorb collision forces, as well as providing more space between the occupant and the point of impact.

The first CAFE standards, according to a 2002 National Research Council study, resulted in 13,000 to 26,000 more Americans suffering incapacitating injuries on the roads in 1993, a typical year, because cars were lighter.[4] If any pharmaceutical product had killed that many patients, the manufacturer would have gone bankrupt. Families can sue Merck, but not Uncle Sam.

The saddest aspect of moral superiority is that it is neither moral nor superior. The relatives of the thousands of dead American motorists might need some convincing that the loss of their loved ones was a needed sacrifice for our energy policy, particularly one that claims moral superiority as a foundation.

After dead motorists, the biggest losers from higher standards would be Americans who prefer large vehicles to carry families, equipment, and pets on daily trips or long vacations. Other major losers would be the domestic car manufacturers, General Motors (GM), Ford, and Chrysler, which have invested in plants that make large sedans and light trucks, Americans' preference. Automakers are already restructuring to try to reduce labor costs; higher CAFE standards would be the nail in the automobile industry's coffin.

In other words, for the government, saving fuel is more important than saving lives. It prefers to pay in blood to save oil. People are willing to pay for less fuel-efficient vehicles because of the added safety, but are being prohibited from doing so because of government regulation. Despite being bad economic policy, this is also morally reprehensible.

And it does not stop there. According to estimates by the Center for Automotive Research (CAR),

A 56 mpg standard would impose on consumers a net loss (sticker price increase minus fuel savings) of $2,858 over five years if gasoline prices average $3.50/gallon. The 62 mpg that CARB, green groups, and (very likely) Obama preferred would impose a net loss of $6,525.

For most consumers, this is an unwanted expense. For others, the feelings of moral superiority justify the savings.

It is well known that Obama, Congress, and environmentalists all take great pleasure in playing dice with other peoples' money, but as the CAFE example shows, they have taken it a step too far, playing a game of Russian roulette with human lives.

The new fuel-efficiency standard beautifully outlines all of the inherent sophistries of green initiatives discussed in this book. Costs on top of unnecessary costs are strewn in this initiative with few-to-no real benefits save a chest-thumping pride that we are saving the world from all the evil, carbon-belching fat-cat corporations. Though our initiatives will have a profoundly negative effect on Americans' lives through higher traffic fatalities, livelihoods, and wealth, at least we will pat ourselves on the back knowing that we are the most morally superior nation in the world.

Another absurd example of our preferring that warm feeling in our chests over reason and practicality is a new fad to make the U.S. military green. Yes, the Army has green uniforms, but this greenery would extend to the Air Force and the Navy.

In response to pressure from the executive branch, both the Air Force and Navy have announced plans to get half their fuel from renewable sources by 2020. "We have already tested the F-18 Hornet on biofuels, the Green Hornet," Secretary of the Navy Ray Mabus explained in a speech in 2010. "The biofuel it used was made from camelina, a member of the mustard family. . . . [T]he Marines, who are not known as leaders of the environmental movement, have embraced this wholeheartedly."[5]

In his 1979 book *Soft Energy Paths*, environmental guru Amory Lovins proposed getting one-third of the country's fuel oil from domestic crops. All it would take to achieve this, he says, would be building a distillery complex only ten times the size of the plants of the combined beer and wine industries.[6] In 2004, the Department of Defense (DOD) paid Lovins to write *Winning the Oil Endgame*, in which he proposes running the entire electrical grid on wind and solar energy, and our transportation sector on natural gas and biofuels.[7] However, Lovins completely forgets to calculate how much land would be needed to grow these crops. Robert James, a retired rear admiral and a former branch chief for the Central Intelligence Agency (CIA), gives Lovins a helping hand in the estimate:

> We would need an area three times the size of the continental United States to replace one-third of our oil requirements. These figures are confirmed in that we now employ one-third of the corn harvest—our biggest crop—to replace only 3 percent of our oil consumption. [Further], in *Winning the Oil Endgame* . . . Mr. Lovins predicated his scenario on inventing cars that get 125 miles to the gallon.[8]

In our green jobs fantasyland, costs and feasibilities are irrelevant. Like a five-year-old in Toys-R-Us, it is all "I want, I want," without any sense of reality.

Reporter Elisabeth Rosenthal writes that "[S]enior commanders have come to see overdependence on fossil fuel as a big liability," and "renewable technologies . . . [are] providing a potential answer. . . . The Marines are exploring . . . a small-scale, truck-based biofuel plant that could transform local crops, like illegal poppies, into fuel."[9] How many acres of poppies would be necessary? Robert James cites Lester Brown, the renowned environmentalist who has turned against biofuels, who concludes that "the grain required to fill a 25-gallon SUV gas tank with ethanol will feed one person for a year."[10]

Although shipping diesel and gasoline to remote battlefields is costly, using renewable energy has its own set of challenges. It takes massive amounts of land to gather very diluted energy streams. Recharging a laptop with a fold-up solar panel is plausible, but larger devices would require more substantial panels, or even windmills, that could be spotted by the enemy.

The Rand Corporation recently reported to the secretary of defense that "the use of alternative fuels offers the armed services no direct military benefit. . . ." and "the military is best served by efforts directed at using energy more efficiently in weapons systems and at military installations."[11] Gambling taxpayer dollars, Americans' livelihoods, and the lives of drivers is bad enough, but certainly even the greenest of environmentalists can admit that it has gone too far when the lives of American soldiers overseas become the playground of the environmentalists.

Another prime example of our moral superiority is the myth that mandatory recycling is somehow beneficial for society. There is no actual evidence in favor of mandatory recycling programs, which squander valuable resources, but they sound good and that is enough for most people to buy into it. Contrary to popular opinion, more toxic substances are actually released in recycling processes than in new paper processing. The polluting effect of recycling is not least due to curbside pick-up, which is mandated by many governments throughout the country. Instead of one truck picking up forty or more pounds of rubbish, separate trucks must be sent out to pick up four to eight pounds of recyclables. Therefore, it could take up to twice as many oil-guzzling trucks on the road in any particular city to perform the recycling-pickup duty.

As Clemson University economics professor Daniel K. Benjamin relates, "This means more iron ore and coal mining, more steel and rubber manufacturing, more petroleum extracted and refined for fuel—and of course all that extra air pollution" caused by hundreds of extra trucks on the road.[12] Needless to say, proponents of recycling conveniently forget that such tradeoffs exist. Advocates of recycling and other green initiatives simply and mysteriously cannot fathom the principle that costs as well as benefits follow from every economic decision made.

Public service campaigns in favor of recycling exaggerate the benefits while pointing the fingers at evil economists who think otherwise. There is no shortage of misinformation provided. According to Benjamin, "Bottle and can deposit laws, which effectively misinform people about the true value of used beverage containers, induce people to waste resources collecting and processing items that appear to be worth five (or even ten) cents, given their redemption prices, but in fact are worth a penny or less to society."[13]

Further, people also waste scarce resources by recycling to excess, thanks to costly government programs that pick up recycling at no charge. These programs appear to save the government money when in reality they are consuming scarce resources that could be put to hundreds of better uses. It is no overstatement to say that society is indeed poorer because of our obsession with posing as world leaders of morality.

Even if we were to assume that every green initiative made by federal, state, and local governments were cost-efficient, these initiatives would not be effective in combating global warming if China and India did not follow along. China and India are both rapidly developing countries, and combined they make up nearly 37 percent of the world's total population. As we have seen in Chapter 8, China only appears to be going green. In reality, it depends on fossil fuels rather than renewables.

The Chinese government understands that using renewable energy is not cost-effective, and its main objective is to take advantage of both its low-cost labor and the Western obsession with environmentalism to become the world's leading producer of renewables. In other words, China is intent on strengthening its economy rather than fighting the possibility of manmade global warming. Even if America were to become 100 percent green, this would not cause a significant drop in worldwide carbon emissions.

Likewise, in India, renewables such as geothermal, solar, and wind power hold little importance in its electric power generation.[14] But why is this the case? Do not China and India know that a green way of life would be a bargain? Perhaps these countries read a recent United Nations report that admitted that going green would cost not $600 billion a year for the next decade, as the United Nations claimed two years ago, but triple that: $1.9 trillion per year for forty years, or $76 trillion over the forty-year period in order to "solve" climate change. [15] This sum is more than five times the entire GDP of the United States, which was $15 trillion in 2011.

In supporting our government's green policies, we are consenting to live in a poorer world with less wealth. Clean air and green forests are indisputably desirable, but $76 trillion can buy many goods and services, medical care, clean water, and trash collection. Taking pride in moral rectitude is important, but it is not worth $76 trillion, especially if individuals will not choose to spend the $76 trillion of their own volition.

Unfortunately, the United Nations' World Economic and Social Survey 2011 has little to do with fighting climate change. For instance, the press release for the report discusses the need "to achieve a decent living standard for people in developing countries, especially the 1.4 billion still living in extreme poverty, and the additional 2 billion people expected worldwide by 2050."[16] The main objective of this U.N.-led economic revolution is to redistribute the world's wealth, not to fight global warming. The report says that "One half of the required investments would have to be realized in developing countries."[17] Going green somehow entails the developed world donating $38 trillion to the developing world.

Further, "The *Survey* estimates that incremental green investment of about 3 per cent of world gross product (WGP) (about $1.9 trillion in 2010) would be required to overcome poverty, increase food production to eradicate hunger without degrading land and water resources, and avert the climate change catastrophe."[18]

Overcoming poverty . . . eradicating hunger . . . averting climate change. Since when are the problems of poverty and hunger part of global warming? If the environmental agenda is a global socialist redistribution of wealth, so be it. At least tell it as it is, though, and do not pretend that the main objective is to fight climate change.

The next time a government official sanctimoniously tells you to buy a smaller car or install solar panels so that green energy will save America, you too can feel morally superior. As a consequence of green jobs policies, some Americans may die, others may lose their jobs, our economy may crater, our quality of life will diminish, our own lives may become nastier and more bitter, and yet apparently it will all be worthwhile, because we will be following the instructions of the morally superior.

PART IV

CONCLUSION

10

FOSSIL FUELS: FROM SIN TO REDEMPTION

Green jobs policies are delivering less than government promised. But due to changes in technology, particularly the development of hydraulic fracturing, America is discovering new reserves of oil and natural gas.

Oil and natural gas reserves keep expanding as new exploration occurs and new recovery technologies are devised. Just in the last several years, huge deposits of natural gas have been discovered from Texas to Louisiana to Pennsylvania and New York. Natural gas prices have fallen below any prior expectations.

As this book went to press, North Dakota, home of a shale oil boom, has the lowest unemployment rate in the nation, at 3 percent. Recently the U.S. Geological Survey estimated that 84 trillion cubic feet of undiscovered technically recoverable natural gas was contained within the Marcellus Formation in New York, West Virginia, and Pennsylvania.[1] This amounts to 3.5 years of total U.S. consumption. In addition, the area contains 3.4 billion barrels of natural gas liquids.

Some people might think that President Obama would encourage domestic oil and gas development. After all, he favors energy independence, and independence means more domestic oil and gas production. In addition, domestic oil and gas generate hundreds of thousands jobs, directly and indirectly.

But oil has been demonized, and the president, in budget after budget submitted to Congress, has been trying slow oil and gas production by raising taxes on the industry, denying approval of the Keystone XL Pipeline that would deliver oil from Canada, and reducing permits available for exploration. These policies would make the country more dependent, not less, on imported oil.

Although Congress spends billions of dollars on green technologies in a futile attempt to create jobs and promote energy independence, Obama wants to deny access to development of our own oil and gas resources in some of the most geologically promising areas available and to increase the tax costs of developing these resources.

Americans might become greater conservationists, prodded by guilt or by higher fuel prices. But even if they do, they will still need oil and natural gas for driving, home heating, and electricity generation for many years to come.

TAX INCREASES ON OIL AND GAS

The taxes in Obama's 2013 budget would make domestic oil relatively less profitable and tend to raise the country's already high fraction of imports of crude and product. Such taxes would result in the substitution of foreign oil for domestic and curtail well-paying jobs in domestic exploration for and production of oil.

In his 2013 budget, Obama tried to raise $41 billion over the next decade from direct tax increases on oil and gas, more than on any other industry.[2] Plus, a disproportionate share of tax increases on overseas income and higher Superfund levies would have affected the domestic oil industry, raising another $22 billion over ten years.[3] Furthermore, the repeal of last-in, first-out (LIFO) accounting methods would cost the industry another $26 billion over ten years.[4]

It is not just that Obama wanted to remove tax preferences for oil and gas. The second-largest component of his tax increase, $11.6 billion over ten years, would have come from disallowing oil and gas companies to take advantage of a provision that applies to all domestic manufacturing, known as the domestic manufacturing deduction. Currently manufacturers can take a deduction from taxes of 9 percent on their income from domestic production. Oil companies already have a lower deduction of 6 percent.

Obama wanted to completely eliminate the domestic manufacturing deduction for oil and gas companies so that oil companies would be the only domestic manufacturers not to qualify. It makes no sense to punish one industry by removing a tax benefit that applies to all manufacturing. If domestic manufacturing is not worthy of a deduction, it should be repealed for all industries.

Some tax advantages that Obama wanted to repeal, such as expensing of intangible drilling costs and percentage depletion, generally benefit smaller oil companies. Others, such as curtailing credits for taxes, in the form of royalties, paid to foreign governments on production abroad, affect larger companies. Such tax increases would shrink the profitability of American companies vis-à-vis foreign ones. Foreign companies might win out in bidding wars for all phases of U.S. petroleum development because their tax burdens would be lower.

The rules also increase the likelihood of U.S.-based oil companies moving their headquarters to other countries. This has been seen in the oil and gas services industry, with companies including Transocean and Noble moving to Switzerland, Halliburton to Dubai, and Ensco to London. The industry is international. These companies do not need further encouragement to move their headquarters, and their well-paying jobs, to another country.

The ostensible rationale for these tax increases is that the current tax system "distorts markets by encouraging more investment in the oil and gas industry than would occur under a neutral system. To the extent expensing encourages overproduction of oil and gas, it is detrimental to long-term energy security . . ." This reasoning is repeated eight times in the Treasury Department's 2011 Green Book, a description of proposed spending and revenue changes in the budget.[5]

This makes no sense. Furthermore, the idea that reducing oil and gas investment would lead to a rush of capital into the alternative energy sector belies the existence of international capital markets. The only way to increase relative investments in clean energy is to reduce risk, or increase returns, relative to other sectors.

In contrast, Obama wants tax incentives for "clean energy technology," far more expensive than oil and gas, raising households' energy costs and effectively shrinking their income.

Rather than leading towards energy independence, Obama's proposals would drive oil and gas production abroad and make American oil and gas uncompetitive in a global market. The levies would punish domestic American companies and benefit countries with large reserves such as Venezuela, Saudi Arabia, Iran, and Russia.

THE KEYSTONE XL PIPELINE

Green jobs are a frequent conversation topic, but jobs from an oil pipeline seem to have no supporters. The Keystone XL Pipeline, which would create 20,000 jobs, failed to win approval from the State Department.

In September 2008, TransCanada Pipelines, a Canadian company, proposed building a 1,711-mile-long, 36-inch-wide pipeline to carry crude from the oil-rich Lake Athabasca region of Canada to the U.S. Gulf Coast, where it would be refined; since 1,384 miles are to be built in the United States, the application was submitted to the State Department. Even though the State Department gave the project a positive environmental assessment in August 2011, the following November the Department announced that approval would be delayed until the first quarter of 2013, pending the study of alternative routes.

One obstacle came from Nebraska, which objected that the pipeline would go over the Ogallala Aquifer in the State's Sand Hills region. Residents worried that a spill would pollute the aquifer and leave the water unusable for generations. To counter this concern, TransCanada offered several concessions, including a cement pipe coating in areas where the water table is close to the location of the pipe; a $100 million performance bond to the State of Nebraska; and an oil-spill response team, with equipment, in the Sand Hills area.

But Nebraska cannot prevent State Department authorization of the pipeline, which could be approved over Nebraska objections. In fact, Nebraska is working with TransCanada over a different route.

As a condition for extending a reduction in the payroll tax, Congress in December 2011 required the State Department to speed up its decision on the Keystone XL Pipeline and deliver a verdict by mid-February 2012. On January 18, 2012, President Obama again rejected the permit on recommendation of the State Department.

The original cost of the project was $7 billion, and TransCanada has already spent $1.9 billion. The Perryman Group, in a study commissioned by TransCanada, estimated that the project would result in $9.6 billion in domestic product, with $6.5 billion in personal income, and about 119,000 person-years of employment. During construction, the pipeline was estimated to provide $99 million to local governments, $486 million to state governments, and about $5.3 billion in future cumulative property taxes. The federal government's share in tax revenue, assuming a rate of 15 percent, would be around $1.44 billion.

Environmentalists attacked the proposed Keystone XL pipeline because it would expand the use of the oil sands in Alberta, Canada, which is a more carbon-intensive form of oil than that produced from traditional underground reservoirs. Yet in the State Department's environmental review it was noted that "Oil sands mining projects have reduced greenhouse gas emissions intensity by an average of 39 percent between 1990 and 2008 and are working toward further reductions."

Some unions, such as the Service Employees International Union (SEIU), the International Union, United Automobile, Aerospace and Agricultural Implement Workers of America (UAW), and the United Steelworkers (USW) supported the president.[6] The Laborers International Union of North America (LIUNA) opposed him.[7] Days later LIUNA left the BlueGreen Alliance (mentioned in Chapter 4) in outrage at the other Alliance members' support of the job-killing decision.[8]

Currently, a large portion of the heavy oil that Gulf of Mexico refineries receive is from Mexico and Venezuela, whose volume available for import has been dwindling. America's single largest concentration of petrochemical facilities and associated industries, located in the Gulf, would also benefit from new sources of oil. Further, the idea that stopping the pipeline would curtail development of the Canadian oil sands is economically naïve; Canada would just export the oil to Asia, harming Gulf refineries, and benefiting economic competitors.

HYDROFRACTURING: THE NEW OPPORTUNITY

Despite threats of higher taxes, regulatory obstacles, and subsidies for green energy, fossil fuel production in America is increasing, led by new technologies. Hydrofracturing is being used from Pennsylvania to North Dakota to extract oil and gas from the ground.

Fracking is a method of extracting natural gas and oil from shale formations and packed sand. Wells are drilled 4,000 to 5,000 feet below the surface and then sometimes curve to drill horizontally. Fluids are then pushed into the well to separate the gas from the shale and sand and so make it extractable.

Due to the irregular distribution of natural gas underground (small pockets are spread unevenly within the tight rock, like bubble wrap) the only way to remove the gas from the shale is through hydrofracturing and horizontal drilling. Fracking techniques have been known since the 1940s but have recently become more widespread, and therefore controversial, as the long, upward trend of oil prices has made shale formations of natural gas look more profitable.

Fracking has made trillions of cubic feet potentially available, and has driven the price of natural gas down to its current 2012 level of $2.41 per million British thermal units from $7 or $8 per million British thermal units between 2004 and 2009. As a result, estimates of recoverable U.S. natural gas have climbed dramatically, from 1,100 trillion cubic feet in 1990 to 2,214 trillion cubic feet today.[9] America is forecast to produce 24 trillion cubic feet of marketed natural gas this year, 15 percent more than in 2001, and 5 percent more than in 2010. About 25 percent of this gas comes from fracking.

Government and industry data show that natural gas production has been increasing rapidly and is on a path to continue. America has 200 years of natural gas supplies. As more remote deposits become harder to drill, other large shale fields with more easily recoverable oil are available for drilling. Estimates of recoverable U.S. natural gas, made by the Energy Information Administration (EIA), have climbed dramatically, from 1,100 trillion cubic feet in 1990 to 2,587 trillion cubic feet today. Shale gas production is expected to triple between 2009 and 2035. According to EIA chief Richard Newell, natural gas is expected to account for 60 percent of the 223-gigawatt addition to U.S. energy capacity projected to occur between 2009 and 2035.

In May 2011 the International Energy Agency suggested that the world might be entering "a golden age of gas" and projected that world gas usage might rise by more than 50 percent from 2010 levels and account for more than 25 percent of world energy use by 2035. Melanie Kenderdine, executive director of the Massachusetts Institute of Technology Energy Initiative, projects that 500 trillion cubic feet of shale gas are available, with a cost of less than $7 per thousand cubic feet.

Natural gas is a cleaner-burning fossil fuel with about half of the carbon emissions of coal. Emissions from natural gas burning automobiles are 25 percent cleaner than are those from gasoline or diesel engines, so one would think that natural gas would be popular with environmentalists.

But environmentalists do not like hydrofracturing because they are concerned about water contamination. Because wells pass through clean water aquifers, some fear that the chemicals used in a hydrofracturing job will be released into the earth and contaminate the aquifer.

Another concern is the disposal of water used in the drilling process. Typically 25 percent of the water is recycled back up to the surface. Many skeptics worry that the water brought to the surface is dumped directly into rivers and streams, that the lined pits used to hold recycled water contaminate the soil, or that accidents involving the trucks carrying the recycled water could cause irrevocable environmental damage. The 75 percent of hydro-fracked water that remains underground worries people because of possible contamination of the aquifer. Lastly, water usage itself is a point of contention. The critics point out that hydrofracturing jobs deplete large amounts of water, with large jobs using four to five million gallons.

Some of these worries, while conscientious, are misguided. Natural gas deposits, at 4,000 to 5,000 feet below ground, are well below the 500 to 700 feet depth of the water tables. Dense shale rock lies in between the two strata. The rare but well-publicized cases of water-table contamination occurred due to poor casing jobs or improper drilling techniques and were immediately prosecuted by the governmental authorities.

Wastewater from the fracking process is trucked away or piped to Environmental Protection Agency (EPA)-certified treatment facilities. Until then, companies store it in steel or earthen-lined pits, with steel pits providing the most protection. States could require steel pits to be used as a condition of granting permits.

Some water is recycled and used again for other drilling operations. Flowback from hydrofracturing fluids has never contaminated an underground aquifer or above-ground water source.

A large hydrofracturing project may require 4 to 5 million gallons of water. This seems large, but it is small in comparison to total household consumption. For example, Pennsylvania residents use more than 300 billion gallons (62,800 gallons per household) a year. Tax revenues from natural gas exploration can be used to improve state parks and rivers, rendering the environment cleaner than it would have been otherwise.

If New York were to permit fracking, the Empire State would see new jobs, a surge of economic activity, and more tax revenues. One study by Timothy Considine of the University of Wyoming, estimates that in 2015 New York State could enjoy $1.7 billion in additional economic activity and $214 million in extra tax revenue if its natural gas reserves were developed.[10] Over the period 2011 to 2020, New York State could gain $11.4 billion in economic output and $1.4 billion in tax revenues.

Neighboring Pennsylvania produces over 80 billion cubic feet of natural gas a year. It has 296 wells in the Marcellus Shale, a geologic formation that stretches into New York and West Virginia. A 2010 study found that the Marcellus gas operations in Pennsylvania added about $2 billion to Pennsylvania's economy.[11]

Although Pennsylvania, Texas, and Arkansas, among others, are successfully using hydraulic fracturing to tap into their gas reserves, New York has effectively banned the process, at least for the present, on environmental grounds. In 2010, then-Governor David Paterson issued Executive Order 41, which bans new drilling permits until the New York Department of Environmental Conservation issues a new Supplemental Generic Environmental Impact Statement (SGEIS). The public comment period on the revised draft ended in January 2012 and the DEC plans to issue both the final SGEIS and final regulations before the end of 2012.[12]

According to Considine's analysis of the Pennsylvania Department of Environmental Protection data, between 2008 and 2010, 7.9 percent of wells had serious violations of the stringent regulations placed upon them by the state.[13] Considine and his team classified serious violations as major spills, cement and casing violations, blowouts and venting, and stray gas.[14] The majority of these violations occurred not because of the process of hydrofracturing itself, but rather because of improper drilling or poor casing jobs.

In other words, fracking itself is not the villain. Sloppy drilling and casing are problems, but such problems are neither inevitable nor pervasive. Considine calculates that the economic damage resulting from the environmental effects of a typical shale well came to $14,000, which is low when compared with the benefits per well of $4 million. It is impossible to have costless manufacturing of any product or human activity, and the benefits far outweigh the costs.

New York faces serious budget challenges. It had to close a budget deficit of $8.5 billion in fiscal year 2011, and it faces continued budget deficits in future years. For fiscal health, New York should emulate Pennsylvania and develop its natural gas reserves.

Some suggest that hydrofracturing is a bubble, like the dot-com bubble in the late 1990s or the housing bubble that burst in the first decade of this century. But evidence is against a gas bubble because of strong U.S. and global demand for energy. Gas demand will remain strong due to the administration's phase-out of coal, which now produces 36 percent of our electricity. New administration rules under review would make it more costly to burn coal, due to emissions, and to mine it, due to mine dust. If the administration continues on its current path, additional coal-fired power plants will close, and electricity will become more expensive. At least 100 coal-fired plants have closed since January 1, 2010.[15]

America now imports 7 percent of its natural gas consumption, down from 16 percent in 2001.[16] There is scope for getting rid of imports completely and perhaps for exporting gas through liquefaction.

America is increasing its share of electricity from natural gas. Over 250 new natural gas power electricity generation plants will be built by 2016. Those generators represent the addition of 37,718 megawatts of potential capacity. The additions are coming because of low natural gas prices. However, simply looking at additions does not give a complete picture to the extent that the demand for natural gas is increasing from power companies.

Furthermore, the costs of using fossil fuels to generate electricity are significantly lower than the costs of doing so with renewable energy sources. In an estimation of the total levelized costs of different types of power plants entering service in 2017, the U.S.

Energy Information Administration found that natural gas-fired plants have average costs of $68.6 per megawatt-hour. Meanwhile, solar photovoltaic sources have average costs of $156.9 per megawatt-hour, wind sources $96.8 per megawatt-hour, and biomass plants $120.2 per megawatt-hour.[17]

The overall costs of using natural gas to generate electricity are significantly lower than the costs of doing so with renewable energy sources. Table 10-1 shows a consolidation of a projection by the U.S. Energy Information Administration of the total costs of different types of power plants entering service in 2017. With costs that are 25 percent less than the next cheapest type of energy, natural gas-fired plants are much cheaper than any other type of power plant.

In 2011 natural gas demand from electrical power plants increased 8.2 percent from 2010,[18] even though total electrical generation declined by half of 1 percent over the same period.[19] The trend within the unseasonably warm December 2011 was even starker. Overall generation between December 2011 and December 2010 declined by about 7 percent. Coal-fired generation declined 21 percent over the same time period, and electrical generation from natural gas rose about 12 percent. This change meant that for December 2011 natural gas represented 26 percent of total electricity generation, up from 22 percent in the same month the year before. At the same time coal generation dropped from 46 percent of total generation to 39 percent.

The increase in demand for natural gas was much greater than the incremental increase that was caused by the increase of the natural gas electrical generation fleet. From 2000 to 2005, partly due to the construction boom, 163 gigawatts of net summer electrical generating capacity were added to the fleet, fueled by natural gas. That expansion happened because of the adoption of natural gas combined cycle generators, which replaced a large amount of the older natural gas power plants. Over 16 gigawatts

TABLE 10-1
U.S. Average Levelized Costs for Plants Entering Service in 2017

Fuel Type	Total System Levelized Cost ($/MWh)
Natural Gas-Fired (Conventional Combined Cycle)	68.6
Conventional Coal	99.6
Advanced Nuclear	112.7
Geothermal	99.6
Biomass	120.2
Wind	96.8
Wind (Offshore)	330.6
Solar PV	156.9
Solar Thermal	251.0
Hydro	89.9

Source: U.S. Energy Information Administration, "Levelized Cost of New Generation Resources in the Annual Energy Outlook 2012," last modified January 23, 2012, http://www.eia.gov/forecasts/aeo/electricity_generation.cfm.

of net summer natural gas fired generating capacity were lost from 2002 to 2005 due to the closure of older plants. In short, the United States has a lot of new natural gas units.

The natural gas fleet is the largest part of electrical-generating capacity. In 2010 it represented around 40 percent of net summer capacity.[20] Included in natural gas are combined cycle gas plants that represent around 16.5 percent of all capacity.[21] These are plants that have high thermal efficiencies and are designed with the capability to meet base-load demand. The remainder of the fleet is made up of single-cycle gas plants and steam plants, which have lower thermal efficiencies and thus require more energy to create a proportional amount of electricity. However, these plants are necessary for an electrical grid operator to meet intermediate and peak demand, as they can be quickly dispatched to meet demand.

Prior to the last several years, the fleet was significantly underutilized, which was explained by the sharp increase in prices that occurred in the United States around the time all of these plants were being brought online. Table 10-2 shows capacity factors, actual output divided by total generation capacity, that the EIA estimates every year for different fuel sources. These show that natural gas plants are underutilized.

Over the past several years, utilization of combined cycle natural gas plants has increased substantially. Estimates from other sources have put capacity factors for combined cycle natural gas plants at around 46 percent for the year 2011.[22] Given the previously discussed large annual increases in natural gas for electricity generation, it is likely that utilization is higher. To get some idea of potential utilization, consider that combined cycle plants are typically designed to operate at capacity factors around 85 percent.[23]

Table 10-2 confirms that natural gas plants are operating well below capacity and could easily increase electricity production. It is also worth noting that increasing use of renewables, which produce power intermittently, will increase the need for fossil fuel powered plants to make up shortfalls in supply. Renewables have a higher outage rate since they depend on certain weather conditions to produce power, so when the wind is not blowing or the sun not shining, power from another source must be quickly dispatched to meet the shortfall. A continued environment of low natural gas prices, versus other fuel sources—mainly coal—will lead to an exacerbation of the current switch that is underway as older coal power plants are retired in favor of newer, more thermally efficient, natural gas plants, and the current fleet is increasingly utilized. Utilization of the existing fleet has been the main driver recently and will likely continue to be in the near-term, given the fact that no additional capital investment is required and prices for natural gas allow for extremely favorable marginal generation costs when compared to coal. In the longer-term, increased base load capacity is expected to be used, with the EIA

TABLE 10-2
Capacity of Power Plants by Fuel Type, 2003–2009 (percentage)

Year	Coal	Petroleum	Natural Gas Combined Cycle	Natural Gas other	Nuclear	Hydro Conventional	Other Renewables	All Energy Sources
2003	72	22.4	33.5	12.1	87.9	40	50	47.7
2004	71.9	23.3	35.5	10.7	90.1	39.4	50.5	47.9
2005	73.3	23.8	36.8	10.6	89.3	39.8	47	48.3
2006	72.6	12.6	38.8	10.7	89.6	42.4	45.7	48
2007	73.6	13.4	42	11.4	91.8	36.3	40	48.7
2008	72.2	9.2	40.6	10.6	91.1	37.2	37.3	47.4
2009	63.8	7.8	42.2	10.1	90.3	39.8	33.9	44.9

Source: "Table 5.2 Electrical Power Annual 2009," United States Energy Information Administration, revised November 2011, http://205.254.135.7/electricity/annual/archive/03482009.pdf.

forecasting combined cycle generation plants' net summer generation capacity to increase at an annualized rate of 1.4 percent from year-end 2010 to 2035.[24]

NOT JUST GAS

As natural gas prices have remained at a relatively low levels, and oil at historically high levels, producers have moved into "liquids-rich" areas. This phrase simply refers to areas where oil, natural gas condensates, or natural gas liquids are a high percentage of production.

These areas, known as "plays," are geographically and geologically varied. One of the most mature plays, in terms of development, is the Bakken Formation in the Williston Basin, stretching from Montana to North Dakota and into Canada. One of the first major fields that demonstrated the potential of this reservoir was the Elm Coulee field, which is located in eastern Montana and was first horizontally drilled in 2000, and subsequently hydrofracturing was performed by Halliburton.[25] This demonstrated the production possibility of a "good" horizontal well that is fractured. [26]

As with most developments, a confluence of factors has allowed production in reservoirs such as Bakken. Development required not only high oil prices but also developments in drilling and well-completion technology, including fracturing. Most of these methods were not truly "discovered," because geologists had been aware of them before. For instance, the Bakken Formation had been previously drilled, but the application of horizontal drilling with hydraulic fracturing had to be developed before the play became what it is today, a major oil field.

Currently the Williston Basin, location of the Bakken Formation, is extremely active, with the majority of the production concentrated in western North Dakota. The Bakken Formation drove North Dakota oil production to 609,373 barrels per day in April

2012, from 351,261 barrels per day in April 2011.[27] This increase has helped offset declines in the drop in production that followed the moratorium on drilling in the Gulf of Mexico. North Dakota has caught up to Alaska and California to become the second-largest crude oil producing state.

The development has been an economic boon for the state of North Dakota. The Department of Mineral Resources has estimated that based on current prices the average Bakken well in North Dakota would produce 575,000 barrels of oil. That production would result in $4,250,000 in taxes and $6,900,000 in royalties to mineral owners.[28]

Production is continuing to increase, with estimates of an average of 199 drilling rigs running in May 2012, compared with 162 in May 2011.[29]

Although the Bakken Formation is the most prolific oil production area, many other areas contain liquids. Producers in the Marcellus are continuing to focus on the western area of the play because of the liquid content of the gas.[30] Other areas where booms are occurring include the Eagle Ford Shale in south Texas and the Granite Wash in the Texas panhandle.

Recently, producers have been expanding into areas including the Utica Shale, largely in Ohio, and the Niobrara Shale. The Niobrara shale development is focused in two distinct areas, the Powder River Basin in Wyoming and the Denver-Julesburg Basin in north central and northeastern Colorado. Anadarko recently announced a large field in northeastern Colorado that may hold 1 billion barrels of recoverable oil from the Niobrara Formation.[31] Producers are also examining the New Albany Shale, mainly in Indiana and Kentucky, to determine the size and commercial potential of the play.

Significant work is occurring in America's most active onshore basin, the Permian Basin, which is located in west Texas and eastern New Mexico. Formations under development include the Wolfcamp Shale, the Avalon Shale, and the Bone Spring Formation. The Cana Woodford Shale in western Oklahoma has sparked interest because of the high liquids content of production. Oklahoma is also witnessing large producer interest in the nascent Mississippi Lime play in northern Oklahoma. The behemoth that was made up by the Haynesville and Bossier Shales in far eastern Texas and western Louisiana has slowed, but it may pick up if natural gas prices rise because of the prolific wells that have been drilled there. The same is true of the Fayetteville Shale in Arkansas, and areas like the Arkoma and Anadarko Basins in Oklahoma, and the Piceance Basin in western Colorado.

California would likely see more exploration if the state could find a faster way to approve permits, given the historic production in the prolific, long-producing fields in Kern County and the Monterrey Shale, still in the very early stages of development. California's environmental lobby is all-powerful, but in November 2011 Governor Jerry Brown, a Democrat, announced that he was replacing the two individuals who were directly responsible for overseeing oil and gas permits, in an attempt to speed up the process.[32] Occidental, the largest leaseholder in the Monterrey Shale, has noted that it would do more hydrofracturing if the permitting process would speed up.[33]

Many producers focus on areas where they do not have to deal with federal regulators because much federal land is either off-limits or tied up in red tape. Almost all substantial U.S. onshore oil and gas development has been on private lands. That is not saying that geology is the main reason; rocks really do not care about who owns the land above them. Areas of North Dakota where the oil boom is taking place are privately owned, as are areas in Pennsylvania. If Wyoming, Utah, and Alaska had more private property, they would be able to put into place a streamlined development approval process.

Coupled with substantial discoveries made in the deep-water Gulf of Mexico, the United States has the potential to undergo significant petroleum production over the next several decades. Furthermore, when one considers the large investments in the oil sands in Alberta, North America is seeing sustained increases in petroleum for the first time since the 1980s oil industry bust.

Lucian Pugliaresi, president of the Energy Policy Research Foundation, has written extensively about the importance not only of supply and demand for setting energy prices, but also of expectations about future events, such as world demand, availability of supplies, and government policies. He states, "In many cases, the immediate loss in output from any number of unexpected events has much less effect on the world market than the resulting shift in expectations about the ability to expand output over the next 5–10 years."[34]

That is why an aggressive oil and gas development program would signal to buyers and sellers that America is serious about bringing supplies to market. It would open up a resource base to American innovation and result in lower prices.

As America ponders the failure of green jobs policies and cronyism, the oil and gas industry is ratcheting up supplies of energy, together with employment, which has risen from 298,500 workers in April 2006 to 457,100 in April of 2012.[35] Sometimes, unplanned industrial activity trumps industrial policy.

CONCLUSION

Many people believe that government "investment" in green jobs helps Americans and America's economy, and that such "investment" will enable America to keep pace with China. Neither concept is true. Rather, spending to promote green jobs harms the economy by raising energy prices. Such higher prices act in the same way as a tax, reducing production and employment. Some green jobs may be created, but many more manufacturing and energy-intensive jobs are eliminated or driven offshore. This makes Americans worse off, rather than better off, and puts America at a disadvantage compared to China and other countries.

Green jobs are the most recent reappearance of a perennial idea—industrial policy to promote certain industries. Industrial policy has failed in the past, in America, Japan, Russia, and numerous other countries across the globe and across the centuries. Today, green jobs initiatives result in a higher cost of energy to businesses, driving them to locate in other countries, and to households, who can afford fewer goods.

In his State of the Union Address on January 24, 2012, President Barack Obama declared, "Some technologies don't pan out; some companies fail. But I will not walk away from the promise of clean energy . . . I will not cede the wind or solar or battery industry to China or Germany because we refuse to make the same commitment here."[36]

No matter that Germany has announced an end to its solar subsidies by 2017 or that it imports energy from France and the Czech Republic because its solar panels do not produce electricity in the overcast winter months. Or that China generates less than 2 percent of its electricity from non-hydropower renewables.

The bipartisan support of green jobs has become an excuse for reforming the economy with expensive industrial policies. Spending on green jobs now includes tax subsidies and direct grants for broadband, electric cars, renewable energy (such as wind, solar, and biofuels), mass transit, high-speed rail, and environmental rehabilitation.

But government-subsidized projects often fail. Chevy's electric car, the Volt, has caught fire for catching fire. The plug-in hybrid car's batteries apparently burst into flames after some government crash tests. In March 2012, a five-week suspension of the Volt's production was announced in reaction to low sales numbers. Meanwhile, within the same week, Chrysler and General Motors (GM) announced plans to produce pick-up trucks with dual fuel tanks, capable of running on both natural gas and gasoline—without a government program.

Many new green jobs—manufacturing solar panels, wind turbines, and electric batteries, for instance—are being created in China and South Korea rather than in the United States. But the Chinese do not use the solar panels they produce to power their electricity; they use old-fashioned coal, an inexpensive way to operate their power plants. Rather, they export the renewable equipment to America, raising our costs of production.

Studies showing that green jobs policies create jobs and innovation in the economy are fundamentally flawed. Green jobs are not well defined—some are in construction, some exist already but are reclassified, and some are temporary. Studies come up with inconsistent results. One study, by the Center for American Progress, estimates that an "investment" of $100 billion will result in 2 million new jobs over two years.[37] Another, by the Center for Energy Efficiency and Renewable Technologies, calculates that "investing" $50 billion a year will result in 500,000 new jobs annually.[38]

These studies contain little analysis of jobs destroyed through green industrial policy, such as jobs in coal production, oil exploration and refining, traditional auto production, and incandescent electric light bulbs.

Nor do the studies consider the disparate geographical effects of green jobs industrial policies. Although these policies raise energy prices, lower production, and increase unemployment nationally, they have different effects on different states. Regulation of carbon will be especially harmful to the economies of Pennsylvania, Ohio, Kentucky, West Virginia, and Tennessee, which produce coal and rely on it to generate electricity. The failure of the

Interior Department to resume permits for drilling in the Gulf of Mexico has slowed business in the Gulf states.

If green jobs policies are not creating employment, how about traditional fossil fuels? The renewed emergence of fossil fuels can power the economy. Over the past few years, new hydrofracturing techniques have resulted in a boom in oil and natural gas development, lowering the price of energy and creating domestic jobs. Lower energy costs are attracting manufacturing back to America from overseas.

In America, policies are not cast in stone. The pendulum, having swung one way, can swing back. We have reformed welfare programs, which used to pay teenagers unlimited amounts to have babies out of wedlock. We have lowered taxes from a top rate of 90 percent to 35 percent because high rates are economically destructive. We have abandoned the construction of large public housing projects, which bred crime and delinquency. We can also move away from expensive, inefficient, green jobs policies when we find they are counter to economic growth and are a wasteful way of meeting our objectives.

ENDNOTES

Chapter 1

1. U.S. Office of the Press Secretary "President Bush Signs H.R. 6, the Energy Independence and Security Act of 2007," December 19, 2007, http://georgewbush-whitehouse.archives.gov/news/releases/2007/12/20071219-6.html.

2. "Energy Independence and Security Act of 2007," H.R. 6, 110th Congress, December 13, 2007. Section 1002 (2) (D) (ii) and Section 1002 (3) (A) (vi), http://frwebgate.access.gpo.gov/cgi-bin/getdoc.cgi?dbname=110_cong_bills&docid=f:h6eas2.txt.pdf.

3. Ibid., Section 431 and 432.

4. United Nations, Online Inventory of UN System Activities on Climate Change, 2008, http://www.un.org/climatechange/project-search/proj_details.asp?projID=155&ck=XpzmpoEa3yid8Nd.

5.   American Institute of Physics, "The Carbon Dioxide Green-house Effect," February 2011, http://www.aip.org/history/climate/co2.htm.

6.   Paul Crutzen, "Albedo Enhancement by Stratospheric Sulfur Injections: A Contribution to Resolve a Policy Dilemma?" Vol. 77, No. 3(August 1, 2006): 211–220, http://dx.doi.org/10.1007/s10584-006-9101-y.

7.   Philip J. Rasch et al., "An Overview of Geoengineering of Climate using Stratospheric Sulphate Aerosals," Vol. 366, No. 1882–4037 (November 2008), http://rsta.royalsocietypublishing.org/content/366/1882/4007.full.

8.   Marc Gunther, "Brighten Clouds, Cool the Air, Save the Planet," June 12, 2011, http://www.marcgunther.com/2011/06/12/brighten-clouds-cool-the-air-save-the-planet/.

9.   Darren Quick, "Computer Modeling Indicates White Roofs May Be a Cool Idea," January 28, 2010, http://www.gizmag.com/white-roofs-climate-change/14021/.

10.   J. Eric Bickel and Lee Lane, "An Analysis of Climate Engineering as a Response to Climate Change," ed. Bjorn Lomborg (Cambridge: Cambridge University Press, 2010), http://www.aei.org/files/2009/08/07/AP-Climate-Engineering-Bickel-Lane-v.3.0.pdf.

11.   Ibid.

12.   Office of Management and Budget, U.S. Government Printing Office, Washington, DC, 2012, http://www.whitehouse.gov/sites/default/files/omb/budget/fy2013/assets/budget.pdf.

13.   "Climate Change: A Coordinated Strategy Could Focus Federal Geoengineering Research and Inform Governance Efforts," U.S. Government Accountability Office Report to the Chairman, Committee on Science and Technology, House of Representatives, GAO-10-903, September 2010, Table 1, p. 19, http://www.gao.gov/new.items/d10903.pdf.

14.   U.S. Department of Energy, Loan Programs Office, https://lpo.energy.gov/?page_id=45.

15. "Remarks by the President in Holland, Michigan on Investing in Clean Energy" White House Press Release, July 15, 2010, http://www.whitehouse.gov/the-press-office/remarks-president-holland-michigan-investing-clean-energy.

Chapter 2

1. Frédéric Bastiat, "That Which Is Seen and That Which Is Not Seen," *Selected Essays on Political Economy.* Seymour Cain, trans. (Library of Economics and Liberty, 1995), http://www.econlib.org/library/Bastiat/basEss1.html.

2. Ibid.

3. Ibid.

4. G. Alvarez et al., "Study on the Effect on Employment of Public Aid to Renewable Energy Sources," Universidad Rey Juan Carlos, March 2009, http://www.juandemariana.org/pdf/090327-employment-public-aid-renewable.pdf.

5. U.S. Energy Information Administration, International Statistics, 2011, http://www.eia.gov/cfapps/ipdbproject/iedindex3.cfm?tid=2&pid=36&aid=12&cid=regions&syid=2005&eyid=2009&unit=BKWH.

6. "Experts: Salazar Misrepresents Our Position," *Marine Log,* June 11, 2011, http://www.marinelog.com/DOCS/NEWSMMIX/2010jun00112.html.

7. "Gulf Oil Spill: New Moratorium Explained," *Los Angeles Times,* July 12, 2010. http://latimesblogs.latimes.com/greenspace/2010/07/gulf-oil-spill-new-moratorium-explained.html.

8. U.S. Energy Information Administration, *2011 Outlook for Hurricane Related Production in the Gulf of Mexico,* June 2011, https://docs.google.com/viewer?a=v&q=cache:UhLUG6fBEicJ:205.254.135.24/forecasts/steo/special/pdf/2011_sp_02.pdf+&hl=en&gl=us&pid=bl&srcid=ADGEESjymuqbcqiCL17aKRy UbQKwYddm2Ftfcbj8ZIo-FAJ05KVq11gQCDjoNJYPBM447GeBEl2AKWFmEYj3VCzsz57sfS-odyGE4 VSsNCfBfZG7ucL3fw8_tXWtySVvqxvXdMVW4ntSRS&sig=A HIEtbQt7HteqU67kyoVFObAooRr7uooew.

9. U.S. Energy Information Administration, *Monthly Crude Oil Production by US PAD District and State,* November 29, 2011, http://www.eia.gov/dnav/pet/pet_crd_crpdn_adc_mbbl_m.htm.

10. "US to Reap Fruits of Deepwater Labor," *Rigzone,* March 26, 2010, http://www.rigzone.com/news/article.asp?a_id=90122.

11. "BP Announces Giant Oil Discovery in the Gulf of Mexico," BP Investor Relations, September 2, 2009, http://www.bp.com/genericarticle.do?categoryId=2012968&contentId=7055818.

12. "ExxonMobil Announces Three Discoveries in the Deepwater Gulf of Mexico," ExxonMobil Investor Relations, June 08, 2011, http://www.businesswire.com/news/home/20110608005901/en/ExxonMobil-Announces-Discoveries-Deepwater-Gulf-Mexico.

13. Baker Hughes Rotary Rig Count, June 8, 2012, http://investor.shareholder.com/bhi/rig_counts/rc_index.cfm?showpage=na.

14. Matt Wolfe, "GPI+ — Gulf Permit Index — as of April 30," Gulf Permit Index, Greater New Orleans Inc. http://gnoinc.org/news/publications/press-release/gpi-gulf-permit-index-as-of-april-30/

15. Ibid.

16. American Clean Energy and Security Act of 2009. H.R. 2454,. http://thomas.loc.gov/cgi-bin/bdquery/D?d111:9:./temp/~bdYGLT::|/home/LegislativeData.php?n=BSS;c=111|.

17. Joseph Lieberman website, "Kerry, Lieberman: American Power Act Bill Will Secure America's Energy, Climate Future," Press Release, May 5, 2010, http://lieberman.senate.gov/index.cfm/news-events/news/2010/5/kerry-lieberman-american-power-act-bill-will-secure-americas-energy-climate-future.

18. Ed Markey website, "House Passes Historic Waxman-Markey Clean Energy Bill," Press Release, June 26, 2009, http://markey.house.gov/press-release/june-26-2009-house-passes-historic-waxman-markey-clean-energy-bill.

19. Nancy Pelosi website, "Pelosi: 'Remember These Four Words For What This Legislation Means: Jobs, Jobs, Jobs, and Jobs," Press

Release, June 26, 2009, http://www.democraticleader.gov/news/press?id=1254.

20. Congressional Budget Office, "H.R. 2454 American Clean Energy and Security Act of 2009," Cost Estimate, June 5, 2009, pp. 35–37 http://www.cbo.gov/ftpdocs/102xx/doc10262/hr2454.pdf.

21. U.S. Congressional Research Service, "H.R.2454 CRS Summary," pp. 1–4, http://thomas.loc.gov/cgi-bin/bdquery/D?d111:2:./temp/~bdALge:@@@D&summ2=m&|/home/LegislativeData.php?n=BSS;c=111|.

22. Stephen Davis and John Haltiwanger, "Sectoral Job Creation and Destruction Responses to Oil Price Changes," *Journal of Monetary Economics*, Vol. 48, No. 3 (December 2001):465–512, http://www.sciencedirect.com/science/article/pii/S0304393201000861.

23. Congressional Budget Office, "How Policies to Reduce Greenhouse Gas Emissions Could Affect Employment" (Brief), May 5, 2010, http://www.cbo.gov/ftpdocs/105xx/doc10564/05-05-CapAndTrade_Brief.pdf.

24. Ibid., p. 1.

25. Ibid., p. 2.

26. Ibid., p. 3.

27. W. David Montgomery, Prepared testimony of W. David Montgomery, Ph.D., before the Committee on Environment and Public Works Subcommittee on "Green Jobs and the New Economy," United States Senate Hearing on Green Jobs and Trade *Proceedings of the Green Jobs and Trade,* Washington, DC, http://www.epw.senate.gov/public/index.cfm?FuseAction=Files.View&FileStore_id=5abed004-c3d2-4f28-a721-734ad78cdd99.

28. Barack Obama, "Statement by the President on the Ozone National Ambient Air Quality Standards," White House Office of the Press Secretary, Press Release, September 2, 2011, http://www.whitehouse.gov/the-press-office/2011/09/02/statement-president-ozone-national-ambient-air-quality-standards.

29. U.S. Bureau of Labor Statistics, "The Employment Situation—August 2011," September 2, 2011, http://www.bls.gov/news.release/archives/empsit_09022011.pdf.

30. U.S. Bureau of Labor Statistics, "The Employment Situation—October 2011," September 2, 2011, http://www.bls.gov/news.release/archives/empsit_11042011.pdf.

31. Barack Obama, "Statement by the President on the Ozone National Ambient Air Quality Standards," White House Office of the Press Secretary, Press Release, September 2, 2011, http://www.whitehouse.gov/the-press-office/2011/09/02/statement-president-ozone-national-ambient-air-quality-standards.

32. U.S. Environmental Protection Agency, Office of Air Quality Planning and Standards, "March 2008 Final National Ambient Air Quality Standards for Ground-level Ozone," pp. 1–8 http://www.epa.gov/apti/Materials/Ozone%20Final%20NAAQS%20Presentation.version%20for%20Lydia%20broadcast.draft.pdf.

33. John Broder, "E.P.A. Seeks Stricter Rules to Curb Smog," *The New York Times*, January 7, 2010, http://www.nytimes.com/2010/01/08/science/earth/08smog.html.

34. U.S. Environmental Protection Agency, "S2: Supplemental Regulatory Impact Analysis of Alternative Standards 0.055 and 0.060 ppm for the Ozone NAAQS Reconsideration," November 5, 2009, pp. 18–20, http://www.epa.gov/ttn/ecas/regdata/RIAs/s2-suppmental_analysis-060%2605_55_11-5-09.pdf. See also "Final Ozone NAAQS Regulatory Impact Analysis," http://www.epa.gov/ttnecas1/regdata/RIAs/452_R_08_003.pdf

35. U.S. Environmental Protection Agency Office of Air Quality Planning and Standards, "Latest Findings on National Air Quality." January 2008, http://epa.gov/airtrends/2007/report/trends_report_full.pdf.

36. Lara Akinbami,"The State of Childhood Asthma, United States, 1980–2005,"Advance Data from Vital and Health Statistics No.

381, Centers for Disease Control and Prevention, December 12, 2006, http://www.cdc.gov/nchs/data/ad/ad381.pdf.

37. "Harman/Upton Amendment to Title I," House Energy Commerce Committee website, http://democrats.energycommerce.house.gov/images/stories/Documents/Markups/PDF/HARMON-UPTON.pdf.

38. U.S. Government Printing Office, "Energy Independence and Security Act of 2007," pp. 1573–1577, December 19, 2007, http://www.gpo.gov/fdsys/pkg/PLAW-110publ140/pdf/PLAW-110publ140.pdf.

39. Ibid.

40. "Locations: Winchester & Lexington, Kentucky," Sylvania website, http://www.sylvania.com/en-us/about/Pages/locations.aspx.

41. "Neptun Light complies with "Buy American" Program and ARRA Funds for Induction Lights," Neptun Press Release, June 25, 2010, http://www.neptunlight.com/press_release_details/118.

42. U.S. Environmental Protection Agency, "Cleaning Up a Broken CFL," http://www.epa.gov/cfl/cflcleanup.html.

43. National Electrical Manufacturers Association, "Shipments of Incandescent Lamps Illuminate at the Close of 2011." Press Release, March 15, 2012, http://www.nema.org/media/pr/20120315a.cfm.

44. Peter Whoriskey, "Government-Subsidized Green Light Bulb Carries a Costly Price Tag," *The Washington Post*, March 8, 2012, http://www.washingtonpost.com/business/economy/government-subsidized-green-light-bulb-carries-costly-price-tag/2012/03/07/gIQAFxODoR_story.html.

45. Colin Bird, "End of Ethanol Subsidies Could Increase Gas Prices Marginally," *The Chicago Tribune*, January 4, 2012, http://blogs.cars.com/kickingtires/2012/01/end-of-ethanol-subsidies-could-increase-gas-prices-marginally.html.

46. "Alcohol and Cellulosic Biofuel Fuels Credit," IRS Form 6478, http://www.irs.gov/pub/irs-pdf/f6478.pdf.

47. U.S. Environmental Protection Agency, Office of Transportation and Air Quality, "EPA Finalizes 2012 Renewable Fuel Standards,"

December 2011, http://www.epa.gov/otaq/fuels/renewablefuels/
documents/420f11044.pdf.

48. Ibid.

49. Matthew Wald, "A Fine for Not Using a Biofuel That Doesn't
Exist," *The New York Times,* January 9, 2012, http://www.nytimes.
com/2012/01/10/business/energy-environment/companies-face-fines-
for-not-using-unavailable-biofuel.html.

50. U.S. Environmental Protection Agency, "Civil Enforcement of
the Renewable Fuels Standard (RFS) Program," http://www.epa.gov/
compliance/civil/caa/fuel-novs.html.

51. H.R. 3010: Regulatory Accountability Act of 2011, 112th Congress, 2011–2012, http://www.govtrack.us/congress/bills/112/hr3010/
text.

Chapter 3

1. Charles A. Reich, The Greening of America (New York: Ran-
dom House, 1970).

2. U.S. Department of Labor, Bureau of Labor Statistics, http://
bls.gov/green/green_definition.pdf.

3. List of NAICS codes, and whether industry qualifies as green,
August 24, 2010, http://www.bls.gov/green/final_green_def_8242010_
pub.xls.

4. Ibid.

5. U.S. Department of Labor, Bureau of Labor Statistics, "News
Release: Employment in Green Goods and Services-2010," March 22,
2012, http://www.bls.gov/news.release/pdf/ggqcew.pdf.

6. U.S. Department of Agriculture, "World Agriculture Supply
and Demand Estimates," November 9, 2011, http://www.usda.gov/oce/
commodity/wasde/latest.pdf.

7. U.S. Department of Labor, Bureau of Labor Statistics, "Measuring Green Jobs," http://www.bls.gov/green/#faqs.

8. List of NAICS codes, and whether industry qualifies as green,
http://www.bls.gov/green/final_green_def_8242010_pub.xls.

9. U.S. Green Buildings Council, *LEED Rating System Development,* 2012, http://www.usgbc.org/DisplayPage. aspx?CMSPageID=2360.

10. U.S. Environmental Protection Agency and U.S. Department of Energy, *About Energy Star,* Energystar.gov website, 2011, http://www. energystar.gov/index.cfm?c=about.ab_index.

11. Brett McMahon, Testimony on "The Green Jobs Debacle: Where Has All of the Taxpayers' Money Gone?" before the Subcommittee on Regulatory Affairs, Stimulus Oversight and Government Spending, November 2, 2011, http://oversight.house.gov/images/stories/ Testimony/11-2-11_RegAffairs_McMahon_Testimony.pdf.

12. "Carbon Calculator," The Carbon Fund, http://www.carbonfund.org/site/pages/carbon_calculators/category/Assumptions.

13. "Solicitation for Grant Applications—Labor Market Improvement Green Job Grants Consortium States Submittal Summary," Employment Security Department, Washington State, July 2009, http://www.wtb.wa.gov/Documents/LMEAconsortiumapps.pdf.

14. "The Northern Plains and Rocky Mountain Consortium Final Report," *Northern Plains and Rocky Mountain Consortium,* 2011, http:// researchingthegreeneconomy.org/docfolder/publications/The%20 Northern%20Plains%20&%20Rocky%20Mountain%20Consortium%20Final%20Report.pdf.

15. *MARC Regional Green Jobs* website, *What is a Green Job,* http:// www.marcgreenworks.com/gsipub/index.asp?docid=398.

16. "The Greening of Louisiana's Economy: Summary of Survey Results," *Louisiana Workforce Commission,* September 2011, http://lwc. laworks.net/sites/LMI/GreenJobs/Reports/Louisiana_Survey_Results. pdf#Method.

17. "Alabama Green Definitions," Alabama Department of Industrial Relations website, http://www.greenjobsinalabama.com/gsipub/ index.asp?docid=417.

18. "The Pennsylvania Green Jobs Report Part 1," Pennsylvania Workforce Development Commission,

http://www.portal.state.pa.us/portal/server.pt/directory/
center_for_green_careers/134700?DirMode=1.

19. "The Greening of Oregon's Workforce: Jobs, Wages and Training," *Oregon Employment Department Workforce and Economic Research
Division*, June 2009, http://www.qualityinfo.org/pubs/green/greening.
pdf.

20. "Green Jobs," *New Jersey Next Stop . . . Your Career* website,
accessed November 8, 2011, http://www.state.nj.us/njnextstop/home/
greenjobs/.

21. "WI Department of Commerce Accepting Applications Now
for Manufacturing Renewable and Energy Efficiency Projects," Wisconsin Department of Commerce, http://energyindependence.wi.gov/
docview.asp?docid=18370&locid=160.

22. "Green Goods and Services Industries by NAICS Code," Federal Register Notice for Public Comment: September 21, 2010, http://
www.bls.gov/green/final_green_def_8242010_pub.pdf.

23. Elliot Lewis (Assistant Inspector General, U.S. Department
of Labor), Testimony on "The Green Jobs Debacle: Where Has All of
the Taxpayers' Money Gone?" before the Subcommittee on Regulatory
Affairs, Stimulus Oversight and Government Spending, November 2,
2011.

24. Ibid.

25. Jane Oates (Assistant Secretary for Employment and Training),
U.S. Department of Labor. *Response to Senator Grassley Regarding Green
Jobs Training Grants*. Letter, April 4, 2012.

26. Jane Oates (Assistant Secretary for Employment and Training, U.S. Department of Labor) Testimony on "Addressing Concerns
about the Integrity of the U.S. Department of Labor's Jobs Reporting"
before the U.S. House of Representatives Committee on Oversight and
Government Reform, June 6, 2012, http://oversight.house.gov/hear-
ing/addressing-concerns-about-the-integrity-of-the-u-s-department-of-
labors-jobs-reporting/

27. Connection Research, "Who Are the Green Collar Workers?" commissioned by the Environment Institute of Australia & New Zealand, St. Leonard's, Australia, 2009, http://www.eianz.org/sb/modules/news/attachments/71/Green%20Collar%20Worker%20report%20Final.pdf.

28. U.K. House of Commons, *Green Jobs and Skills: Government Response to the Committee's Second Report*, First Special Report of Session 2009–2010. Environmental Audit Committee, March 15, 2010, p. 5. http://www.publications.parliament.uk/pa/cm200910/cmselect/cmenvaud/435/435.pdf.

29. U.K. House of Commons, *Green Jobs and Skills: Government Response to the Committee's Second Report*, First Special Report of Session 2009–2010. Environmental Audit Committee, March 15, 2010, http://www.publications.parliament.uk/pa/cm200910/cmselect/cmenvaud/435/435.pdf.

30. U.K. House of Commons, *Green Jobs and Skills Second Report of Session 2008–2009*, Environmental Audit Committee, December 16, 2009, http://www.publications.parliament.uk/pa/cm200910/cmselect/cmenvaud/159/159i.pdf.

31. "Green Worker Program," National Parks of Japan, accessed November 15, 2011, http://www.env.go.jp/en/nature/nps/park/support/gw.html.

32. "Green Jobs: Toward Decent Work in a Sustainable, Low Carbon World," United Nations Environment Programme, Nairobi, Kenya, 2008, http://www.ilo.org/wcmsp5/groups/public/@ed_emp/@emp_ent/documents/publication/wcms_158727.pdf.

33. C. Martinez-Fernandez et al. *Green Jobs and Skills: The Local Labour Market Implications of Addressing Climate Change*, February 8, 2010, working document, CFE/LEED, OECD, http://www.oecd.org/dataoecd/54/43/44683169.pdf?contentId=44683170.

34. Allister Slingenberg et al., *Environment and Labour Force Skills*, European Commission DG Environment. ECORYS. Rotterdam 2008,

http://ec.europa.eu/environment/enveco/industry_employment/pdf/
labor_force.pdf.

Chapter 4

1. Arthur Conan Doyle, "Silver Blaze," *Memoirs of Sherlock Holmes* (London, George Newnes, 1894).

2. Reich, *The Greening of America*, p. 89.

3. A. Durning, *Green Collar Jobs* (Seattle: Northwest Environment Watch, 1999).

4. "Apollo Alliance Advisory Board of Directors," Apollo Alliance website, http://apolloalliance.org/about/board/.

5. BlueGreen Alliance, "Apollo Alliance Project," http://www.bluegreenalliance.org/apollo.

6. New Energy for America: The Apollo Jobs Report, January 2004, http://www.apolloalliance.org/downloads/resources_ApolloReport_022404_122748.pdf.

7. Bracken Hendricks, *Take Back America Conferences, Campaign for America's Future, Plenary session: An Apollo Project for Energy Independence*, June 5, 2003, http://www.ourfuture.org/files/z_historic/tba05/hendricks.pdf.

8. J. Inslee and B. Hendricks, *Apollo's Fire: Igniting America's Clean Energy Economy* (Washington. DC: Island Press, 2007).

9. See R. Pinderhughes, *Green Collar Jobs,* 2007, http://bss.sfsu.edu/raquelrp/documents/v13fullreport.pdf.

10. Apollo Alliance, "Cleveland Rocks New Energy Economy," 2007.

11. Pinderhughes, *Green Collar Jobs.*

12. Ibid.

13. J. Grossfeld, "Leo the Linchpin," *The American Prospect*, September 24, 2007, http://prospect.org/cs/articles?article=leo_the_linchpin.

14. U.S. Department of Labor, Bureau of Labor Statistics, "May 2011 National Industry-Specific Occupational Employment and Wage

Estimates," Occupation Employment Statistics, http://www.bls.gov/oes/current/oes472221.htm#nat.

15. J. Grossfeld, "Leo the Linchpin," *The American Prospect*, September 24, 2007, http://prospect.org/cs/articles?article=leo_the_linchpin.

16. Laborers International Union of North America (LIUNA), "Job Killers, 2; American Workers," Press Release, January 18, 2012, http://www.liunabuildsamerica.org/news/story/766.

17. Communication Workers of America, "Environmental Groups, Unions Support President's Decision on Keystone XL," Press Release, January 18, 2012, http://www.cwa-union.org/news/entry/environmental_groups_unions_support_presidents_decision_on_keystone_xl.

18. Ibid.

19. AFL-CIO, *Greening the Economy*, March 4, 2008, http://www.aflcio.org/About/Exec-Council/EC-Statements/Greening-the-Economy.

20. Ibid.

21. J. Brecher, "Labor's War on Global Warming," *The Nation*, March 24, 2008, http://www.thenation.com/article/labors-war-global-warming.

22. "BlueGreen Alliance and Apollo Alliance Merge to Strengthen Green Economy," Environment News Service, May 26, 2011, http://www.ens-newswire.com/ens/may2011/2011-05-26-091.html.

23. As reported in a 2008 article by *The Nation*. The collaboration has since grown to unite 14 million members, including numerous labor unions and environmental groups, whose motto is "In pursuit of good jobs, a clean environment and a green economy." See also BlueGreen Alliance, *About the BlueGreen Alliance*, 2011, http://www.bluegreenalliance.org/about.

24. BlueGreen Alliance, *Issues*, 2011, http://www.bluegreen-alliance.org/about_us?id=0003.

25. E. Saner, " What is a Green-Collar job?" *The Guardian*, January 28, 2008, http://www.guardian.co.uk/environment/2008/jan/28/ethicalliving.ethicalbusiness.

26. Brecher, "Labor's War on Global Warming."

27. Ibid.

28. Centers for Disease Control and Prevention, *Green, Safe and Healthy Jobs*, August 26, 2010, http://www.cdc.gov/niosh/topics/PtD/greenjobs.html.

29. Calculation made by the author using data at "Overview of Funding: Contract, Grant and Loan Programs," Recovery.gov, http://www.recovery.gov/Transparency/fundingoverview/Pages/contracts-grantsloans-details.aspx#Transportation.

30. LIUNA, "LIUNA Leaves BlueGreen Alliance," Press Release, January 20, 2012, http://www.liunabuildsamerica.org/news/story/767.

31. E. Strickland, "The New Face of Environmentalism," *East Bay Express*, November 2, 2005, http://www.eastbayexpress.com/gyrobase/the-new-face-of-environmentalism/Content?oid=1079539&showFullTex t=true.

32. D. Roberts, "Van Jones: 'I feel like I'm just get-ting started'," *Grist*, March 25, 2010, http://www.grist.org/article/2010-03-25-van-jones-i-feel-like-im-just-getting-started.

33. Elliot Michael, "Heroes of the Environment 2008: Activists, Van Jones." *TIME*, September 24, 2008, http://www.time.com/time/specials/packages/article/0,28804,1841778_1841781_1841811,00.html.

34. Green For All explains the virtues of a green economy: "A clean-energy economy will move America past some of its most press-ing challenges. By making us energy independent, it will improve our national and economic security. By radically reducing the pollution that causes global warming, it will improve the health of our families and neighborhoods. And by creating millions of quality jobs and careers, it will pull America out of the current recession, strengthen our middle class, and better protect us from future economic turmoil."

35. pp. 21, 23.

36. p. 1

37. V. Jones, *The Green Collar Economy*, (New York: HarperOne, 2008), p. 184.

38. Ibid., p. 186.

39. Frédéric Bastiat, *Selected Essays on Political Economy*, trans. Seymour Cain (Irvington-on-Hudson, NY: Library of Economics and Liberty, 1995), http://www.econlib.org/library/Bastiat/basEss1.html.

40. To be sure, this book must not be taken to imply that markets work perfectly and are *always* better than government involvement. Far from it. The free market has numerous failings, and there is always room for political input, so far as respected economists are involved in the discussions. Problems arise, however, when non-economists and social activists deceive themselves into believing that they can success-fully plan an economy that is made up of billions of transactions daily. Their intentions may be noble, but being economically illiterate, they fail to recognize that it is humanly impossible to gather the billions of ever-changing pieces of information needed to run an economy. The failure of the Soviet Union should be ample proof of the futility of such an endeavor. To read an excellent essay on the theory of the self-regulating nature of the *invisible hand* of the market, see Leonard E. Read, "I, Pencil: My Family Tree as told to Leonard E. Read" (Irvington-on-Hudson, NY: Library of Economics and Liberty, 1999), http://www.econlib.org/library/Essays/rdPncl1.html.

41. K. Schneider, "Recovery Bill Is Breakthrough on Clean Energy, Good Jobs," *Apollo Alliance*, February 17, 2009, http://apolloalliance.org/feature-articles/at-last-federal-government-signs-up-for-clean-energy-economy/.

42. Apollo Alliance, "Mission," 2011, http://apolloalliance.org/about/mission/.

43. Apollo Alliance, "Achievements," 2011, http://apolloalliance.org/about/achievements/.

44. Schneider, "Recovery Bill Is Breakthrough on Clean Energy, Good Jobs."

45. D. Stone, "What Green Jobs?" *Newsweek*, July 28, 2009, http://www.newsweek.com/2009/07/27/what-green-jobs.html.

46. Durning, A. "Climate Fairness." *Sightline Daily*. January 24, 2008. http://daily.sightline.org/daily_score/archive/2008/01/24/climate-fairness

47. Eduardo Galeano, *Open Veins of Latin America* (New York: Monthly Review Press, 1973), p. 1.

48. A. Durning "Climate Fairness," *Sightline Daily*, January 24, 2008, http://daily.sightline.org/daily_score/archive/2008/01/24/climate-fairness.

49. E. de Place, "Best Post Ever?" *Sightline Daily*, April 14, 2008, http://daily.sightline.org/daily_score/archive/2008/04/14/best-post-ever.

50. A. Durning, " Climate and Race," *Sightline Daily*, January 14, 2010, http://daily.sightline.org/daily_score/archive/2010/01/14/climate-and-race.

51. U.S. Congressional Budget Office, *Estimated Impact of the American Recovery and Reinvestment Act,* November 2011, http://www.cbo.gov/ftpdocs/125xx/doc12564/11-22-ARRA.pdf.

52. According to Tom Krolik of the Bureau of Labor Statistics, as of November 2011, 8,838,00 jobs had been lost since payroll employment peaked in January of 2008, and since then only 2,947,000 jobs have been regained.

53. Congressional Budget Office, "How Policies to Reduce Greenhouse Gas Emissions Could Affect Employment" (Brief), May 5, 2010, http://www.cbo.gov/ftpdocs/105xx/doc10564/05-05-CapAndTrade_Brief.pdf.

54. A. Durning, "Rebutting CBO's Climate Policy and Jobs Paper," *Sightline Daily*, May 6, 2010, accessed December 1, 2011, http://daily.sightline.org/daily_score/archive/2010/05/06/rebutting-cbos-climate-job-killer-paper.

55. Ibid.

56. Ibid.

Chapter 5

1. J. Heintz et al., *New Jobs—Cleaner Air: Employment Effects under Planned Changes to EPA's Air Pollution Rules*, Ceres and PERI, February 2011, http://www.ceres.org/resources/reports/new-jobs-cleaner-air.

2. Bastiat, *Selected Essays on Political Economy*.

3. Ibid., p. 2.

4. Ibid.

5. Richard Shamalensee and Robert Stavins, "A Guide to Economic and Policy Analysis of EPA's Transport Rule," March 2011, http://www.supportcleanair.com/resources/studies/file/4-15-11-Schmalensee-Stavins-Guide-to-EPAs-Transport-Rule.pdf.

6. Ibid., p. 15.

7. R. Pollin et al., *Green Recovery: A Program to Create Good Jobs and Start Building a Low-Carbon Economy*, Department of Economics and Political Economy Research Institute (PERI), University of Massachusetts-Amherst, and Kit Batten and Bracken Hendricks, Project Managers, Center for American Progress (CAP), September 2008, http://www.americanprogress.org/issues/2008/09/pdf/green_recovery.pdf, p. 4.

8. Global Insight (GI), "U.S. Metro Economies Current and Potential Green Jobs in the U.S. Economy," October 2008, http://www.usmayors.org/pressreleases/uploads/greenjobsreport.pdf.

9. Ibid., p. 2.

10. Ibid., p. 14.

11. Montgomery, Prepared testimony before the Committee on Environment and Public Works Subcommittee on "Green Jobs and the New Economy."

12. Andrew David, *Shifts in U.S. Wind Turbine Equipment Trade in 2010*, United States International Trade Commission, Office of Industries, June 2011, http://www.usitc.gov/publications/332/executive_briefings/wind_EBOT_commission_review_final2.pdf.

13. Ibid.

14. Andrew David, *Industry and Trade Summary*, U.S. International Trade Commission, Office of Industries Publication ITS-02, June 2009, http://www.usitc.gov/publications/332/ITS-2.pdf.

15. R. Pollin et al., op. cit.

16. Global Insight (GI), "U.S. Metro Economies Current and Potential Green Jobs in the U.S. Economy," p. 13.

17. T. Carper, Sen. *Carper Reacts to "New Jobs-Cleaner Air: Employment Effects Under Planned Changes to EPA's Air Pollution Rules" Report.* February 8, 2001, http://senate.gov/press/record.cfm?id=330970.

18. J. Heintz et al., *New Jobs—Cleaner Air: Employment Effects under Planned Changes to EPA's Air Pollution Rules.*

19. Seth Masia, "New EPA Rules May Create 1.45 Million Jobs," *Solar Today*, February 11, 2011, http://www.ases.org/index.php?option=com_myblog&show=New-EPA-rules-may-create-1.45-million-jobs.html&Itemid=27.

20. Dale W. Jorgenson and Peter J. Wilcoxen, "Reducing U.S. Carbon Dioxide Emissions: The Cost of Different Goals," in J.R. Moroney (ed.), *Advances in the Economics of Energy and Resources*, Vol. 7 (Greenwich, CT: JAI Press, 1992) pp. 125–158.

21. "Green Jobs: A Review of Recent Studies," Center for Energy Economics, Bureau of Economic Geology, Jackson School of Geosciences, the University of Texas at Austin, December 2008, http://www.beg.utexas.edu/energyecon/documents/CEE_Green_Jobs_Review.pdf.

22. Montgomery, Prepared testimony before the Committee on Environment and Public Works Subcommittee on "Green Jobs and the New Economy."

23. Pollin et al. *Green Recovery: A Program to Create Good Jobs and Start Building a Low-Carbon Economy*, p. 2.

24. Elliot Lewis, Testimony on "The Green Jobs Debacle: Where has all of the Taxpayers' Money Gone?" before the Subcommittee on Regulatory Affairs, Stimulus Oversight and Government Spending.

25. K. Gordon, Testimony for the U.S. Senate Committee on Environment and Public Works Subcommittee on Green Jobs and the New Economy, *Green Jobs and Trade*, Washington, DC, 2011. http://epw.senate.gov/public/index.cfm?FuseAction=Files. View&FileStore_id=9a2a8be6-5bc2-4b71-80ed-e47f1fa8cb66.

26. Ibid.

27. Amar Bhidé, *The Venturesome Economy: How Innovation Sustains Prosperity in a More Connected World*, (Princeton, NJ: Princeton University Press, 2008).

28. K. Gordon, Testimony for the U.S. Senate Committee on Environment and Public Works Subcommittee on Green Jobs and the New Economy. http://epw.senate.gov/public/index.cfm?FuseAction=Files. View&FileStore_id=9a2a8be6-5bc2-4b71-80ed-e47f1fa8cb66.

Chapter 6

1. U.S. Congress, *Revised Continuing Appropriations Resolution,* 2007, H.J. Res. 20. 110th Congress, 2007. http://www.gpo.gov/fdsys/pkg/BILLS-110hjres20enr/pdf/BILLS-110hjres20enr.pdf.

2. U.S. Congress, *Omnibus Appropriations Act, 2009*, H. R. 1105 111th Congress, 2009, http://www.gpo.gov/fdsys/pkg/BILLS-111hr1105enr/pdf/BILLS-111hr1105enr.pdf.

3. George Bush, "Bush Remarks on Climate," Transcript, *The Washington Post*, April 16, 2008, http://www.washingtonpost.com/wp-dyn/content/article/2008/04/16/AR2008041603084.html

4. "History," U.S. Department of Energy Loan Program Office website, https://lpo.energy.gov/?page_id=134.

5. "LGP (1703 and 1705) FAQ," Department of Energy Loan Program Office website, 2011, https://lpo.energy.gov/?page_id=368.

6. Nichola Groom, "Fisker Announces Layoffs, Renegotiates Loan," *Reuters*, February 2, 2012. http://www.reuters.com/article/2012/02/07/us-fisker-idUSTRE8161BE20120207.

7. Carol D. Leonnig, Joe Stephens, and Alice Crites, "Obama's Focus on Visiting Clean-Tech Companies Raises Questions," *The*

Washington Post, June 25, 2011, http://www.washingtonpost.com/ politics/obamas-focus-on-visiting-clean-tech-companies-raises-questions/2011/06/24/AGSFu9kH_story.html.

8. Solyndra, "Timeline," Solyndra website, 2012, http://www. solyndra.com/about-us/timeline/.

9. Credit Committee Recommendation from Chairman Loan Guarantee Credit Committee to Director Loan Guarantee Program Office, Subject: Credit Committee Recommendation re: Solyndra Fab 2 LLC, solar photovoltaic power panel project for a loan guarantee of $535,000,000, January 9, 2009, http://republicans.energycommerce. house.gov/Media/file/Hearings/Oversight/091411/DocumentsEntered-IntoRecord.pdf.

10. E-mail from Lachlan Steward to [Name redacted], Subject: Solyndra meeting, January 13, 2009, http://republicans.energycommerce.house.gov/Media/file/Hearings/Oversight/091411/DocumentsEnteredIntoRecord.pdf.

11. E-mail from Senior Advisor to the Secretary of Energy for Recovery Act Spending to [Name Redacted], March 10, 2009, http:// republicans.energycommerce.house.gov/Media/file/Hearings/Oversight/091411/DocumentsEnteredIntoRecord.pdf

12. E-mail from [Name redacted] to [Name Redacted], Subject: Re: Solar co loan announcement in northern California, Match 10, 2009, http://republicans.energycommerce.house.gov/Media/file/Hearings/ Oversight/091411/DocumentsEnteredIntoRecord.pdf.

13. E-mail from [Name redacted] to [Name redacted], subject: Final Solyndra Credit Subsidy Cost, August 27, 2009, http://republicans. energycommerce.house.gov/Media/file/Hearings/Oversight/091411/ DocumentsEnteredIntoRecord.pdf

14. E-mail from [Name redacted] to [Name redacted], Subject: Solyndra, August 19, 2009, http://republicans.energycommerce. house.gov/Media/file/Hearings/Oversight/091411/DocumentsEntered-IntoRecord.pdf. Note: (A/R stands for accounts receivable.)

15. E-mail from [Name redacted]@hq.doe.gov to [Name redacted], Subject: Solyndra Closing Date, August 27, 2009, http://republicans. energycommerce.house.gov/Media/file/Hearings/Oversight/091411/ DocumentsEnteredIntoRecord.pdf.

16. E-mail from Office of Management and Budget official to Terrell P. McSweeny, subject: DOE announcement, August 31, 2009, http://republicans.energycommerce.house.gov/Media/file/Hearings/ Oversight/111711_solyndra/footnotes.pdf.

17. Jonathan Stempel, "Solar Company Solyndra's Survival in Doubt Pre-IPO," Reuters, April 2, 2010, http://www.reuters. com/article/2010/04/02/us-solyndra-ipo-goingconcern-idUS-TRE6311C320100402. Note: A deficit means a company's liabilities are greater than its assets, whereas an operating loss occurs when the cost of producing a good exceeds its revenue.

18. E-mail from Steve Westly to Valerie Jarrett, May 24, 2010, http://republicans.energycommerce.house.gov/Media/file/Hearings/ Oversight/111711_solyndra/footnotes.pdf.

19. E-mail from Valerie Jarrett to Ronald Klain, May 24, 2010, http://republicans.energycommerce.house.gov/Media/file/Hearings/ Oversight/111711_solyndra/footnotes.pdf.

20. E-mail from [Name redacted] to [Name redacted], Subject: Solydra optics, January 31, 2011. http://republicans.energycommerce. house.gov/Media/file/Hearings/Oversight/091411/DocumentsEntered-IntoRecord.pdf

21. Solyndra, Press Release, September 2009, http://www.solyn-dra.com/2009/09/megawatt-solar/.

22. Susan S. Richardson, "Solyndra Restructuring Memorandum," Office of the Chief Counsel of the Department of Energy Loan Pro-grams Office, http://republicans.energycommerce.house.gov/Media/ file/Hearings/Oversight/101411/memotogc.pdf.

23. Eric Meltzer, e-mail exchange, November 23, 2011.

24. Dan Primack, "Solyndra 'Repayment' Debate was Worthless," *CNN Money*, March 7, 2012, http://finance.fortune.cnn.com/2012/03/07/solyndra-repayment-debate-was-pointless/?iid=SF_F_LN.

25. "White House Visitor Access Records," White House, 2011, http://www.whitehouse.gov/briefing-room/disclosures/visitor-records.

26. "BOK Financial Bios of Officers and Directors," BOK Financial, 2012, http://investor.bokf.com/od.aspx?iid=100003.

27. "History of TCF," Tulsa Community Foundation, 2010,http://www.tulsacf.org/index.php?option=com_content&view=article&id=48&Itemid.

28. E-mail from Ken Levit to Steve Mitchell, Subject: Re: KPMG, February 27, 2010, http://republicans.energycommerce.house.gov/Media/file/Letters/112th/110911KaiserEmails.pdf.

29. E-mail from George Kaiser to Steve Mitchell, March 5, 2010, http://republicans.energycommerce.house.gov/Media/file/Letters/112th/110911KaiserEmails.pdf.

30. E-mail from Steve Mitchell to George Kaiser, October 6, 2010, released by House Energy Commerce Committee, accessed November 16, 2011, http://democrats.energycommerce.house.gov/sites/default/files/documents/Email_MitchelKaiser_Footnote13_10.06.10.pdf.

31. E-mail from Steve Mitchell to George Kaiser, October 3, 2010, release by House Energy Commerce Committee, http://democrats.energycommerce.house.gov/sites/default/files/documents/Email_MitchelKaiser_Footnote13_10.06.10.pdf.

32. Phone call with Michelle Bean of 1366 Technologies, November 15, 2011.

33. Evergreen Solar, "Evergreen Solar to Close Devens Manufacturing Facility," Press Release, January 11, 2011, http://evergreensolar.com/en/2011/01/evergreen-solar-to-close-devens-manufacturing-facility/index.html

34. Dawn McCarty, "Evergreen Energy Files for Bankruptcy, Cites Lack of Financing," *Bloomberg*, January 24, 2012, http://www.bloomberg.com/news/2012-01-23/evergreen-energy-files-for-bankruptcy-liquidation-1-.html.

35. Beacon Power, "About Flywheel Energy Storage," 2012, http://www.beaconpower.com/products/about-flywheels.asp.

36. Beacon Power, *Form 10-K (Annual Report) for the Period Ended December 31, 2010*, March 16, 2011, http://files.shareholder.com/downloads/BCON/1480955423x0xS1047469-11-2225/1103345/filing.pdf.

37. Beacon Power, *Form 10-G (Quarterly Report) for the Period Ended June 30, 2011*, August 9, 2011, http://investors.beaconpower.com/secfiling.cfm?filingID=1104659-11-45359&CIK=1103345.

38. Bill Capp, "Statement from Beacon Power Corporation," November 1, 2011, http://beaconpower.com/files/Beacon-Media-Statement.pdf.

39. Rockland Capital, "Beacon Power Assets to Be Sold to Rockland Capital," Press Release, February 6, 2012, http://www.rockland-capital.com/newsmedia.htm.

40. George Stephanopoulos, Transcript: "George Stephanopoulos' ABC News / Yahoo! News Exclusive Interview with President Obama," October 3, 2011, http://abcnews.go.com/Politics/transcript-george-stephanopoulos-abc-news-yahoo-news-exclusive/story?id=14659193&singlePage=true#.TxByyG-Pn8c.

41. Jonathan Silver, Testimony before the House Committee on Energy and Commerce, Subcommittee on Oversight and Investigations on "Solyndra and the DOE Loan Program," September 14, 2011, http://republicans.energycommerce.house.gov/Media/file/Hearings/Oversight/091411/Silver.pdf.

42. "Annual Energy Outlook 2011: With Projections to 2035," U.S. Department of Energy, Energy Information Agency, April 2011, http://www.eia.gov/forecasts/aeo/pdf/0383(2011).pdf.

43. "International Energy Outlook: 2011" U.S. Department of Energy, Energy Information Agency, September 2011, http://205.254.135.24/forecasts/ieo/pdf/0484(2011).pdf.

44. Ben Blanchard, "At Least 32 Die in East China High-Speed Train Crash," *Reuters*, July 23, 2011, http://www.reuters.com/article/2011/07/23/us-china-train-idUSTRE76M26T20110723.

45. Mark Murro and Jonathan Rothwell, "Why the U.S. Should Not Abandon Its Clean Energy Lending Programs," *Brookings*, November 3, 2011, http://www.brookings.edu/opinions/2011/0927_solyndra_muro_rothwell.aspx.

Chapter 7

1. Department of Energy Awards $43 Million to Spur Offshore Wind Energy, September 8, 2011, http://energy.gov/articles/department-energy-awards-43-million-spur-offshore-wind-energy.

2. Based on data provided by the Treasury Department and author calculations, approximately 40 percent of total grants for wind, through the DOE section 1603 grants, were given to wind projects where there is a foreign owner and/or operator. http://www.treasury.gov/initiatives/recovery/Documents/Section%201603%20Awards%20%2011.16.11.xlsx.

3. BENTEK Energy, *The Wind Power Paradox*, July 19 2011, http://www.bentekenergy.com/documents/BENTEK_TheWind-PowerParadox_071911_Sample.pdf.

4. Ibid.

5. Robert Bryce, "A New Study Takes The Wind Out Of Wind Energy," *Forbes.com*, July 19, 2011, http://www.forbes.com/2011/07/19/wind-energy-carbon.html.

6. BENTEK Energy, *The Wind Power Paradox*.

7. Ibid.

8. Ibid.

9. Ibid.

10. James Murray, "US 2012 Carbon Price to Hit $13.70 - 02 Mar 2009," *BusinessGreen,* March 2, 2009, http://www.businessgreen.com/bg/news/1800695/us-2012-carbon-price-hit-usd1370.

11. BENTEK Energy, *The Wind Power Paradox.*

12. Robert Bryce, *The High Cost of Wind Energy as a Carbon-Dioxide Reduction Method,* Issue Brief No. 11, October 2011, http://www.manhattan-institute.org/html/ib_11.htm.

13. Robert Bryce, "America's Worst Wind-Energy Project," *National Review Online,* October 12, 2011, http://www.nationalreview.com/articles/279802/america-s-worst-wind-energy-project-robert-bryce.

14. Robert Bryce, "Texas Wind Fails, Again," *National Review Online,* August 29, 2011, http://www.manhattan-institute.org/html/miarticle.htm?id=7406.

15. Robert Mendick, "Firms Paid to Shut Down Wind Farms When the Wind Is Blowing," *The Telegraph,* June 19, 2010, http://www.telegraph.co.uk/earth/energy/windpower/7840035/Firms-paid-to-shut-down-wind-farms-when-the-wind-is-blowing.html.

16. Lee Van der Loo, "BPA Decision May Prompt Wind Shutdown Soon," *Sustainable Business Oregon* of the *Portland Business Journal,* May 16, 2011, http://www.sustainablebusinessoregon.com/articles/2011/05/bpa-decision-may-prompt-wind-shutdown.html.

17. "Northern N.B. Wind Farm Slowed by Ice Again," February 18, 2011, http://www.cbc.ca/news/canada/new-brunswick/story/2011/02/15/nb-caribou-wind-farm-ice.html.

18. Robert Bryce, "The Blowback Against Big Wind," *CounterPunch.com,* February 13, 2012, http://www.counterpunch.org/2012/02/13/the-blowback-against-big-wind/.

19. Ontario Wind Resistance website, 2012, http://ontario-wind-resistance.org/.

20. Bob Drogin, "Massachusetts Tribes Aim to Take the Wind Out of a Wind Farm," *The Los Angeles Times,* March 26, 2010, http://articles.latimes.com/2010/mar/26/nation/la-na-wind26-2010mar26.

21. American Wind Energy Association (AWEA), *U.S. Wind Industry Year-End 2010 Market Report,* January 2011, http://www.awea.org/learnabout/publications/upload/4Q10_market_outlook_public.pdf.

22. American Wind Energy Association, "Industry Statistics," http://www.awea.org/learnabout/industry_stats/index.cfm.

23. Iberdorola Renewables, "Major US Wind Power Installer Hails Recovery Act As Driver of Job Creation, Ongoing Domestic Investment," Iberdorola Renewables Press Release, October 14, 2010, accessed December 1, 2011, http://www.iberdrolarenewables.us/rel_10.10.14.html.

24. Energy Center of Wisconsin, "Parts of a Turbine," http://www.ecw.org/windpower/web/cat2a.html.

25. Andrew David, *Impact of Wind Energy Installations on Direct Manufacturing and Trade,* U.S. International Trade Commission, Office of Industries, July 2010, http://www.usitc.gov/publications/332/working_papers/ID-25.pdf.

26. Domestic content is calculated by taking the amount spent on each component and multiplying it by what the AWEA calculated to be the domestically manufactured content of each component.

27. Andrew S. David, "Impact of Wind Energy Installations on Domestic Manufacturing and Trade, " Office of Industries: U.S. International Trade Commission, July 2010, http://www.usitc.gov/publications/332/working_papers/ID-25.pdf

28. Vestas Americas, "Vestas Finishes 2010 With Record Order Intake in North America," January 5, 2011, http://www.vestas.com/files//Filer/EN/Press_releases/Local/2011/AM_110105_NR_UK.pdf.

29. Siemens, "New facility in Hutchinson," December 3, 2010, http://www.siemens.com/press/en/presspicture/?press=/en/presspicture/2010/renewable_energy/2010-11-wind/ere201012022-01.htm

30. Keith Bradsher, "China Wins in Wind Power, by Its Own Rules," *The New York Times,* December 14, 2010, http://www.nytimes.com/2010/12/15/business/global/15chinawind.html?ref=windpower.

31. Ibid.

32. Andrew David, *Shifts in U.S. Wind Turbine Equipment Trade in 2010*, June 2011, http://www.usitc.gov/publications/332/executive_briefings/wind_EBOT_commission_review_final2.pdf.

33. Xiangyi Dang, "Development of Wind Power Generation—Reflections on Chinese Power Generation," Tsinghua University, October 4, 2010, http://wenku.baidu.com/view/9fe8bfbfc77da26925c5b035.html.

34. Bradsher, "China Wins in Wind Power, by Its Own Rules."

35. Tom Zeller Jr. and Keith Bradsher, "China's Push into Wind Worries U.S.," *The New York Times,* December 2010, http://www.nytimes.com/2010/12/16/business/global/16wind.html.

36. Ibid.

37. Rebecca Smith, "Chinese-Made Turbines to Fill U.S. Wind Farm," *The Wall Street Journal,* October 30, 2009, http://online.wsj.com/article/SB125683832677216475.html.

38. Ibid.

39. Zeller and Bradsher, "China's Push into Wind Worries U.S. Industry."

40. As of February 2011 China's wind power capacity was 44,733 megawatts, while the United States' capacity was 40,180 megawatts. According to recent data released by the Chinese Renewable Energy Industry Association (CREIA), China had installed a total of 41.8 gigawatts (GW) of wind capacity by the end of 2010, just ahead of the U.S. total of 40.2 gigawatts.

41. Haibing Ma, "Beyond the Numbers: A Closer Look at China's Wind Power Success," *Revolt, the Worldwatch Institute's Climate and Energy Blog,* Worldwatch Institute, February 28, 2011, http://blogs.worldwatch.org/revolt/beyond-the-numbers-a-closer-look-at-china%E2%80%99s-wind-power-success/ (see also http://nyj.ndrc.gov.cn/ggtz/t20110128_393339.htm).

42. Ibid.

43. Ibid.

44. Ibid.

45. G. Alvarez et al., *Study on the Effects on Employment of Public Aid to Renewable Energy Sources.*

46. Ibid.

47. Royal Decree 2366/1994, http://www.iflr.com/Article/2025527/Spain-The-regulation-of-renewables.html.

48. Subsequent legislation increased Spain's commitment to the green agenda. In 2004, Royal Decree 234/2004 provided an economic outline for government assistance to renewables. The law set a precedent for reimbursement above a "mean reference rate' (an artificial rate set by the government) for the purchase of green technologies.

49. 661/2007.

50. Based on the U.S. Euro/USD closing price on June 1, 2007, the day that Royal Decree Royal 661/2007 went into effect.

51. Ibid., citation xxxvi.

52. Javier Santos, "Spain: The Regulation of Renewables," *IFLR The Global Practice Service*, October 1, 2008, http://www.iflr.com/Article/2025527/Channel/193438/Spain-The-regulation-of-renewables.html.

53. Based on the December 30, 2011, Euro/USD at U.S. close, of $1.295 per Euro.

54. Gabriel C. Alvarez, Raquel M. Jara, and Juan R. Julian, *Study on the Effects on Employment of Public Aid to Renewable Energy Sources,* Universidad Rey Juan Carlos, March 2009, http://www.juandemariana.org/pdf/090327-employment-public-aid-Renewable.pdf.

55. Ibid.

56 National Institute of Statistics (Spain), "Economically Active Population Survey (EAPS) First quarter of 2012," April 27, 2012, http://www.ine.es/en/daco/daco42/daco4211/epao112_en.pdf.

57. "Help for Spain's Regions Will Not Harm Rating, Minister Says," *El Pais*, May 21, 2012, http://elpais.com/elpais/2012/05/21/inenglish/1337628321_713419.html.

58. Michael Snyder, "9 Reasons Spain Is a Dead Economy Walking," *Business Insider*, June 15, 2010, http://www.businessinsider.com/why-spain-is-a-dead-economy-walking-2010-6.

59. Barbara Kollmeyer, "Spain Predicts higher budget deficit in 2011," *Marketwatch.com*, December 30, 2011, http://www.marketwatch.com/story/spain-predicts-higher-budget-deficit-in-2011-2011-12-30.

60. Anthony Faiola, "Spain's Answer to Unemployment: Go Greener," *The Washington Post*, September 24, 2009, http://www.washingtonpost.com/wp-dyn/content/article/2009/09/23/AR2009092302152.html?sid=ST2009092302161.

61. David Roman, "Spain Approves 30% Cut to Solar Subsidies, "*The Wall Street Journal*, December 23, 2010, http://online.wsj.com/article/SB10001424052748704278404576037343359005376.html.

62. Ben Stills, "Spain Halts Renewable Subsidies to Curb $31 Billion of Debts," *Bloomberg*, January 27, 2012, http://www.bloomberg.com/news/2012-01-27/spain-suspends-subsidies-for-new-renewable-energy-plants.html.

63. Kenneth P. Green, *The Myth of Green Energy Jobs: The European Experience*, American Enterprise Institute, February 2011, http://www.aei.org/files/2011/02/15/EEO-2011-02-No-2-updated-g.pdf.

64. Ibid.

65. Ibid.

66. Reuters, "German Bundestag approves solar incentive cuts," May 6, 2010, http://www.reuters.com/article/2010/05/06/germany-solar-idUSBAT00541720100506.

67. "German Solar Subsidy Cut Not Good For Yingli, Solar Industry," *Forbes.com*, January 25, 2012, http://www.forbes.com/sites/greatspeculations/2012/01/25/german-solar-subsidy-cut-not-good-for-yingli-solar-industry/.

68. Anthony Watts, "Quote of the Week—I Feel Duped." *Watts Up With That?* February 8, 2012, http://wattsupwiththat.com/2012/02/08/quote-of-the-week-i-feel-duped/.

69. Andrew David, *Growth in Wind Turbine Manufacturing and Trade,* March 2009, http://www.usitc.gov/publications/332/Executive_Briefings/USITC_EB_WindTurbines_David.pdf.

70. David, *Shifts in U.S. Wind Turbine Equipment Trade in 2010.*

71. Ibid.

72. In Center for Politiske Studier, *Wind Energy, The Case for Denmark,* September 2009, accessed November 29, 2011, http://www.cepos.dk/fileadmin/user_upload/Arkiv/PDF/Wind_energy_-_the_case_of_Denmark.pdf.

73. Ibid.

74. Ibid.

75. "Electricity Households," *Europe's Energy Portal,* June 2011, accessed November 29, 2011, http://www.energy.eu/.

76. Kenneth P. Green, *The Myth of Green Energy Jobs: The European Experience,* American Enterprise Institute, February 2011, http://www.aei.org/files/2011/02/15/EEO-2011-02-No-2-updated-g.pdf.

77. Keith Bradsher, "China Wins in Wind Power, by Its Own Rules," *The New York Times,* December 14, 2010, http://www.nytimes.com/2010/12/15/business/global/15chinawind.html?ref=windpower.

78. Brian Romano, "GE Says Wind Turbine Prices Drag on Profits, Sees Better 2012," *ReCharge,* January 23, 2012, http://www.recharge-news.com/business_area/finance/article299174.ece?.

Chapter 8

1. C. Schultze, "Green Energy Policy: Getting the Prices Right," Unpublished paper presented at the "Green Economy Dialogues," a conference hosted by the Business Advisory Council of the OECD, October 12, 2011.

2. Author calculations and OECD, Country Statistical Profile: China 2011–2012, Annual GDP Growth Rate 2006–2010, OECD, December 12, 2011, http://dx.doi.org/10.1787/csp-chn-table-2011-1-en.

3. Angel Gurría and Pier Carlo Padoan, Organisation for Economic Co-operation and Development (OECD), Press Con-

ference, Paris, May 22, 2012, p. 3, http://www.oecd.org/datao-ecd/44/58/49995435.pdf.

4. U.S. Energy Information Administration, "International Energy Statistics," http://www.eia.gov/cfapps/ipdbproject/IEDIndex3.cfm?tid=6&pid=29&aid=12.

5. Ibid.

6. Ibid.

7. UPDATE "Harmonised Unemployment Rate by Gender—Total," EuroStat Database, http://epp.eurostat.ec.europa.eu/tgm/table.do?tab=table&language=en&pcode=teilm020&tableSelection=1&plugin=1.

8. World Bank Development Indicators, 2011, http://data.worldbank.org/indicator/NY.GDP.MKTP.KD.ZG.

9. U.S. Energy Information Administration, http://www.eia.gov/cfapps/ipdbproject/IEDIndex3.cfm?tid=6&pid=29&aid=12.

10. "International Energy Statistics," U.S. Energy Information Administration, http://www.eia.gov/cfapps/ipdbproject/iedindex3.cfm?tid=2&pid=29&aid=12&cid=AS,BR,CA,CH,FR,GM,IN,IT,JA,MX,RS,SP,UK,US,&syid=2010&eyid=2010&unit=BKWH.

11. "Greenpeace: China Becomes World's Largest Wind-Installation Country, Challenges Remain," January 29, 2011, http://www.ibtimes.com/articles/106571/20110129/greenpeace-china-becomes-world-s-largest-wind-installation-country-challenges-remain.htm.

12. Coco Liu, "China Uses Feed-In Tariff to Build Domestic Solar Market," September 14, 2011, http://www.nytimes.com/cwire/2011/09/14/14climatewire-china-uses-feed-in-tariff-to-build-domestic-25559.html?pagewanted=all.

13. Organisation for Economic Cooperation and Development (OECD), http://www.oecd-ilibrary.org/economics/country-statistical-profiles-key-tables-from-oecd_20752288;jsessionid=2jf603nbo6q7o.delta.

14. Ibid.

15. Liu, "China Uses Feed-In Tariff to Build Domestic Solar Market."

16. "Coal consumption (most recent) by country," http://www. nationmaster.com/country/ch-china/ene-energy.

17. John Lee, "The Greening of China A Mirage," Hudson Institute, September 19, 2011, http://www.hudson.org/index. cfm?fuseaction=publication_details&id=8335.

18. J. Chen, "Renewable Energy in China: A Necessity, Not an Alternative," 2009, http://www.knowledgeatwharton.com.cn/index. cfm?fa=viewArticle&articleID=2054&languageid=1.

19. Ibid.

20. Ibid.

21. Ibid.

22. Ibid.

23. Ibid.

24. "An Overview of China's Renewable Energy Market." *June 16, 2011,* http://www.china-briefing.com/news/2011/06/16/an-overview-of-chinas-renewable-energy-market.html.

25. Ibid.

26. Ibid.

27. Ibid.

28. Martinot, Eric, and Junfeng Li. "Renewable Energy Policy Update For China." July 21, 2010, http://www. renewableenergyworld.com/rea/news/article/2010/07/ renewable-energy-policy-update-for-china.

29. Ibid.

30. Ibid.

31. Central Intelligence Agency (CIA), "Economy: China" May 9, 2012, https://www.cia.gov/library/publications/the-world-factbook/ geos/ch.html.

32. World Bank, 1996–2000, 2001–2005, 2006–2010. World Bank national accounts data, and OECD National Accounts data files,

Catalog Sources World Development Indicators, 2011, http://data.
worldbank.org/indicator/NY.GDP.MKTP.KD.ZG?page=2.

33. Ibid.

34. U.S. Bureau of Labor Statistics, Labor Force Statistics from the
Current Population Survey.

35. International Labour Organization, Catalog Sources World
Development Indicators, 2006–2010, http://data.worldbank.org/indi-
cator/SL.UEM.TOTL.ZS/countries.

Chapter 9

1. Senator Dianne Feinstein website, "Feinstein, Snowe Call
for 'Maximum Feasible' Fuel Economy Standards," Press Release,
July 25, 2011, http://www.feinstein.senate.gov/public/index.cfm/
press-releases?ID=11a953af-6be6-4d9b-a591-268545190512.

2. "President Obama Announces Historic 54.5 mpg Fuel
Efficiency Standard," White House Press Release, July 29,
2011, http://www.whitehouse.gov/the-press-office/2011/07/29/
president-obama-announces-historic-545-mpg-fuel-efficiency-standard.

3. "US Government Announces Deal with Automakers for
Next-Generation CAFE Standards," IHS Global Insight: Country and
Industry Forecasting, August 1, 2011, http://www.ihs.com/products/
global-insight/industry-economic-report.aspx?ID=1065930149.

4. National Highway Traffic Safety Administration (NHTSA),
*Relationship of Vehicle Weight to Fatality and Injury Risk in Model Year
1985-93 Passenger Cars and Light Trucks*, NHTSA Summary Report,
DOT HS 808 569, (Springfield, VA: National Technical Information
Services, 1997). See also National Research Council, "Effectiveness and
Impact of Corporate Average Fuel Economy (CAFÉ) Standards," 2002,
http://www.nhtsa.gov/cars/rules/cafe/docs/162944_web.pdf.

5. Ray Mabus, *Remarks by the Honorable Ray Mabus, Secretary of
the Navy,* Carnegie Council on Ethics in International Relations, New

York, New York, November 9, 2010, http://www.navy.mil/navydata/
people/secnav/Mabus/Speech/Carnegie11910.pdf.

6. Amory Lovins, *Soft Energy Paths*, (New York: Harper and Row,
1979).

7. Amory Lovins, *Winning the Oil Endgame*, (Snowmass, CO:
Rocky Mountain Institute, 2005).

8. James, "Of Mustard Fuel and Marines."

9. Elisabeth Rosenthal, "U.S. Military Orders Less Dependence
on Fossil Fuels," *The New York Times*, October 4, 2010, http://www.
nytimes.com/2010/10/05/science/earth/05fossil.html?pagewanted=all.

10. James, "Of Mustard Fuel and Marines."

11. J. Bartis and Lawrence Van Bibber, *Alternative Fuels for Military
Applications* (RAND National Defense Research Institute, 2011), http://
www.rand.org/content/dam/rand/pubs/monographs/2011/RAND_
MG969.sum.pdf.

12. D.K. Benjamin, *Eight Great Myths of Recycling*, 2003, http://
www.perc.org/pdf/ps28.pdf.

13. Ibid.

14. U.S. Energy Information Adminstration, Independent Statistics and Analysis, *Share of Total Primary Energy Supply in 2008, India*,
http://www.eia.gov/countries/cab.cfm?fips=IN.

15. United Nations, Department of Economic and Social
Affairs, *World Economic and Social Survey 2011*, New York, 2011, p.
xxii. http://www.un.org/en/development/desa/policy/wess/wess_
current/2011wess.pdf.

16. United Nations, "UN Report Calls for Major Investments in New Technologies in Developing Countries to Build
Green Economies," Press Release, United Nations, Geneva, July
5, 2011, http://www.un.org/en/development/desa/policy/wess/
wess_current/2011wesspr_en.pdf.

17. United Nations, *World Economic and Social Survey 2011*, p. 26.

18. Ibid., p. 26.

Chapter 10

1.   United States Geological Survey (USGS), "USGS Releases New Assessment of Gas Resources in the Marcellus Shale, Appalachian Basin," August 23, 2011, http://www.usgs.gov/newsroom/article. asp?ID=2893.

2.   Office of Management and Budget, *Fiscal Year 2013 Budget of the U.S. Government,* U.S. Government Printing Office, Washington, 2012, http://www.whitehouse.gov/sites/default/files/omb/budget/ fy2013/assets/budget.pdf.

3.   Estimate based on API's oil and gas industry share of Modifications of Dual Capacity Rule ($10.7 billion over 10 years) and of Reinstating Superfund Taxes ($10.5 billion over 10 years). See American Petroleum Institute, "FY2013 Budget Calls for Targeted Tax Increase on America's Oil & Natural Gas Producers," February 2012 http://www. api.org/policy-and-issues/~/media/3E404873038D44DA8685086ED0 83C9EF.ashx.

4.   Ibid.

5.   U.S. Department of the Treasury, "General Explanations of the Administration's Fiscal Year 2012 Revenue Proposals," February 2011, http://www.treasury.gov/resource-center/tax-policy/Documents/ General-Explanations-FY2012.pdf.

6.   Communications Workers of America, "Environmental Groups, Unions Support President's Decision on Keystone XL," Press Release, January 18, 2012, http://www.cwa-union.org/news/entry/ environmental_groups_unions_support_presidents_decision_on_keystone_xl#.Tz2B9FyPn8d.

7.   LIUNA, "Job Killers, 2; American Workers."

8.   LIUNA, "LIUNA Leaves BlueGreen Alliance."

9.   Howard Gruenspecht, "The U.S. Natural Gas Market in Focus: Current and Projected Supply and Demand Conditions, U.S. Energy Information Administration," April 17, 2012, Slide 9, https://docs. google.com/viewer?url=http%3A%2F%2F205.254.135.7%2Fpressroom %2Fpresentations%2Fhoward_04172012.ppt.

10. Timothy J. Considine and Robert W. Watson, "The Economic Opportunities of Shale Energy Development," *Energy Policy and the Environment Report No. 9*, Center for the Energy Policy and the Environment at the Manhattan Institute, June 9, 2011, http://www.manhattan-institute.org/html/eper_09.htm.

11. Timothy J. Considine, Robert W. Watson, and Seth Blumsack, "The Economic Impacts of the Pennsylvania Marcellus Shale Natural Gas Play: An Update," Pennsylvania State University, May 24, 2011, p. 10, http://marcelluscoalition.org/wp-content/uploads/2010/05/PA-Marcellus-Updated-Economic-Impacts-5.24.10.3.pdf.

12. New York State Department of Environmental Conservation, "Fact Sheet: High-Volume Hydraulic Fracturing SGEIS Time Line." http://www.dec.ny.gov/docs/materials_minerals_pdf/sgeis-timefs092011.pdf.

13. Considine, Watson, and Blumsack, "The Economic Opportunities of Shale Energy Development," p. 9.

14. Ibid., p. 8.

15. Michael Brune, "Looking Beyond the Numbers," Sierra Club, February 29, 2012, http://sierraclub.typepad.com/michaelbrune/2012/02/100-coal-plants-looking-beyond-the-numbers.html.

16. *EIA Natural Gas Monthly April 2012*, United States Energy Information Agency, May 31, 2012, http://205.254.135.7/naturalgas/monthly/.

17. U.S. Energy Information Administration, "Levelized Cost of New Generation Resources in the Annual Energy Outlook 2012," January 23, 2012. http://www.eia.gov/forecasts/aeo/electricity_generation.cfm.

18. U.S. Energy Information Administration, "Table 2.8.A, Electrical Power Monthly, December 2011," February 29, 2012, http://www.eia.gov/electricity/monthly/epm_table_grapher.cfm?t=epmt_2_8_a.

19. U.S. Energy Information Administration, "Table 1.1, Electrical Power Monthly, December 2011," February 29, 2012, http://www.eia.gov/electricity/monthly/epm_table_grapher.cfm?t=epmt_1_1.

20. U.S. Energy Information Administration, "Table 1.2, Existing Capacity by Energy Source," *Electrical Power Annual 2010,* November 2011, http://www.eia.gov/electricity/annual/pdf/table1.2.pdf.

21. Ibid. In conjunction with U.S. Energy Information Administration, "Annual Energy Outlook Tables, Electricity Generating Capacity," *Annual Energy Outlook 2012* Early Release, March 20, 2012, http://www.eia.gov/oiaf/aeo/tablebrowser/#release=EARLY2012&subject=0-EARLY2012&table=9-EARLY2012&region=0-0&cases=early2012-d121011b.

22. Nuclear Energy Institute, "US Capacity Factors by Fuel Type," April 2011, http://www.nei.org/resourcesandstats/documentlibrary/reliableandaffordableenergy/graphicsandcharts/uscapacityfactorsbyfueltype/.

23. Julianne Klara and John Wimer, "Natural Gas Combined Cycle Plant," U.S. Department of Energy, May 2007, http://www.netl.doe.gov/KMD/cds/disk50/NGCC%20Plant%20Case_FClass_051607.pdf.

24. U.S. Energy Information Administration, "Annual Energy Outlook Tables, Electricity Generating Capacity," *Annual Energy Outlook 2012* Early Release, March 20, 2012, http://www.eia.gov/oiaf/aeo/tablebrowser/#release=EARLY2012&subject=0-EARLY2012&table=9-EARLY2012&region=0-0&cases=early2012-d121011b. See also Rebecca Smith, "Cheap Natural Gas Unplugs US Nuclear Power Revival," *Wall Street Journal,* March 15, 2012, http://online.wsj.com/article/SB10001424052702304459804577281490129153610.html?mod=WSJ_hps_editorsPicks_2.

25. T. Smith, "Insight: A Booming Oil Shale," *OilEdge,* December 30, 2010, http://www.oiledge.com/n/Insight_a_booming_oil_shale/629b3c20.aspx.

26. Ibid.

27. North Dakota Industrial Commission, "North Dakota Oil Production Statistics," Department of Mineral Resources, Oil and Gas Division, https://www.dmr.nd.gov/oilgas/stats/historicaloilprodstats.pdf.

28. North Dakota Department of Mineral Resources, Presentation on June 28, 2011, https://www.dmr.nd.gov/oilgas/presentations/IOGCC2011-06-28.pdf.

29. Baker Hughes. "Rigs by State- Current & Historical," December 9, 2011. http://investor.shareholder.com/bhi/rig_counts/rc_index.cfm?showpage=na.

30. Range Resources, Presentation to the Bank of America Merrill Lynch 2011 Global Energy Conference, November 15, 2011, http://phx.corporate-ir.net/External.File?item=UGFyZW50SUQ9NDQ4MTUwfE NoaWxkSUQ9NDcyMTUzfFR5cGU9MQ==&t=1.

31. Anadarko Petroleum, "Anadarko Provides Horizontal Niobrara Update," November 14, 2011, http://www.anadarko.com/Investor/Pages/NewsReleases/NewsReleases.aspx?release-id=1630127.

32. Bradley Olson, "California Permit Official Dismissal May Boost Oil Spending," *Bloomberg*, November 7, 2011, http://www.bloomberg.com/news/2011-11-07/california-oil-permit-official-dismissal-may-boost-investment.html.

33. Third Quarter 2011 Earnings Conference Call, Occidental Petroleum Corporation, Transcript by Morningstar, Transcript written on October 27, 2011, http://www.morningstar.com/earnings/earnings-call-transcript.aspx?t=OXY&region=USA.

34. Lucian Pugliaresi, Testimony on "The American Energy Initiative: Oil Supplies, Gasoline Prices, and Jobs in the Gulf of Mexico" before Subcommittee on the Energy and Power, U.S. House of Representatives Committee on Energy and Commerce Hearing, March 17, 2011, http://republicans.energycommerce.house.gov/Media/file/Hearings/Energy/031711/Pugliaresi.pdf

35. U.S. Department of Labor, *Employment, Hours, and Earnings from the Current Employment Statistics Survey (National)*. Bureau of Labor Statistics, NAICS Code 211, oil and gas extraction and NAICS Code 213112 Support activities for oil and gas operations, http://data. bls.gov/pdq/SurveyOutputServlet;jsessionid=3952FEA7D59EB7BCCC8 76BCADF9B88F5.tc_instance5.

36. Barack Obama, "Remarks by the President in State of Union Address." The White House, Office of the Press Secretary, Washington, DC, January 24, 2012, http://www.whitehouse.gov/ the-press-office/2012/01/24/remarks-president-state-union-address.

37. Pollin et al., *Green Recovery: A Program to Create Good Jobs and Start Building a Low-Carbon Economy*.

38. Peter Asmus, *Harvesting California's Renewable Energy Resources: A Green Jobs Business Plan*, Center for Energy Efficiency and Renewable Technologies (CEERT), Sacramento, California, August 15, 2008, http://www.energy.ca.gov/2009publications/CEERT-1000-2009-022/CEERT-1000-2009-022.PDF.

ACKNOWLEDGMENTS

First and foremost, I would like to thank the Manhattan Institute for providing a warm, collegial, and supportive environment. Larry Mone, Howard Husock, and Lindsay Young Craig never faltered in their support of the book and in their belief in the importance of the subject matter.

The book benefited from numerous conversations with David Montgomery of National Economic Research Associates and Lee Lane of Hudson Institute on the effects of green policies on the economy. Professor Harvey Rosen of Princeton University generously welcomed me to discuss the concept of green jobs policies as a tax on the economy. John Philipp, a mechanical engineer who built power plants all over the world, read the entire manuscript to check the technical details. Thanks to Lucian Pugliaresi of the

Energy Policy Research Foundation, Inc., for his wealth of information on America's growing production and reserves of oil and natural gas and the infrastructure that needs to accompany it. Lucian and I together survived grilling by Massachusetts Representative Ed Markey on why America should be exporting petroleum products. Brett McMahon of Miller and Long Construction Company provided exceptional insights into precisely how jobs were being relabeled as green in the construction industry, including subtleties of Lo-Flo versus traditional toilets. Eric Meltzer of Telecom Capital Corp. used his venture capital experience to decipher the financial situations of firms that received government guaranteed loans. Karlyn Bowman of the American Enterprise Institute shortened the book proposal, explaining that people now like to read less, rather than more. Special thanks go to Irwin and Cita Stelzer of Hudson Institute, who suggested the cover photo and who were always ready with information and advice in Washington, London, and Aspen. Editors Edward Cowan and Robert Asahina provided invaluable suggestions on the manuscript. I am grateful for research funding in initial stages of the project from the Searle Freedom Trust.

It was a true pleasure working with Roger Kimball, the dynamic editor of Encounter Books, who appears to work all the time and responds rapidly to queries, even on weekends. The Encounter Books team, Heather Ohle, Lauren Miklos, and Sam Schneider were a model of efficiency as they shepherded the book to completion.

My research associate, Claire Rogers, checked and rechecked countless references. I was also ably assisted by my researchers Christopher Bien, Zachary Javitt, Leah Loversky, Cindy Luu, Kristopher Munger, Alexander Ray, Joshual Sheppard, and Chi Zhang.

My husband, Harold, and my children, Leon and his wife Deborah, Francesca, Jeremy, Godfrey, Theodore, and Richard, endured my work on the book on so-called "family vacations" and encouraged me during countless evenings and weekends at the computer. They know far more about green jobs policies than they need.

Above all, I am grateful to my parents from bringing me here from Britain as a child, enabling me to meet Harold, have six children, and pursue a career in economic policy. Back in the 1960s, living in London, my father had a job interview in America. He called home to my mother and said, "We have to move here, they heat the bathrooms." There is nothing like growing up in Britain to make someone appreciate the value of warm houses (including heated bathrooms), clothes dryers, large refrigerators, large cars, easy availability of parking, and long hot high pressure showers— all the result of inexpensive energy. It is for this reason, among many others, that I dedicate the book to them.

BIBLIOGRAPHY

A.E. Feldman Associates. "Jobs in the Renewable Energy
  Sector to Explode Under Obama." *A.E. Feldman*. January 28, 2009. http://blog.aefeldman.com/2009/01/28/
  jobs-in-the-Renewable-energy-sector-to-explode-under-obama/
Akinbami, Lara. "The State of Childhood Asthma, United States,
  1980–2005."*Advance Data from Vital and Health Statistics No. 381*.
  Centers for Disease Control and Prevention. December 12, 2006.
  http://www.cdc.gov/nchs/data/ad/ad381.pdf
Alabama Department of Industrial Relations. *Alabama Green Definitions*. http://www.greenjobsinalabama.com/gsipub/index.
  asp?docid=417
Alvarez, Gabriel C., Raquel M. Jara, and Juan R. Julian. *Study on the
  Effects on Employment of Public Aid to Renewable Energy Sources.*

Universidad Rey Juan Carlos, March 2009. http://www.juande-mariana.org/pdf/090327-employment-public-aid-Renewable.pdf

American Clean Energy and Security Act of 2009. H.R. 2454. http://thomas.loc.gov/cgi-bin/bdquery/D?d111:9:./temp/~bdYGLT::|/home/LegislativeData.php?n=BSS;c=111

American Federation of Labor and Congress of Industrial Organizations (AFL-CIO). "Greening the Economy." AFL-CIO.org. http://www.aflcio.org/aboutus/thisistheaflcio/ecouncil/eco3042008m.cfm

American Institute of Physics. *The Carbon Dioxide Greenhouse Effect.* February 2011. http://www.aip.org/history/climate/co2.htm

American Wind Energy Association (AWEA). *U.S. Wind Industry Year-End 2010 Market Report.* January 2011. http://www.awea.org/learnabout/publications/loader.cfm?csModule=security/getfile&PageID=5083

Anadarko Petroleum. "Anadarko Provides Horizontal Niobrara Update." Press Release. November 14, 2011, http://www.anadarko.com/Investor/Pages/NewsReleases/NewsReleases.aspx?release-id=1630127

Apollo Alliance. "Achievements." 2011. http://apolloalliance.org/about/achievements/

Apollo Alliance. "Apollo Alliance Advisory Board of Directors." http://apolloalliance.org/about/board/

Apollo Alliance. "Mission." 2011. http://apolloalliance.org/about/mission/

Asmus, Peter. *Harvesting California's Renewable Energy Resources: A Green Jobs Business Plan.* Center for Energy Efficiency and Renewable Technologies (CEERT), Sacramento, California. August 15, 2008. http://www.energy.ca.gov/2009publications/CEERT-1000-2009-022/CEERT-1000-2009-022.PDF

Baker Hughes. *Baker Hughes Rotary Rig Count, Rigs by State.* December 9, 2011. http://investor.shareholder.com/common/download/download.cfm?companyid=BHI&fileid=527423&filekey=C366

20CE-AE90-45D5-809A-1F85C4CA8625&filename=Rigs_by_
State_120911.xls

Bartis, J. and Lawrence Van Bibber. *Alternative Fuels for Military Applications*. Arlington, VA: RAND National Defense Research Institute, 2011. http://www.rand.org/content/dam/rand/pubs/monographs/2011/RAND_MG969.sum.pdf

Bastiat, Frédéric. *Selected Essays on Political Economy*. Trans. Seymour Cain. Irvington-On-Hudson, NY: Library of Economics and Liberty, 1995. http://www.econlib.org/library/Bastiat/basEss1.html

Beacon Power. "About Flywheel Energy Storage." 2012. http://www.beaconpower.com/products/about-flywheels.asp

Beacon Power. *Form 10-G (Quarterly Report) for the Period Ended June 30, 2011*. August 9, 2011. http://investors.beaconpower.com/secfiling.cfm?filingID=1104659-11-45359&CIK=1103345

Beacon Power. *Form 10-K (Annual Report) for the Period Ended December 31, 2010*. March 16, 2011. http://files.shareholder.com/downloads/BCON/1480955423x0xS1047469-11-2225/1103345/filing.pdf

Benjamin, D.K. *Eight Great Myths of Recycling*. 2003. http://www.perc.org/pdf/ps28.pdf

Bentek Energy. *The Wind Power Paradox*. July 19, 2011. http://www.bentekenergy.com/

Bhidé, Amar. *The Venturesome Economy: How Innovation Sustains Prosperity in a More Connected World*. Princeton, NJ: Princeton University Press, 2008.

Bickel, J. Eric and Lee Lane. "An Analysis of Climate Engineering as a Response to Climate Change," *Smart Climate Solutions*. Ed. Bjorn Lomborg. Cambridge: Cambridge University Press, 2010.

Bird, Colin. "End of Ethanol Subsidies Could Increase Gas Prices Marginally." *The Chicago Tribune*. January 4, 2012. http://www.chicagotribune.com/classified/automotive/sns-end-of-ethanol-subsidies-could-increase-gas-p-20120104,0,2499937.story.

BlueGreen Alliance. "About the Bluegreen Alliance." 2011. http://www.bluegreenalliance.org/about_us?id=0001

BlueGreen Alliance. "Issues." 2011. http://www.bluegreenalliance.org/ about_us?id=0003

BOK Financial Corporation. "BOK Financial Bios of Officers and Directors." BOK Financial website. 2012. http://investor.bokf.com/ od.aspx?iid=100003

Bradsher, K. "China Leading Global Race to Make Clean Energy." *The New York Times.* January 30, 2010. http://www.nytimes. com/2010/01/31/business/energy-environment/31renew.html

Bradsher, Keith. "China Wins in Wind Power, by Its Own Rules" *The New York Times.* December 14, 2010. http://www. nytimes.com/2010/12/15/business/global/15Chinawind. html?ref=windpower

Brecher, J. "Labor's War on Global Warming." *The Nation.* March 24, 2008. http://www.thenation.com/article/ labors-war-global-warming

British Petroleum (BP). "BP Announces Giant Oil Discovery in the Gulf of Mexico," BP Investor Relations. September 2, 2009. http:// www.bp.com/genericarticle.do?categoryId=2012968&conten tId=7055818

Broder, John. "E.P.A. Seeks Stricter Rules to Curb Smog." *The New York Times.* January 7, 2010. http://www.nytimes.com/2010/01/08/sci-ence/earth/08smog.html

Bryce, Robert. "A New Study Takes The Wind Out of Wind Energy." *Forbes.com.* July 19, 2011. http://www.forbes.com/2011/07/19/ wind-energy-carbon.html

Bryce, Robert. *Power Hungry: The Myths of "Green" Energy and the Real Fuels of the Future.* New York: PublicAffairs Books, 2010.

Bryce, Robert. *The High Cost of Wind Energy as a Carbon-Dioxide Reduc-tion Method.* Issue Brief No. 11. October 2011. http://www.manhat-tan-institute.org/html/ib_11.htm

Capp, Bill. "Statement from Beacon Power Corporation." November 1, 2011. http://beaconpower.com/files/Beacon-Media-Statement.pdf

The Carbon Fund. "Carbon Calculator." 2012. http://www.carbonfund. org.

Carper, T. "Sen. Carper Reacts to 'New Jobs-Cleaner Air: Employment Effects Under Planned Changes to EPA's Air Pollution Rules' Report." February 8, 2001. http://carper.senate.gov/press/record. cfm?id=330970

CBC News. "Northern N.B. Wind Farm Slowed by Ice Again." February 18, 2011. http://www.cbc.ca/news/canada/new-brunswick/ story/2011/02/15/nb-caribou-wind-farm-ice.html

Center for Energy Economics. *Green Jobs: a Review of Recent Studies.* Bureau of Economic Geology, Jackson School of Geosciences, the University of Texas at Austin. December 2008. http://www.beg. utexas.edu/energyecon/documents/CEE_Green_Jobs_Review.pdf

Center for Politiske Studier. *Wind Energy, the Case for Denmark.* Copenhagen, Denmark, September 2009. http://www.cepos.dk/ fileadmin/user_upload/Arkiv/PDF/Wind_energy_-_the_case_of_ Denmark.pdf

Chen, J. "Renewable Energy in China: A Necessity, Not an Alternative." *Knowledge@Wharton.* 2009. http://www.knowledgeatwharton. com.cn/index.cfm?fa=viewArticle&articleID=2054&languageid=1

China Briefing. *An Overview of China's Renewable Energy Market.* June 16, 2011. http://www.China-briefing.com/news/2011/06/16/an-Overview-of-Chinas-Renewable-energy-market.html

Communication Workers of America. "Environmental Groups, Unions Support President's Decision on Kaystone XL." Press Release. January 18, 2012. http://www.cwa-union.org/news/entry/environmen-tal_groups_unions_support_presidents_decision_on_keystone_xl

Connection Research. "Who Are the Green Collar Workers?" Environment Institute of Australia and New Zealand, St. Leonard's, Australia, 2009. http://www.eianz.org/sb/modules/news/attach-ments/71/Green%20Collar%20Worker%20report%20Final.pdf

Considine, Timothy J. and Robert W. Watson. "The Economic Opportunities of Shale Energy Development." *Energy Policy and the*

Environment Report No. 9. Center for the Energy Policy and the Environment at the Manhattan Institute. June 9, 2011. http://www.manhattan-institute.org/html/eper_09.htm

Considine, Timothy J., Robert W. Watson, and Seth Blumsack. "The Economic Impacts of the Pennsylvania Marcellus Shale Natural Gas Play: An Update." Pennsylvania State University. May 24, 2011. http://Marcelluscoalition.org/wp-content/uploads/2010/05/PA-Marcellus-Updated-Economic-Impacts-5.24.10.3.pdf

CQ Transcripts. "Bush Remarks on Climate." Transcript. *The Washington Post.* April 16, 2008. http://www.washingtonpost.com/wp-dyn/content/article/2008/04/16/AR2008041603084.html

Credit Committee Recommendation from Chairman Loan Guarantee Credit Committee to Director Loan Guarantee Program Office. *Subject: Credit Committee Recommendation re: Solyndra Fab 2 LLC, solar photovoltaic power panel project for a loan guarantee of $535,000,000.* January 9, 2009. http://republicans.energycommerce.house.gov/Media/file/Hearings/Oversight/091411/DocumentsEnteredIntoRecord.pdf

Crutzen, Paul. "Albedo Enhancement by Stratospheric Sulfur Injections: A Contribution to Resolve a Policy Dilemma?" *Climatic Change.* Vol. 77, No. 3 (August 1, 2006): 211–220. http://dx.doi.org/10.1007/s10584-006-9101-y

Dang, Xiangyi. "Development of Wind Power Generation—Reflections on Chinese Power Generation." http://wenku.baidu.com/view/9fe8bfbfc77da26925c5b035.html

David, Andrew. "Growth in Wind Turbine Manufacturing and Trade." U.S. International Trade Commission, Office of Industries. *USITC Executive Briefings on Trade.* March 2009. http://www.usitc.gov/publications/332/Executive_Briefings/USITC_EB_WindTurbines_David

David, Andrew. *Industry and Trade Summary.* U.S. International Trade Commission, Office of Industries. Publication ITS-02. June 2009.

David, Andrew. *Shifts in U.S. Wind Turbine Equipment Trade in 2010.* U.S. International Trade Commission, Office of Industries. June 2011. http://www.usitc.gov/publications/332/executive_briefings/wind_EBOT_commission_review_final2.pdf

De Place, E. "Best Post Ever?" *Sightline Daily.* April 14, 2008. http://daily.sightline.org/daily_score/archive/2008/04/14/best-post-ever

Dignan, Larry. "GE: Wind Market Hits Rough Patch, but Rebound Expected." *SmartPlanet.* July 22, 2011. http://www.smartPlanet.com/blog/smart-takes/ge-wind-market-hits-rough-patch-but-rebound-expected/17846

Doyle, Arthur Conan. "Silver Blaze," *Memoirs of Sherlock Holmes.* 1st edition. London: George Newnes, 1894.

Durning, A. "Climate and Race." *Sightline Daily.* January 14, 2010. http://daily.sightline.org/daily_score/archive/2010/01/14/climate-and-Race

Durning, A. "Climate Fairness." *Sightline Daily.* January 24, 2008. http://daily.sightline.org/daily_score/archive/2008/01/24/climate-fairness

Durning, A. "Rebutting CBO's Climate Policy and Jobs Paper." *Sightline Daily.* May 6, 2010. http://daily.sightline.org/daily_score/archive/2010/05/06/rebutting-cbos-climate-job-killer-paper

Durning, A. *Green Collar Jobs.* Seattle: Northwest Environment Watch, 1999.

Energy Center of Wisconsin. "Parts of a Turbine." http://www.ecw.org/windpower/web/cat2a.html

E-mail from Lachlan Steward to [Name redacted], Subject: Solyndra meeting, January 13, 2009, http://republicans.energycommerce.house.gov/media/file/Hearings/Oversight/091411/DocumentsEnteredIntoRecord.pdf

E-mail from [Name redacted]@hq.doe.gov to [Name redacted], Subject: Solyndra Closing Date, August 27, 2009, http://republicans.energycommerce.house.gov/Media/file/Hearings/Oversight/091411/DocumentsEnteredIntoRecord.pdf

E-mail from [Name redacted] to [Name redacted], Subject: Solyndra, August 19, 2009, http://republicans.energycommerce.house.gov/Media/file/Hearings/Oversight/091411/DocumentsEnteredIntoRecord.pdf

E-mail from [Name redacted] to Mary Miller, Subject: Re: DOE Loan Guarantees, August 16, 2011, http://republicans.energycommerce.house.gov/Media/file/Hearings/Oversight/101411/submitteddocs.pdf

E-mail from [Name redacted] to [Name redacted], Subject: Final Solyndra Credit Subsidy Cost, August 27, 2009, http://republicans.energycommerce.house.gov/Media/file/Hearings/Oversight/091411/DocumentsEnteredIntoRecord.pdf

E-mail from [Name redacted] to [Name Redacted], Subject: Re: Solar co loan announcement in northern California, Match 10, 2009, http://republicans.energycommerce.house.gov/Media/file/Hearings/Oversight/091411/DocumentsEnteredIntoRecord.pdf.

E-mail from Office of Management and Budget official to Terrell P. McSweeny, subject: DOE announcement, August 31, 2009, http://republicans.energycommerce.house.gov/Media/file/Hearings/Oversight/111711_solyndra/footnotes.pdf

E-mail from Senior Advisor to the Secretary of Energy for Recovery Act Spending to [Name Redacted], March 10, 2009, http://republicans.energycommerce.house.gov/Media/file/Hearings/Oversight/091411/DocumentsEnteredIntoRecord.pdf

Energy Independence and Security Act of 2007. H.R. 6, 110th Congress, December 13, 2007. Section 1002 (2) (D) (ii) and Section 1002 (3) (A) (vi) http://frwebgate.access.gpo.gov/cgi-bin/getdoc.cgi?dbname=110_cong_Bills&docid=f:h6eas2.txt.pdf

Europe's Energy Portal. *Electricity Households*. June 2011. http://www.energy.eu/

European Commission. "Harmonised Unemployment Rate by Gender—Total." *EuroStat Database*. http://epp.eurostat.ec.europa.eu/

tgm/table.do?tab=table&language=en&pcode=teilm020&tableSEle
ction=1&plugin=1

Evergreen Solar. "Evergreen Solar to Close Devens Manufacturing Facility." Press Release. January 11, 2011. http://evergreensolar.com/
en/2011/01/evergreen-solar-to-close-devens-manufacturing-facility/

ExxonMobil. "ExxonMobil Announces Three Discoveries in the Deepwater Gulf of Mexico," ExxonMobil Investor Relations. June 8, 2011. http://www.
businesswire.com/news/home/20110608005901/en/
ExxonMobil-Announces-DiscOveries-Deepwater-Gulf-Mexico

Faiola, Anthony. "Spain's Answer to Unemployment: Go Greener."
The Washington Post. September 24, 2009. http://www.
washingtonpost.com/wp-dyn/content/article/2009/09/23/
AR2009092302152.html?sid=ST2009092302161

Fehrenbacher, Katie. "Was the DOE Loan Guarantee for Solyndra a
Mistake?" *GigaOM*. May 27, 2010. http://gigaom.com/Cleantech/
was-the-doe-Loan-Guarantee-for-solyndra-a-mistake/

Feinstein, Dianne. "Feinstein, Snowe Call for 'Maximum Feasible' Fuel Economy Standards." Senator
Dianne Feinstein website. Press Release. July 25, 2011.
http://www.feinstein.senate.gov/public/index.cfm/
press-releases?ID=11a953af-6be6-4d9b-a591-268545190512.

Fowler, T. "Return to the Gulf: Big Oil Grabs Leases," *The Wall Street
Journal*. December 15, 2011. http://online.wsj.com/article/SB10001
424052970203893404577098773281211592.html

Gainor, D. "Even U.N. Admits that Going Green Will Cost $76
Trillion." *Fox News*. July 6, 2011. http://www.foxnews.com/
opinion/2011/07/06/even-un-admits-that-going-green-will-Cost-
76-trillion/#ixzz1RLVXSRUg

Garber, K. "Why Clean Coal is Years Away." *US News and World
Report*. March 17, 2009. http://www.usnews.com/news/energy/
articles/2009/03/17/why-Clean-coal-is-years-away?PageNr=3

"German Solar Subsidy Cut Not Good For Yingli, Solar Industry." *Forbes.com*. January 25, 2012. http://www.forbes.com/sites/greatspeculations/2012/01/25/german-solar-subsidy-cut-not-good-for-yingli-solar-industry/

Global Insight. "U.S. Metro Economies Current and Potential Green Jobs in the U.S. Economy." Prepared by Global Insight (GI) for the United States Conference of Mayors and the Mayors Climate Protection Center. October 2008. http://www.usmayors.org/press-releases/uploads/greenjobsreport.pdf

Gordon, K. Testimony for the U.S. Senate Committee on Environment and Public Works Subcommittee on "Green Jobs and the New Economy." Green Jobs and Trade. Washington, DC, 2011. http://epw.senate.gov/public/index.cfm?FuseAction=Files.View&FileStore_id=9a2a8be6-5bc2-4b71-80ed-e47f1fa8cb66

Green, Kenneth P. *The Myth of Green Energy Jobs: The European Experience*. American Enterprise Institute. February 2011. http://www.aei.org/docLib/EEO-2011-02-No-2-updated-g.pdf

Green, Kenneth. *The Green Jobs Myth: Proceedings of the Statement before the Committee on Science, Space and Technology*. American Enterprise Institute, 2011. http://www.aei.org/speech/100219

Greenspace. "Gulf Oil Spill: New Moratorium Explained." *Los Angeles Times*. July 12, 2010. http://latimesblogs.latimes.com/greenspace/2010/07/gulf-oil-spill-new-moratorium-explained.html

Groom, Nichola. "Fisker Announces Layoffs, Renegotiates Loan." *Reuters*. February 2, 2012. http://www.reuters.com/article/2012/02/07/us-fisker-idUSTRE8161BE20120207

Grossfeld, J. "Leo the Linchpin." *The American Prospect*, September 24, 2007. http://prospect.org/cs/articles?article=leo_the_linchpin

Gunther, M. "Brighten Clouds, Cool the Air, Save the Planet," *Marcgunther.com*. June 12, 2011. http://www.marcgunther.com/2011/06/12/brighten-clouds-cool-the-air-save-the-Planet/

Heintz, James, Heidi Garret-Peltier, and Ben Zipperer. *New Jobs—Cleaner Air: Employment Effects under Planned Changes to EPA's Air*

Pollution Rules. Ceres and Political Economy Research Institute (PERI). February 2011. http://www.ceres.org/resources/reports/new-jobs-Cleaner-air

Iberdorola Renewables. "Major US Wind Power Installer Hails Recovery Act As Driver of Job Creation, Ongoing Domestic Investment." Iberdorola Renewables Press Release. October 14, 2010. http://www.iberdrolaRenewables.us/rel_10.10.14.html

IHS, Inc. "US Government Announces Deal with Automakers for Next-Generation CAFE Standards." IHS Global Insight: Country and Industry Forecasting. August 1, 2011. http://www.ihs.com/products/global-insight/industry-economic-report.aspx?ID=1065930149

Inslee, J. and B. Hendricks. *Apollo's Fire: Igniting America's Clean Energy Economy.* Island Press, 2007.

International Business Times. "Greenpeace: China Becomes World's Largest Wind Installation Country, Challenges Remain." January 29, 2011. http://www.ibtimes.com/articles/106571/20110129/greenpeace-China-becomes-world-s-largest-wind-installation-country-challenges-remain.htm

International Energy Agency. *Share of Total Primary Energy Supply in 2008, People's Republic of China.* 2009. http://www.iea.org/stats/pdf_graphs/CNTPESPI.pdf

International Energy Agency. *Share of Total Primary Energy Supply in 2008, United States of America.* 2009. http://www.iea.org/stats/pdf_graphs/USTPESPI.pdf

Institute for America's Future and The Center On Wisconsin Strategy. *New Energy for America. The Apollo Jobs Report: Good Jobs and Energy Independence.* Apollo Alliance, 2004. http://www.apolloalliance.org/downloads/resources_ApolloReport_022404_122748.pdf

International Labour Organization. *Key Indicators of the Labour Market Database.* Catalog Sources, World Development Indicators, 2006–2010. http://data.worldbank.org/indicator/SL.UEM.TOTL.ZS/countries

James, R. "Of Mustard Fuel and Marines." *The Wall Street Journal.* August 2, 2011. http://online.wsj.com/article/SB10001424052748 70452920457625713095828852zhtml

Jones, Van. *The Green Collar Economy.* New York: HarperOne, 2008.

Jorgenson, Dale W. and Peter J. Wilcoxen, "Reducing U.S. Carbon Dioxide Emissions: The Cost of Different Goals," J.R. Moroney, ed. *Advances in the Economics of Energy and Resources.* Vol. 7. Greenwich, CT: JAI Press, 1992. pp. 125–158.

Juan, Du. "China to Build New Hydroelectric Power Plants." *China Daily.* June 23, 2011. http://www.chinadaily.com.cn/business/2011-06/23/content_12759091.htm

Laborers International Union of North America (LIUNA). "Job Killers, 2; American Workers, 0." Press Release. January 18, 2012. http://www.liunabuildsamerica.org/news/story/766

Lee, John. "The Greening of China A Mirage." *The Australian.* Hudson Institute. September 19, 2011. http://www.hudson.org/index.cfm?fuseaction=publication_details&id=8335

Leonnig, Carol D., Joe Stephens, and Alice Crites. "Obama's Focus on Visiting Clean-tech Companies Raises Questions." *The Washington Post.* June 25, 2011. http://www.washingtonpost.com/politics/obamas-focus-on-visiting-Clean-tech-companies-raises-questions/2011/06/24/AGSFu9kH_story.html

Lewis, Elliot. Testimony on "The Green Jobs Debacle: Where Has All of the Taxpayers' Money Gone?" before the Subcommittee on Regulatory Affairs, Stimulus Oversight and Government Spending. November 2, 2011.

Lewis, M. "Mandated Mischief: Obama's 54.5 mpg Standard." July 29, 2011. http://pajamasmedia.com/blog/mandated-mischief-obama%e2%80%99s-54-5-mpg-Standard/?singlepage=true.

Lieberman, Joe. "Kerry, Lieberman: American Power Act Bill Will Secure America's Energy, Climate Future" Senator Lieberman website. Press Release, May 5, 2010. http://lieberman.senate.gov/

index.cfm/news-events/news/2010/5/kerry-lieberman-american-
power-act-Bill-will-secure-americas-energy-climate-future

Louisiana Workforce Commission. *The Greening of Louisiana's Economy:
Summary of Survey Results.* September 2011. http://lwc.laworks.
net/sites/LMI/GreenJobs/Reports/Louisiana_Survey_Results.
pdf#Method

Lovins, Amory. *Soft Energy Paths.* New York: Harper and Row, 1979.

Lovins, Amory. *Winning the Oil Endgame.* Snowmass, CO: Rocky
Mountain Institute, 2005.

Ma, H. *Beyond the Numbers: A Closer Look at China's Wind Power
Success.* Worldwatch Institute. February 28, 2011. http://blogs.
worldwatch.org/revolt/beyond-the-numbers-a-closer-look-at-
China%E2%80%99s-wind-power-success/

Ma, H. *China's Statistical Challenges Stymie Accountable Development.*
Worldwatch Institute. May 20, 2011. http://blogs.worldwatch.org/
revolt/China%e2%80%99s-statistical-challenges-stymie-account-
able-development/

Ma, H. *Data Challenges In Green Economy and Green Jobs Research in
China.* Worldwatch Institute. June 29, 2011. http://blogs.world-
watch.org/revolt/data-challenges-in-green-economy-and-green-
jobs-research-in-China/

Mabus, Ray. *Remarks by the Honorable Ray Mabus, Secretary of the Navy.*
Carnegie Council on Ethics in International Relations, New York,
New York. November 9, 2010. http://www.navy.mil/navydata/
people/secnav/Mabus/Speech/Carnegie119110.pdf

Marine Log. *Experts: Salazar Misrepresents Our Position.* June 11, 2011.
http://www.marinelog.com/DOCS/NEWSMMIX/2010jun00112.
html

Markey, Ed. "House Passes Historic Waxman-Markey Clean Energy
Bill." Congressman Markey website. Press Release. June 26, 2009.
http://markey.house.gov/index.php?option=content&task=view&id
=3748&Itemid=125

Martinez-Fernandez, C., C. Hinojosa, and G. Miranda. *Green Jobs and Skills: The Local Labour Market Implications of Addressing Climate Change.* Working document, CFE/LEED, Organisation for Economic Cooperation and Development. February 8, 2010. http://www.oecd.org/dataoecd/54/43/44683169. pdf?contentId=44683170

Martinot , E. and L. Junfeng. "An Overview of China's Renewable Energy Market." *China Briefing.com*, June 16, 2011. http://www. China-briefing.com/news/2011/06/16/an-Overview-of-Chinas-Renewable-energy-market.html

Martinot, E. and L. Junfeng. *Renewable Energy Policy Update for China.* July 21, 2010. http://www.Renewableenergyworld.com/rea/news/article/2010/07/Renewable-energy-policy-update-for-China

Masia, Seth. "New EPA Rules May Create 1.45 Million Jobs." *Solar Today.* February 11, 2011. http://www.ases.org/index. php?option=com_myblog&show=New-EPA-rules-may-create-1.45-million-jobs.html&Itemid=27

McCarty, Dawn. "Evergreen Energy Files for Bankruptcy, Cites Lack of Financing." *Bloomberg.* January 24, 2012. http://www.bloomberg. com/news/2012-01-23/evergreen-energy-files-for-bankruptcy-liqui-dation-1-.html

McMahon, Brett. Testimony on "The Green Jobs Debacle: Where Has All of the Taxpayers' Money Gone?" before the Subcommittee on Regulatory Affairs, Stimulus Oversight and Government Spending. November 2, 2011. http://Oversight.house.gov/images/sto-ries/Testimony/11-2-11_RegAffairs_McMahon_Testimony.pdf

Mendick, Robert. "Firms Paid to Shut Down Wind Farms When the Wind is Blowing." *The Telegraph.* June 19, 2010. http://www. telegraph.co.uk/earth/energy/windpower/7840035/Firms-paid-to-shut-down-wind-farms-when-the-wind-is-blowing.html

Michael, Elliot. "Heroes of the Environment 2008: Activists, Van Jones." *TIME.* September 24, 2008. http://www.time.com/time/

specials/packages/article/0,28804,1841778_1841781_1841811,00.
html

Mid-Atlantic Regional Collaborative (MARC). *What is a Green Job?*
MARC Regional Green Jobs website. 2012. http://www.marcgreen-
works.com/gsipub/index.asp?docid=398

Mitchell, Steve. E-mail to George Kaiser. October 6, 2010. Release by
House Energy Commerce Committee. http://democrats.energy-
commerce.house.gov/sites/default/files/documents/Email_Mitch-
elKaiser_Footnote13_10.06.10.pdf

Montgomery, W. David. Testimony on "Green Jobs and
Trade" before the U.S. Senate Committee on Environment and Public Works, Subcommittee on Green Jobs
and the New Economy. Washington, DC, 2011. http://
www.epw.senate.gov/public/index.cfm?FuseAction=Files.
View&FileStore_id=5abed004-c3d2-4f28-a721-734ad78cdd99

Murrow, Mark and Jonathan Rothwell. "Why the U.S. Should Not
Abandon Its Clean Energy Lending Programs." *Brookings.* September 27, 2011. http://www.brookings.edu/opinions/2011/0927_
solyndra_muro_rothwell.aspx

National Institute of Statistics (Spain). *Economically Active Population
Survey (EAPS).* Third Quarter of 2011. Press Release. October 28,
2011. http://www.ine.es/en/daco/daco42/daco4211/epao311_en.pdf

National Parks Department (Japan.) *Green Worker Program.* http://www.
env.go.jp/en/nature/nps/park/support/gw.html

National Research Council. *Effectiveness and Impact of Corporate Average Fuel Economy (CAFE) Standards.* 2002. http://www.nhtsa.gov/
cars/rules/cafe/docs/162944_web.pdf

NationalMaster.com. *Coal Consumption (Most Recent) By
Country.* 2011. http://www.nationmaster.com/graph/
ene_coa_con-energy-coal-consumption

New York State Department of Environmental Conservation. *Proposed
Express Terms 6 NYCRR Parts 750.1 and 750.3 Obtaining A SPDES*

Bibliography

Permit and High-Volume Hydro Fracturing (HVHF). September
    2011. http://www.dec.ny.gov/regulations/77383.html
National Highway Traffic Safety Administration (NHTSA). *Relationship
    of Vehicle Weight to Fatality and Injury Risk in Model Year 1985–93
    Passenger Cars and Light Trucks*. NHTSA Summary Report, DOT
    HS 808 569. Springfield, VA: National Technical Information,
    1997.
North Dakota Department of Mineral Resources, North Dakota Oil and
    Gas Commission, and North Dakota Geological Survey. Presenta-
    tion. June 28, 2011. https://www.dmr.nd.gov/oilgas/presentations/
    IOGCC2011-06-28.pdf
North Dakota Industrial Commission, Department of Mineral
    Resources, Oil and Gas Division. *North Dakota Oil Production
    Statistics*. 2012. https://www.dmr.nd.gov/oilgas/stats/historicaloil-
    prodstats.pdf
Northern Plains and Rocky Mountain Consortium. *The Northern
    Plains and Rocky Mountain Consortium Final Report*. 2011. http://
    researchingthegreeneconomy.org/docfolder/publications/The%20
    Northern%20Plains%20&%20Rocky%20Mountain%20Consor-
    tium%20Final%20Report.pdf
Obama, Barack. "Remarks by the President in State of Union Address."
    White House Office of the Press Secretary. Press Release. January
    25, 2011. http://www.whitehouse.gov/the-press-office/2011/01/25/
    remarks-president-state-union-address
Obama, Barack. "Statement by the President on the Ozone
    National Ambient Air Quality Standards." White House,
    Office of the Press Secretary. Press Release. September 2, 2011.
    http://www.whitehouse.gov/the-press-office/2011/09/02/
    statement-president-ozone-national-ambient-air-quality-Standards
Occidental Petroleum Corporation, Third Quarter 2011 Earnings
    Conference Call, Transcript by Morningstar, Transcript. October
    27, 2011. http://www.morningstar.com/earnings/earnings-call-
    transcript.aspx?t=OXY&region=USA

Olson, Bradley. "California Permit Official Dismissal May Boost Oil Spending," *Bloomberg.* November 7, 2011. http://mobile.bloomberg.com/news/2011-11-07/california-oil-permit-official-dismissal-may-boost-investment

Oregon Employment Department Workforce and Economic Research Division. *The Greening of Oregon's Workforce: Jobs, Wages and Training.* June 2009. http://www.qualityinfo.org/pubs/green/greening.pdf

Organisation for Economic Cooperation and Development (OECD). *Country Statistical Profile: China 2011–2012, Annual GDP Growth Rate 2006–2010.* December 12, 2011. http://dx.doi.org/10.1787/csp-chn-table-2011-1-en

Organisation for Economic Cooperation and Development (OECD). *Country Statistical Profiles: Key Tables.* n.d. http://www.oecd-ilibrary.org/economics/country-statistical-profiles-key-tables-from-oecd_20752288;jsessionid=2jf603nbo6q70.delta

Pelosi, Nancy. "Pelosi: 'Remember These Four Words For What This Legislation Means: Jobs, Jobs, Jobs, and Jobs." Nancy Pelosi Website. Press Release. June 26, 2009. http://www.democraticleader.gov/news/press?id=1254

Pennsylvania Workforce Development Commission. *The Pennsylvania Green Jobs Report Part 1.* http://www.portal.state.pa.us/portal/server.pt/directory/center_for_green_careers/134700?DirMode=1

Pinderhughes, R. "Green Collar Jobs." *Race, Poverty, and the Environment.* Vol. 13, No. 1 (2006). http://urbanhabitat.org/node/528

Pinderhughes, R. *Green Collar Jobs.* 2007. http://bss.sfsu.edu/raquelrp/documents/v13fullreport.pdf

POET. "DOE grants final approval on POET Cellulosic Ethanol Loan Guarantee." POET Press Release. September 23, 2011. http://www.poet.com/discOvery/releases/showRelease.asp?id=295.com

Pollin, Robert, Heidi Garrett-Peltier, James Heintz, and Helen Scharber. *Green Recovery: A Program to Create Good Jobs and Start Building a Low-Carbon Economy.* Department of Economics and Political

Economy Research Institute (PERI), University of Massachusetts at
Amherst, and Kit Batten and Bracken Hendricks, Project Managers, Center for American Progress (CAP). September 2008. http://
www.americanprogress.org/issues/2008/09/pdf/green_Recovery.
pdf

Pollin, Robert, James Heintz, and Heidi Garrett-Peltier. *The Economic
Benefits of Investing in Clean Energy.* Center for American Progress
and Political Economy Research Institute (PERI). June 2009.
http://www.americanprogress.org/issues/2009/06/pdf/peri_
report.pdf

Pollin, Robert and Jeannette Wicks-Lim. *Job Opportunities for the Green
Economy: A State-by-State Picture of Occupations That Gain From
Green Investments.* Political Economy Research Institute (PERI),
University of Massachusetts at Amherst. June 2008. http://www.
americanprogress.org/issues/2008/06/pdf/green_jobs.pdf

Pugliaresi, Lucian. Testimony on "The American Energy Initiative: Oil
supplies, Gasoline prices, and Jobs in the Gulf of Mexico" before
the Subcommittee on the Energy and Power, U.S. House of Representatives Committee on Energy and Commerce Hearing, March
17, 2011. http://republicans.energycommerce.house.gov/Media/
file/Hearings/Energy/031711/Pugliaresi.pdf

Quick, Darren. "Computer Modeling Indicates White Roofs May be a
Cool Idea." *Gizmag.com.* January 28, 2010. http://www.gizmag.
com/white-roofs-climate-change/14021/

Range Resources. Presentation to the Bank of America Merrill Lynch
2011 Global Energy Conference. November 15, 2011. http://phx.
corporate-ir.net/External.File?item=UGFyZW50SUQ9NDQ4MTU
wfENoaWxkSUQ9NDcyMTUzfFR5cGU9MQ==&t=1

Rasch, Philip J., Simone Tilmes, Richard P. Turco, Alan Robock,
Luke Oman, Chih-Chieh (Jack) Chen, Georgiy L. Stenchikov, and
Rolando R. Garcia. "An Overview of Geoengineering of Climate
Using Stratospheric Sulphate Aerosals." *Philosophical Transactions
of the Royal Society A: Mathematical, Physical and Engineering Sci-*

ences. Vol. 366, No. 1882 4007-4037 (November 13, 2008). http://rsta.royalsocietypublishing.org/content/366/1882/4007.full

Read, Leonard E. "I, Pencil: My Family Tree as told to Leonard E. Read." Irvington-On-Hudson, NY: Library of Economics and Liberty, 1999. http://www.econlib.org/library/Essays/rdPncl1.html

Reuters. "German Bundestag Approves Solar Incentive Cuts." May 6, 2010. http://www.reuters.com/article/2010/05/06/germany-solar-idUSBAT00541720100506

Richardson, Susan S. *Solyndra Restructuring Memorandum*. Office of the Chief Counsel of the Department of Energy, Loan Programs Office. February 15, 2011. http://republicans.energycommerce.house.gov/Media/file/Hearings/Oversight/101411/memotogc.pdf

Rigzone Staff. "U.S. to Reap Fruits of Deepwater Labor." *Rigzone*. March 26, 2010. http://www.rigzone.com/news/article.asp?a_id=90122

Roberts, D. "Van Jones: 'I feel like I'm just getting started.'" *Grist*. March 25, 2010. http://www.grist.org/article/2010-03-25-van-jones-i-feel-like-im-just-getting-started

Rockland Capital. "Beacon Power Assets to Be Sold to Rockland Capital." Press Release. February 6, 2012. http://www.rocklandcapital.com/newsmedia.htm

Roman, David. "Spain Approves 30% Cut to Solar Subsidies." *The Wall Street Journal*. December 23, 2010. http://online.wsj.com/article/SB10001424052748704278404576037343359005376.html

Romano, Brian. "GE Says Wind Turbine Prices Drag on Profits, Sees Better 2012." *ReCharge*. January 23, 2012. http://www.recharge-news.com/business_area/finance/article299174.ece?

Santos, Javier. "Spain: The Regulation of Renewables." *International Financial Law Review*. October 1, 2008. http://www.iflr.com/Article/2025527/Spain-The-regulation-of-Renewables.html

Schneider, K. *Recovery Bill is Breakthrough on Clean Energy, Good Jobs*. February 17, 2009. http://apolloalliance.org/feature-articles/at-last-federal-gOvernment-signs-up-for-Clean-energy-economy/

Schultze, C. "Green Energy Policy: Getting the Prices Right." Unpublished paper presented at the "Green Economy Dialogues," a conference hosted by the Business Advisory Council of the OECD, October 12, 2011.

Schwartz, A. "China Is Overtaking U.S. in the Clean Energy Race." *Fast Company*. March 26, 2010. http://www.fastcompany. com/1598340/China-is-Overtaking-us-in-the-Clean-energy-Race

Schwartz, Louis. "The Power Grid and the Wind Industry in China: An Update." *Renewable Energy World.com*. May 11, 2010. http:// www.renewableenergyworld.com/rea/news/article/2011/05/ the-power-Grid-and-the-wind-industry-in-China-an-update

Schweizer, P. *Throw Them All Out*. Boston: Houghton Mifflin, 2011. http://biggovernment.com/whall/2011/11/16/robert-kennedy-jr-s-green-company-scored-1-4-Billion-taxpayer-bailout/

Sempra Energy Utility. *Smart Grid Deployment Plan Costs*. 2011. http:// www.sdge.com/regulatory/documents/a-11-06-006/Cost%20Esti-mates.pdf

Shamalensee, Richard and Robert Stavins. "A Guide to Economic and Policy Analysis of EPA's Transport Rule." March 2011. http://www. supportCleanair.com/resources/studies/file/4-15-11-Schmalensee-Stavins-Guide-to-EPAs-Transport-Rule.pdf

Shepardson, S. "President, Automakers Hail New Fuel Efficiency Pact." *The Detroit News*, July 29, 2011. http://www. detnews.com/article/20110729/AUTO01/107290411/1148/ President--automakers-hail-new-Fuel-Efficiency-pact

Silver, Jonathan. Testimony before the House Committee on Energy and Commerce, Subcommittee on Oversight and Investigations on "Solyndra and the DOE Loan Program." September 14, 2011. http://republicans.energycommerce.house.gov/Media/file/Hear-ings/Oversight/091411/Silver.pdf

Slingenberg, Allister, Koen Rademaekers, Ekim Sincer, and Ruud van der Aa. *Environment and Labour Force Skills*. European Commission DG Environment. ECORYS. Rotterdam, 2008. http://

ec.europa.eu/environment/enveco/industry_employment/pdf/
labor_force.pdf

Smith, Rebecca. "Chinese-Made Turbines to Fill U.S. Wind Farm."
The Wall Street Journal. October 30, 2009. http://online.wsj.com/
article/SB125683832677216475.html

Smith, T. "Insight: A Booming Oil Shale," OilEdge. December 30,
2010. http://www.oiledge.com/n/Insight_a_booming_oil_
shale/629b3c20.aspx

Solyndra. "Solyndra Breaks Ground on New 500 Megawatt Solar
Plant." Press Release. 2009. http://www.solyndra.com/2009/09/
megawatt-solar/

Solyndra. "Timeline." http://www.solyndra.com/about-us/timeline/

State of New Jersey. *Green Jobs*. New Jersey Next Stop . . . Your Career
website. 2012. http://www.state.nj.us/njnextstop/home/greenjobs/

Stempel, Jonathan. "Solar Company Solyndra's Survival in Doubt Pre-IPO." *Reuters*. April 2, 2010.
http://www.reuters.com/article/2010/04/02/
us-solyndra-ipo-goingconcern-idUSTRE6311C320100402

Stephanopolous, George. ABC News / Yahoo! News Exclusive Interview with President Obama. Interview Transcript. October 3, 2011.
http://abcnews.go.com/Politics/transcript-george-stephanopoulos-
abc-news-yahoo-news-exclusive/story?id=14659193&singlePage=t
rue#.TxByyG-Pn8c

Steward, Lachlan. E-mail to to [Name redacted], Subject: Solyndra
meeting, January 13, 2009, http://republicans.energycommerce.
house.gov/Media/file/Hearings/Oversight/091411/DocumentsEn-
teredIntoRecord.pdf

Stills, Ben. "Spain Halts Renewable Subsidies to Curb $31 Billion of
Debts." *Bloomberg*. January 27, 2012. http://www.bloomberg.com/
news/2012-01-27/spain-suspends-subsidies-for-new-renewable-
energy-plants.html

Strickland, E. "The New Face of Environmentalism." *East Bay Express*.
November 2, 2005. http://www.eastbayexpress.com/gyrobase/the-

new-face-of-environmentalism/content?oid=1079539&showFullT
ext=true

World Bank. *Annual GDP Growth Rate, 1996–2000, 2001–2005,
2006–2010.* World Bank national accounts data, and OECD
National Accounts data files. Catalog Sources World Development
Indicators. 2011. http://data.worldbank.org/indicator/NY.GDP.
MKTP.KD.ZG?page=2

Three Gorges Dam Hydroelectric Power Plant, China. 2010. http://www.
power-technology.com/projects/gorges/

Tubb, R. "Billions Needed to Meet Long-Term Natural Gas Infrastructure Supply, Demands." *Pipeline and Gas Journal.* Vol. 236, No. 4
(2009).

Tulsa Community Foundation. "History of TCF." 2010. http://www.
tulsacf.org/index.php?option=com_content&view=article&id=48&
Itemid

U.K. House of Commons. *Green Jobs and Skills: Government Response
to the Committee's Second Report.* First Special Report of Session
2009–2010. Environmental Audit Committee, House of Commons. March 15, 2010. http://www.publications.parliament.uk/pa/
cm200910/cmsElect/cmenvaud/435/435.pdf

U.K. House of Commons. *Green Jobs and Skills. Second Report of Session
2008–2009.* Environmental Audit Committee, House of Commons.
December 16, 2009. http://www.publications.parliament.uk/pa/
cm200910/cmsElect/cmenvaud/159/159i.pdf

U.S. Centers for Disease Control and Prevention. *Green, Safe and
Healthy Jobs.* August 26, 2010. http://www.cdc.gov/niosh/topics/
PtD/greenjobs.html

U.S. Congressional Budget Office. *Estimated Impact of the American
Recovery and Reinvestment Act.* November 2011. http://www.cbo.
gov/ftpdocs/125xx/doc12564/11-22-ARRA.pdf

U.S. Congressional Budget Office. *How Policies to Reduce Greenhouse
Gas Emissions Could Affect Employment.* Brief. May 5, 2010. http://

www.cbo.gov/ftpdocs/105xx/doc10564/05-05-CapAndTrade_Brief.
pdf

U.S. Congressional Budget Office. *The Effects of Renewable or Clean
Electricity Standards.* July 2011. http://www.cbo.gov/ftpdocs/121xx/
doc12166/07-26-Energy.pdf

U.S. Congressional Research Service. *H.R.2454 CRS Summary.*
Accessed through Library of Congress THOMAS website.

U.S. Department of Energy, Energy Information Administration. *Direct
Federal Financial Interventions and Subsidies in Energy in Fiscal
Year 2010.* August 1, 2011. http://www.eia.gov/analysis/requests/
subsidy/

U.S. Department of Energy, Energy Information Administration, *2011
Outlook for Hurricane Related Production in the Gulf of Mexico.* June
2011. https://docs.google.com/viewer?a=v&q=cache:UhLUG6fBE
icJ:205.254.135.24/forecasts/steo/special/pdf/2011_sp_02.pdf+&h-
l=en&gl=us&pid=bl&srcid=ADGEESjymuqbcqiCLl7aKRyUbQKwY
ddm2Ftfcbj8ZIoFAJo5KVq11gQCDjoNJYPBM447GeBEl2AKWFm
EYj3VCzsz57sfSodyGE4VSsNCfBfZG7ucL3fw8_txWtySVvqxvXd
MVW4ntSRS&sig=AHIEtbQt7HteqU67kyoVFObAooRr7uooew

U.S. Department of Energy, Energy Information Administration.
Annual Energy Outlook 2011: With Projections to 2035. April 2011.
http://www.eia.gov/forecasts/aeo/pdf/0383(2011).pdf

U.S. Department of Energy, Energy Information Administration. *Brazil, Analysis.* 2011. http://www.eia.gov/countries/cab.cfm?fips=BR

U.S. Department of Energy, Energy Information Administration. *International Energy Outlook: 2011.* September 2011.
http://205.254.135.24/forecasts/ieo/pdf/0484(2011).pdf

U.S. Department of Energy, Energy Information Administration.
Monthly Crude Oil Production by US PAD District and State. November 29, 2011. http://www.eia.gov/dnav/pet/pet_crd_crpdn_adc_
mbbl_m.htm

U.S. Department of Energy. Energy Information Administration. *International Energy Statistics.* 2011. http://www.eia.gov/cfapps/ ipdbproject/IEDIndex3.cfm?tid=6&pid=29&aid=12

U.S. Department of Energy. Energy Information Administration. *Share of Total Primary Energy Supply in 2008, India.* 2008. http://www.eia. gov/countries/cab.cfm?fips=IN

U.S. Department of Energy. Energy Information Administration. International Statistics 2005–2009. http://www.eia.gov/cfapps/ ipdbproject/iedindex3.cfm?tid=2&pid=36&aid=12&cid=regions&sy id=2005&eyid=2009&unit=BKWH

U.S. Department of Energy, Loan Program Office. "LGP (1703 and 1705) FAQ." https://lpo.energy.gov/?page_id=368

U.S. Department of Energy, Loan Programs Office. *Solyndra Restructuring Memorandum.* February 15, 2011. http://republicans.energycommerce.house.gov/Media/file/Hearings/Oversight/101411/ memotogc.pdf

U.S. Department of Labor. "Turning Green Jobs to Gold, Safely." U.S. Department of Labor website. 2012. http://www.dol.gov/dol/ green/

U.S. Department of Labor, Bureau of Labor Statistics. *Employment, Hours, and Earnings from the Current Employment Statistics Survey (National).* NAICS Code 211, Oil and Gas Extraction. 2012. http:// data.bls.gov/timeseries/CES1021100001?data_tool=XGtable

U.S. Department of Labor, Bureau of Labor Statistics. *The Employment Situation-August 2011.* September 2, 2011. http://www.bls.gov/news. release/archives/empsit_09022011.pdf

U.S. Department of Labor, Bureau of Labor Statistics. *The Employment Situation-October 2011.* September 2, 2011. http://www.bls.gov/ news.release/archives/empsit_11042011.pdf

U.S. Department of Labor, Bureau of Labor Statistics. *Green Goods and Services Industries by NAICS Code.* Federal Register Notice for Public Comment. September 21, 2010. http://www.bls.gov/green/ final_green_def_8242010_pub.pdf

U.S. Department of Labor, Bureau of Labor Statistics. *Industries Where Green Goods and Services Are Classified.* 2010. http://www.bls.gov/green/final_green_def_8242010_pub.xls

U.S. Department of Labor, Bureau of Labor Statistics. *May 2010 National Industry-Specific Occupational Employment and Wage Estimates.* BLS Occupation Employment Statistics. 2010. http://www.bls.gov/oes/current/oes472221.htm#nat

U.S. Department of the Treasury. *General Explanations of the Administration's Fiscal Year 2012 Revenue Proposals.* February 2011. http://www.treas.gov/offices/tax-policy/library/greenbk12.pdf

U.S. Energy Information Administration, "Levelized Cost of New Generation Resources in the Annual Energy Outlook 2012." January 23, 2012. http://www.eia.gov/forecasts/aeo/electricity_generation.cfm

U.S. Environmental Protection Agency, Office of Air Quality Planning and Standards *Latest Findings on National Air Quality.* January 2008. http://epa.gov/airtrends/2007/report/trends_report_full.pdf

U.S. Environmental Protection Agency, Office of Air Quality Planning and Standards. *March 2008 Final National Ambient Air Quality Standards for Ground-level Ozone.* March 2008. http://www.epa.gov/apti/Materials/Ozone%20Final%20NAAQS%20Presentation.version%20of%20for%20Lydia%20broadcast.draft.pdf

U.S. Environmental Protection Agency. *S2: Supplemental Regulatory Impact Analysis of Alternative Standards 0.055 and 0.060 ppm for the Ozone NAAQS Reconsideration.* November 5, 2009. http://www.epa.gov/ttn/ecas/regdata/RIAs/s2-suppmental_analysis-060%2605_55_11-5-09.pdf

U.S. Environmental Protection Agency. *What are Clean Energy Jobs?* U.S. Environmental Protection Agency website. 2012. http://www.epa.gov/statelocalclimate/state/topics/Workforce.html

U.S. Environmental Protection Agency and U.S. Department of Energy. *About Energy Star.* Energystar.gov website. 2011. http://www.energystar.gov/index.cfm?c=about.ab_index

U.S. Geological Survey. "USGS Releases New Assessment of Gas Resources in the Marcellus Shale, Appalachian Basin." August 23, 2011. http://www.usgs.gov/newsroom/article.asp?ID=2893

U.S. Government Accountability Office, Report to the Chairman, Committee on Science and Technology, House of Representatives. *Climate Change: A Coordinated Strategy Could Focus Federal Geoengineering Research and Inform Governance Efforts.* GAO-10-903, September 2010. Table 1, p. 19. http://www.gao.gov/new.items/d10903.pdf

U.S. Green Buildings Council. *LEED Rating System Development.* 2012. http://www.usgbc.org/DisplayPage.aspx?CMSPageID=2360

U.S. Office of Management and Budget. *Fiscal Year 2012 Budget of the US Government.* 2011. http://www.whitehouse.gov/sites/default/files/omb/budget/fy2012/assets/budget.pdf

U.S. Office of the Press Secretary. "President Bush Signs H.R. 6, the Energy Independence and Security Act of 2007." White House Press Release. December 19, 2007. http://georgewbush-whitehouse.archives.gov/news/releases/2007/12/20071219-6.html

U.S. Office of the Press Secretary. "President Obama Announces Historic 54.5 mpg Fuel Efficiency Standard." White House Press Release. July 29, 2011. http://www.whitehouse.gov/the-press-office/2011/07/29/president-obama-announces-historic-545-mpg-Fuel-Efficiency-Standard.

United Nations. *Green Jobs Initiative.* United Nations, Online Inventory of UN System Activities on Climate Change. 2008. http://www.un.org/climatechange/projectsearch/proj_details.asp?projID=155&ck=XpzmpoEa3yid8Nd

United Nations. *World Economic and Social Survey 2011.* 2011. http://www.un.org/en/development/desa/policy/wess/wess_current/2011wess.pdf

United Nations, U.N. Environment Programme. *Green Jobs: Toward Decent Work in a Sustainable, Low Carbon World.* Nairobi, Kenya,

2008. http://www.ilo.org/wcmsp5/groups/public/@ed_emp/@
emp_ent/documents/publication/wcms_158727.pdf

Van der Loo, Lee. "BPA Decision may Prompt Wind Shutdown Soon."
Sustainable Business Oregon of the *Portland Business Journal.*
May 16, 2011. http://www.sustainablebusinessoregon.com/arti-
cles/2011/05/bpa-decision-may-prompt-wind-shutdown.html

Washington State Employment Security Department. *Solicitation for
Grant Applications— Labor Market Improvement Green Job Grants
Consortium States Submittal Summary.* July 2009. http://www.wtb.
wa.gov/Documents/LMEAconsortiumapps.pdf

White House. *White House Visitor Access Records.* 2011. http://www.
whitehouse.gov/briefing-room/disclosures/visitor-records

Wisconsin Department of Commerce. *State Energy Program—Recovery Act (SEP-ARRA) —Clean Energy Business Loan Program.* 2011.
http://commerce.wi.gov/BD/BD-SEP-ARRA.html

World Bank Development Indicators. *GDP Growth (Annual).* 2011.
http://data.worldbank.org/indicator/NY.GDP.MKTP.KD.ZG00

World Wind Energy Association. *World Wind Energy Report 2010.*
2011. http://www.wwindea.org/home/images/stories/pdfs/
worldwindenergyreport2010_s.pdf

Zeidenberg, D. *New Report Finds Investments to Clean and Modernize Power Plants will Create Significant U.S. Job Growth.* February
9, 2011. http://www.umass.edu/newsoffice/newsreleases/arti-
cles/121119.php

Zeller, Tom Jr., and Keith Bradsher. "China's Push into Wind Worries
U.S. Industry." *The New York Times.* December 15, 2010. http://
www.nytimes.com/2010/12/16/business/global/16wind.html.

ABOUT THE AUTHOR

Diana Furchtgott-Roth, former chief economist of the U.S. Department of Labor, is a senior fellow at the Manhattan Institute and a contributing editor of RealClearMarkets.com. She is the author of *Women's Figures: An Illustrated Guide to the Economics of Women in America* (Rowman and Littlefield, 2012) and the editor of *Overcoming Barriers to Entrepreneurship in the United States* (Rowman and Littlefield, 2008). She is a columnist for *The Examiner* and *Tax Notes*. Ms. Furchtgott-Roth received degrees in economics from Swarthmore College and Oxford University.

INDEX

corn, 46. *See also* ethanol

Corporate Average Fuel Economy
(CAFE) regulations, 162–64

corporations, 3. *See also specific
industries*

Costantino, Francesca, 147–48

Council of State Governments
(CSG)
"Green Jobs Created or Saved
by the Recovery Act," 57

cronyism, 88, 116–17

Crutzen, Paul, 5

CSG. *See* Council of State
Governments (CSG)

cylindrical panels, 109

Czech Republic, 192

D

Dang, Xiangyi, 134

Darbee, Peter, 7, 8

Davis, Steven, 22–23

Deepwater Horizon, 18–19

Delaware, 15, 95

Democratic Senatorial Campaign
Committee (DSCC), 112

Democrats, 73, 112, 143, 192. *See
also specific people*
green energy and, 103–4

Denmark, 133, 141–43

Denver-Julesburg Basin, 189

Department of Agriculture
(USDA), 46

Department of Defense (DOD),
116–17, 164–66

Department of Energy (DOE), 9,
10, 33, 48, 55–56, 75–76, 147,
219n2
Credit Committee, 106
loan guarantees by, 7–8, 104–
8, 110–13, 117–21, 123
Office of International
Science and Technology
Cooperation, 147
Solyndra and, 106–13
wind energy and, 126

Department of Housing and
Urban Development (HUD), 9

Department of Justice (DOJ), 111,
113

Department of Labor (DOL), 25–
26, 44–45, 47, 54–56, 57
definition of green jobs
(*See also* Bureau of Labor
Statistics (BLS))
definitions of green jobs, 53
Employment and Training
Administration (ETA),
50–51, 54–55
green jobs program, 98
green jobs training program,
54–56
job creation and, 125

Department of Mineral
Resources, 189